MORALS AND POLITICS

# MORALS AND POLITICS
## The Ethics of Revolution

WILLIAM ASH

ROUTLEDGE DIRECT EDITIONS

ROUTLEDGE & KEGAN PAUL
London, Henley and Boston

First published in 1977
by Routledge & Kegan Paul Ltd,
39 Store Street,
London WC1E 7DD,
Broadway House,
Newtown Road,
Henley-on-Thames,
Oxon RG9 1EN and
9 Park Street,
Boston, Mass. 02108, USA
Printed and bound in Great Britain
© William Ash, 1964, 1977

ISBN 0 7100 8558 3

To Reg Birch — lifelong fighter in the ranks of the organised working class and Chairman of the Communist Party of Britain (Marxist-Leninist).

# CONTENTS

# ACKNOWLEDGMENTS

This is a considerably expanded and completely re-worked version
of an earlier book, 'Marxism and Moral Concepts', published by
Monthly Review Press, New York, in 1964. It has been possible
in the present book to do more justice to Mao Tsetung's contributions to Marxist philosophy and to consider in some detail the
ethical implications of the Proletarian Cultural Revolution in
China. An attempt has been made to illustrate particular features
of Marxist moral philosophy by reference to social practice in
socialist countries like China, Albania and Vietnam.

Insofar as this book is an improvement over the earlier edition
I am indebted to comrades in the Communist Party of Britain
(Marxist-Leninist) in argument and discussion with whom, in the
course of political activity, I have gained a deeper understanding
of Marxist philosophy.

# Chapter 1

# VALUES – THE MEANING OF VALUE JUDGMENTS

## INTRODUCTION

When we ask a philosophical question like 'What is value?', there are really two problems involved. In the first place there is the challenge to find a satisfactory answer to such an inquiry when past attempts to do so have already filled many volumes. And in the second place, arising from this very fact, follows the further consideration: 'How can there have been so much confusion about what we mean by our own concepts?' A concern with such questions as why we are puzzled by the idea of 'value' or why completely contradictory opinions about it have been held at the same time and place or why the same arguments about its true meaning have recurred at quite different times and places — questions like these inevitably force us to broaden the scope of our study beyond the confines of academic philosophy and approach the subject from a social and historical point of view. The justification for attacking the problem on a wider front is that often to understand how or why a certain question can be asked is a major step in the direction of being able to answer it.

The guiding principle of this whole inquiry into the nature of ethics is Marxist. The acceptance of such a procedure will naturally be highly provisional on the part of many readers till it shall have been tested practically by providing workable solutions for the problems considered.

By a Marxist approach is meant starting with the proposition 'it is not the consciousness of men that determines their existence, but, on the contrary, their social existence determines their consciousness.' If the way men provide for their practical needs in society profoundly colours their thinking, then there can be no critique of philosophical concepts which does not take fully into account the connection between those concepts and the material conditions of life they reflect.

In saying that philosophical concepts reflect the material conditions of life, it is not meant to suggest that this reflection is passive and mirror-like. On the contrary, it is dynamic, reacting dialectically on the human situation originally imaged. The very realisation that being determines consciousness is itself an alteration in being which must also be registered by consciousness. But an appreciation of the overall sequence by which concrete circumstances precede their conceptualisation furnishes the logical order for investigating the development and significance of ethical ideas.

To argue that the existence of men in society conditions their consciousness is to assume, as opposed to an idealistic point of view, a materialistic point of view which takes several related forms. For one thing it accepts the scientific evidence for the existence of an objective world long before there was any conscious life on it. Awareness, therefore, has been conditioned by the physical context in which it developed; and this fact is crucial for a valid theory of knowledge. The question of how we can know the world around us is not entirely unlike the question of how it is that the food our environment provides happens to agree with our stomachs. Either can become a mystery if we ignore the fact that minds, like stomachs, originated in and have been conditioned by a pre-existent natural order. For another thing a materialistic point of view insists on basing any study of men on their social efforts to satisfy their physical needs. People have to produce the means of their sustenance in order to be able to think about themselves at all. Thinking about society is not a self-sustaining activity: it is bound to be influenced through and through by the preconditional necessity of entering into social relationships for the purpose of maintaining life. When the division of labour which is the basis of social classes does permit certain men to be 'thinkers', to the very extent that they are freed from the necessity of physical work by other men's efforts, their ideas may be 'freed' from relevance to reality. Practical theories about man in society must be rooted in the actual practice of working together in productive ways.

Ethics is the most practical branch of philosophy. It is immediately concerned with men's actions, and since men's actions are largely directed toward securing a livelihood and providing for the continuance of human life, ethics is closely associated with the economic basis of society. In communities like our own, factory and market place are the great concourses of human activity; and the relationships men establish in the process of first producing and then exchanging the goods on which life depends are bound to affect deeply their conception of ethical conduct. It is no mere verbal coincidence that terms like 'values' and 'goods', though with somewhat different connotations, play such an important part in the considerations of both moral philosophy and political economy.

It is this close correspondence between ethical and economic concepts and the fact that the economic sense is the more fundamental which determine the method of approach to such questions as: what is value? what is its relationship, if any, to usefulness? what is the function of value judgments?


VALUE AS DESCRIPTIVE

What, then, is value? One way of trying to understand the nature of value is to see how the most general value word in our language,

'good', is actually used and to attempt to define from such instances what we really mean by the attribution to anything of
'goodness'.  At present we shall only be concerned with this value
word as applied to things — 'a good watch' or 'a good apple'.
It is in value judgments of this type that we can trace most
clearly the link between philosophical and economic interpretations
which is our clue to a better understanding of the nature of value.

Now when we say that a thing is 'good' we might mean that it has
some objective quality which can be so designated or that someone
has an attitude toward it which can be described as favourable.
In either case a factual proposition could be substituted for
the sentence containing a value word without loss of meaning.
This naturalistic account is rejected by many philosophers who
deny that descriptive statements about the thing itself or about
the mental state of someone who approves of it really express the
full significance of calling it 'good'.  According to non-naturalists,
value words do not have so purely empirical a reference.

If the naturalists were correct, value words would raise no
problems because they could be translated without loss into factual
expressions.  Everything that could meaningfully be said could take
the form of descriptive propositions about objects or states of
mind.  To verify the objective use of 'good' we need only examine
anything so described to make sure it has the requisite natural
property.  The subjective use would be proved by ascertaining
whether anyone asserting a thing's 'goodness' actually had a
favourable regard for it.  In each case the meaning of 'goodness'
would be explained by the respective methods of validating sentences
containing it.

Is 'goodness' a property that objects as such can have?
Obviously it is not an immediately discernible property like
'roundness' or 'hardness' or 'yellowness';  and such first-order
properties in themselves are quite irrelevant to the question of
an object's 'goodness'.  Qualities like 'durability' or 'handiness'
or 'brilliantly coloured' do seem to have some bearing on a thing's
value;  and to call an object 'good' may be a kind of shorthand
expression for various characteristics of this latter type.  If
a watch is accurate, sturdy and convenient to carry, then it is a
good watch, and no more is meant by the word 'good' than the sum
of these descriptive phrases.

But although such qualities as 'efficient', 'durable' or
'handy' are all observable, they can be distinguished from physical properties in that they only belong to an object by virtue of
the use or enjoyment someone can get from it.  This distinction
may be denied by idealists who take first-order properties also
to be dependent on the observer, but that is a step onto a slippery
logical slope which can only end in absolute solipsism.  Stones
in a creek bed would have their specific sizes and shapes if the
earth were uninhabited;  but only if a man were looking for something to make into a tool would certain of the stones come to be
designated as good.  It is the purpose he has in mind which dif-
ferentiates good stones from useless ones.  On reflection it seems
that nothing is ever good intrinsically, merely because it is what
it is quite irrespective of a subject who judges and approves it.
We would not say, for example, that a thing was a particularly good

apple because it particularly clearly satisfied some scientific
test of its appleness but because it particularly agreeably satisfied some demand as to its taste, nourishing character or pleasant
odour and appearance — all qualities involving its enjoyment by
someone;  and even if an electronic device is imagined for sorting
good apples from bad, the standard of selection built into the
machine is based on differentiating between ripeness and rotten-
ness according to a human need.  This characteristic of serving a
purpose or satisfying a need as essential to the nature of 'goodness' forces us to abandon the attempt to find the meaning of
value in existential propositions about objects as such.

If 'good', then, cannot be taken as simply qualifying an
object, does it refer instead to the state of one who derives
satisfaction from an object?  Value would thus be purely subjective
and we would not desire a thing because it was good:  it would be
good because we desired it.  To say that something was 'good'
would mean merely that at one time or another by at least someone
it was wanted, approved of or favourably regarded.

But when the question of degrees of goodness is considered, some
of the difficulties with this subjective account of value begin to
appear.  Since we desire some things more than others, we would
presumably say that those things for which we have a greater
desire are better.  But desire for something increases by the
extent that we are deprived of it and under certain circumstances
a crust of bread can be the most desirable thing in the world.
Yet it appears very odd to hold that, since a thing's value can
depend on its not being available, the greater the scarcity of good
things in the world the more value there would be.  Furthermore,
we often disagree over whether one thing is better than another
for a particular purpose and argue about our differences.  Such
an argument makes sense if it concerns a conflict of opinions
about the relative merits of two objects as candidates for preference;  but as a dispute about whether we really have the
respective states of mind we say we have, it would be utterly
pointless.  Comparative judgments of this kind seem to lead us
back to the object again as the referent of value judgments;  but
we have already failed to find any objective property to attach
them to.

Perhaps, then, 'goodness' might refer neither to object nor
subject in themselves but to some causal relationship between
properties of the object and qualities of feeling in the subject.
Value would be the result of the action of a desirable object on
a desiring subject.  Certainly this account avoids some of the
difficulties met with in simpler versions of the descriptive explanation of value.  On the one hand, we are no longer confronted
with the problem of how a thing can have value irrespective of an
evaluator and, on the other,we have eliminated the absurdity of
having to assign maximum value to a world where satisfactory things
are scarcest.  What we have now is a naturalistic formula by which
value resides in the relationship between certain observable
properties of the object like durable, handy, efficient or tasty and
certain recognisable reactions on the part of the subject like wanting, enjoying, liking or approving — in much the same way as
knowledge might be taken to be the result of the action of an

objective physical property like 'yellowness' on a percipient
sensitive to rays of light.

Because, of course, any naturalistic account of value words means
that there is no distinction between value judgments and factual
statements, that questions about value resolve themselves into
epistemological questions concerning our knowledge of reality.  The
view that value is simply a property of the object is equivalent to
naive realism which airily denies that the acquisition of knowledge
presents any problem at all;  the belief that it merely qualifies
the feelings of anyone who enjoys or desires the object represents
subjective idealism;  and the opinion that it is to be found in a
causal relationship between the two is a form of mechanical materialism.  According to this last interpretation, just as natural
objects impinge on our passive awareness and give us our ideas of
reality, so things with certain qualities can satisfy our desires
and by giving us pleasurablé sensations earn the designation 'good'.

It is this causal account of the production of pleasurable states
which underlies the utilitarian ethics of the English empiricists.
Since 'goodness' is considered to be a pleasurable state brought
about by the provision of objects which induce such happiness, then
the supreme good can be expressed as the greatest possible happiness for the greatest number of people and this can be advanced as
the proper goal of personal morality or government policy.

But there are difficulties with this value relationship between
good objects and pleasurable feelings which are analogous to certain
problems encountered in connection with the empiricist theory of
knowledge.  Perceptual illusions can make us suspicious of a
mechanical production of knowledge by way of the senses;  and
even if these errors are corrigible by reasoning based on the evidence of other sense impressions, the process is more sophisticated
than would be allowed for by a theory of the mind as passively
receptive and knowledge itself as the mere result of the association of ideas.  Similarly, there are psychological phenomena which
cast doubt on the efficacy of our formula for the production of
value by pleasurable reactions to objects described as 'good'.
Not only can the same object arouse in us quite different feelings
at different times but, more generally, the very search for happiness by multiplying satisfactions can prove self-defeating.

Epistemologically this discrepancy can lead to a development in
empiricism by which we are assumed to know directly not things themselves but our ideas of things.  Sense data are imposed between
ourselves and the world, shutting us off from it;  and what began
as an objective, materialistic theory of knowledge ends in subjective idealism.  In the same way there is a tendency for the
utilitarian account of value, which seemed to steer a middle
course between objective and subjective extremes, increasingly to
derive the goodness of things from our feelings about them rather
than to assume that because a thing has certain qualities we are
bound to want it.  There is a basic instability in the causal
formula by which value tends to become more and more subjective and
ceases to link in a direct relationship our states of feeling and
specifically good objects.  There is also, as we shall see, a
reason why this shift toward subjectivism occurs.

But the main objection to the naturalistic explanation of value is that it does not permit us to go on to make the kind of statements which are characteristically ethical.  If the supreme good is the greatest happiness of the largest number of people, we expect it to follow that as between possible courses of action we ought to choose the one which most contributes to the maximum realisation of happiness.  But the utilitarian definition of 'good' does not warrant such a prescriptive conclusion.  If 'good' merely describes certain objects or certain reactions or a certain relationship between them, we can only derive from such accounts of the matter statements which are themselves merely descriptive of human behaviour.  We could say that people do tend by and large to seek out things which induce pleasurable sensations and even that they may take pleasure themselves in contributing to the pleasure of others;  but we could not say that they ought to act so as to bring about these effects.  We could say that some forms of pleasure are higher or more lasting than others;  but we could not say that anyone ought to choose them.

The reason for this is simply that, logically, nothing can be extracted from a definition which was not, at least implicitly, given in that definition to begin with.  The naturalistic interpretation of value reduces sentences containing value words like 'good' to factual propositions.  'You ought to choose this' or 'you ought to like that' are not factual propositions.  There is no existential state of affairs which they simply describe;  and therefore they cannot be derived from an account of 'good' which is purely descriptive.  The attempt to do so has been called the naturalistic fallacy.  It is like saying 'There is a pin sticking in you and you really ought to try to feel it.'  The empiricist philosopher, David Hume, who formulated this principle as 'no ought from an is' provides in 'A Treatise of Human Nature' one of the most notorious examples of this very fallacy:  'Reason is, and ought only to be the slave of the passions and can never pretend to any other office than to serve and obey them.'(1) A similar example is provided by Jeremy Bentham's well-known statement:  'Nature has placed mankind under the governance of two sovereign masters, pain and pleasure.  It is for them alone to point out what we ought to do, as well as to determine what we shall do.'(2)


## VALUE AS PRESCRIPTIVE

If, then, the philosophical attempt to make descriptive sentences cover the whole field of experience seems either to deny us the use of characteristic value terms or to try to convince us that when we do use such terms we do not really mean by them what we think we mean, let us look at the problem from the other end. Starting with prescriptive sentences including value terms let us see how description might be logically accommodated also.  Unless a place for descriptive sentences is somehow maintained of course, reason can play no part in value judgments and our prescriptive utterances will be purely arbitrary.

Among the sternest critics of the fallacy by which utilitarians
pass without logical justification from defining 'good' in terms
of some descriptive aspect of object or subject to a use of value
words for persuasion or recommendation are the intuitionists like
G.E. Moore.  They try to avoid the difficulty themselves by denying that 'good' is definable at all.  It is a simple notion with
which we are directly acquainted, an ultimate term which cannot be
analysed into some other property like 'being desired'.  Just as
'yellowness' is immediately perceived as what we see, so 'goodness' is immediately intuited as what we value, as what ought to
be.  It is a non-natural quality and, indeed, a thing need not
actually exist to be accounted good in this sense of ought-to-be-
ness.  The intuitionist would, in fact, argue that the very attempt
to make value judgments conform to the sort of proposition which
links two things that exist instead of recognising them as expressions of 'seeing' something in a special light is to commit
the naturalistic fallacy.

Intuitionists can thus speak legitimately of good things as
those we ought to prefer because the 'ought' is, according to them,
inherent in our apprehension of a thing's 'goodness'.  But do we
actually have this faculty of simply intuiting what ought to be
preferred?  If so, there should be the same general measure of
agreement about what is good as about what is yellow or round and,
just as differences of opinion about physical properties can be
settled by accurate testing of the object or by checking against
a common standard an individual's perceptive sensibilities, so in
arguments about degrees of goodness there should be some criteria
for testing our special apprehension of the ought-to-be-chosen.
But the moment such an appeal to some basis of comparison is allowed,
like suitability for a purpose or pleasure-giving capacity, 'good'
has been defined in terms of something else and the whole intuitionist case is lost.  If, on the other hand, differences about relative degrees of goodness are simply accepted as irreconcilable,
'good' ceases to be objective and the postulation of a special kind
of awareness by which we can be acquainted with the special quality
'goodness' loses any point.

But even if the intuitionists fail to validate their conception
of 'good' as an undefinable, directly apprehensible quality, they
do demonstrate an important aspect of the way a value word like
'good' actually functions.  If we say that a watch, for instance, is
'good' simply because in keeping accurate time it satisfies a need
of its possessor, we find that there is one sense of the word we
cannot account for.  In attributing goodness to a thing we mean
to commend it, but nothing can be commended for merely being what
it is.  Commendation implies that something need not have been
what it is;  and this idea cannot be conveyed by any factual proposition about the observable properties of the object, the current
state of anyone's feelings about it or any immediately recognisable
relationship between the two.  It is not a question of analysing
characteristics of watches or of feelings about watches and, above
a certain level of accuracy or beyond a certain degree of accept-
ability, adding 'good' to the other modifying adjectives.  In
ascribing 'goodness' to something we not only wish to say that such
and such a thing with particular qualities is, in fact, approved by

someone or other but also that it is worthy of approval — a use, as we have already noted, that can never be adequately explained on the basis of a naturalistic interpretation of value words. Descriptive sentences are a passive recognition of what is the case, while the prescriptive use of 'good' is a way of actively advocating what it is thought should be the case.

This active role of value words in commending something or urging others to approve of it would be accounted for by Kant by associating goodness not with passive feelings but with the dynamic will. For him the only thing which is good absolutely is a good will, and by a good will he means one which acts in accord with rational principles irrespective of any inclination toward sensuous gratification. Since the human will is not free from such inclinations, the dictates of reason take the form of commands which the will is obliged to obey in order to be designated good. To call any object 'good', therefore, implies the injunction 'choose this' — not because the choice will bring personal satisfaction but because it conforms to the universal maxims of pure reason. Value does not reside in what is desired;  it is a characteristic of the will which is directed toward what ought to be chosen.

But what is the source of these universal maxims which must guide our acts of choice? They cannot be abstracted from our experience of what things in the past have been conducive to happiness or useful for attaining practical ends because that would mean that value sentences, as the naturalists contend, are ultimately reducible to factual propositions. Kant's answer to this question follows the same line as his proposed solution to the problem of how we can know the world around us. Just as the so-called empirical laws of nature cannot themselves be discovered empirically but must be deduced from the logical categories without which there can be no sensible experience, so the categorical imperative which is reason's demand on the will can only be derived from the self-conscious principles of pure rationality itself, regardless of any consequences such an imperative may entail in the ordinary world of desire and satisfaction. Because man has a kind of double citizenship in both the sensible world and the world of the understanding which it epistemologically presupposes, the practical will can be subject to those maxims of reason incumbent on all rational beings as such. As belonging to the sensible world the will is influenced by natural desires but as belonging also to the intelligible world it is free to act only in such a manner as to be able to prescribe the principle of its action as a universal law. Therefore, willing reasonably can be expressed as an 'ought' and a general rule can be laid down for the selective conduct in respect to a good watch of anyone anywhere ever needing to measure time.

Kant realised, of course, that even if we accept as valid his method of establishing the cogency of universal maxims of choice on the same basis as his deduction of a natural principle like the law of causation from the categories of thought, it is still legitimate to ask why the individual will should conform to these maxims. His work on ethics consists largely of a sincere but hopeless quest for a third term connecting with the rigour of natural law the categorical imperative with the good will. This is another way of saying that he was trying to discover a direct ethical relation-

ship between the world of the understanding whence value judgments
obtain their full prescriptive force and the sensible world where
only descriptions of things are possible.  Without such a relationship there is no way of explaining why anyone ought to choose
what is good in the Kantian sense;  with it choice loses its unique
reference to the concept of duty as such which Kant wished to
maintain as the distinctive characteristic of 'ought' sentences.

The seriousness of Kant's attempt to define the relationship
between prescriptive and descriptive sentences, between 'good' as
a value word and 'good' as a property of things or of people's
attitude toward things, is attested by his never abandoning the
thing-in-itself.  A more thorough-going idealism like Hegel's
which cuts itself free from the material world even in so atten-
uated a form as the thing-in-itself has no difficulty in establishing the non-natural character of value words.  Since we have
the idea of value as that which is worthy of choice and since ideas
are the ultimate reality, then the worthy-of-choice obviously
exists.  The only problem is that on the basis of these idealistic
assumptions our descriptive statements become non-naturalistic too
and all watches, good or bad, become ideal.

Non-naturalist theories of value imply at some stage or other the
possibility of non-empirical knowledge.  This may take the passive
Platonic form of deriving our knowledge of things from pre-existent
ideas like 'yellowness' or 'roundness' or 'thingness' itself and
using this priority of the ideal to explain our direct apprehension
of a quality like 'goodness'.  Or it may take a more dynamic form
of assuming that the human mind enters actively into the process
of experiencing the world by contributing the logical categories
which are a condition of that experience, thus providing us with
an analogy by which we can understand the value we find in the world
as something we put there ourselves through possessing a value-
creative will.

Even though non-naturalistic interpretations of value do not
simply resolve themselves into epistemological theories as must
happen, by definition, with any naturalist account, they do involve
epistemological considerations.  The ethical question of how value
judgments which are not to be reduced to statements of fact can
yet have a content that is in some sense true or false is very
much like the epistemological question of how some proposition can
be at once deductive and informative.  Logically speaking, the whole
non-naturalist case is closely associated with the validity of
synthetic a priori propositions which tell us something but are
not derived from experience.  If such propositions are possible
and meaningful, it is reasonable to suppose that there are also
judgments which can cogently ascribe a non-natural property like
'value' to objects actually existing in the natural world.


VALUE AS NEITHER DESCRIPTIVE NOR PRESCRIPTIVE

Logical positivists divide all meaningful propositions into analytic a priori, which are purely formal tautologies like the laws
of thought or the rules of mathematics, and synthetic a posteriori,
which are empirical hypotheses like our ordinary descriptive

statements.  The former are certain but do not tell us anything
we did not already know implicitly;  the latter are informative
but have only an inductive probability.

Since no other kind of proposition is admitted and since value
judgments are obviously not formal tautologies, they must either
be reducible to descriptive statements, as naturalists like the
utilitarians suppose, or else they are not propositions at all.
A.J. Ayer argues against the reduction of value to non-value
statements on the ground that it is not consistent with the conventions of our actual language.  Value words, as the intuitionists maintain, have an intrinsic signiiicance which prevents us
from translating sentences containing them into empirical propositions.  But since, as a positivist, Ayer cannot accept the
possibility of non-empirical propositions, he must deny that value
judgments have the propositional characteristic of actually stating
anything — either about objects or situations or even about the
minds and attitudes of people who make them.  A word like 'good' may
imply certain descriptive features such as, in the case of watches,
accuracy or compactness;  but in so far as it is used in an ethical
sense of ascribing value to a thing as that which ought to be
chosen or preferred, it is a pseudo-concept which adds nothing to
the meaning of a sentence in which it occurs.  Instead of saying
'This is a good watch' we might as well have said 'watch!' with
a special emphasis.  The evaluative function of 'good' is merely
an emotional sound of approval on the part of the speaker which
could have been conveyed as well by the tone of voice or by writing
an exclamation point after the object word.

The contention that this emotive theory of value is simply a
form of subjectivism is countered by the insistence on the difference between asserting and expressing a feeling.  To argue that
a thing is 'good' because we like it is to determine the validity
of value judgments by the nature of our feelings;  but a shout of
joy has no validity, asserts nothing and thus escapes the objections to a subjective theory of value.  In this way logical positivists can claim to have avoided an illegitimate use of value
words — by the extreme expedient of emptying all meaning from the
idea of value!  And as we shall see, there is a reason for this move.

And yet people go on making what seem to be value judgments and
appearing to mean more by them than they would by a groan or a
chuckle.  They give every impression of arguing about values and
they could not do this logically if an emotive theory of value were
true.  Positivists may insist that such people are really arguing
about facts;  but this is scarcely the case when they debate
whether a watch is really worth what it costs or whether promise-
keeping ought to override all other considerations.  People apparently believe that values can be inculcated and it would be
difficult to maintain that what they actually mean is teaching the
young when a sigh or an expletive is appropriate.  In short this
positivist account is no more consistent with the conventions of
social language than the naturalist account.

Linguistic analysis plays a part in the development of the
logical positivist argument and much recent philosophy has been
concerned with treating problems as the result of confusion about
the language in which such problems are expressed.  But the very

philosophical divisions a linguistic approach was supposed to
circumvent break out afresh.  Some argue from an idealistic
point of view that there are no facts apart from the propositions
asserting them, that language, like the Kantian categories, conditions all experience and that the rules of grammar are a kind of
logical framework of the universe or that language, like the
Hegelian idea, is itself the real in its most comprehensible
manifestation.  These find no difficulty in establishing a non-
naturalistic account of value — but at the cost of any straight-
forward explanation of our factual knowledge since the material
world has vanished in the Word.  Others bring an empiricist attitude
to bear on the expressions people actually use; but not by way of
providing a critique of popular forms of speech nor a study of how
a social product like language developed historically nor a comparison of the characteristic expressions of one type of society
with those of another or of one section of the same society with
those of another section.  Their empiricism consists rather in taking
everyday language as a sort of datum from which they can generalise
about how a particular language works but never why it works that
way.


VALUE AS EITHER DESCRIPTIVE OR PRESCRIPTIVE

When we consider the actual use people make of a word like 'good',
we do find that it may be descriptive, referring either to the
suitability of an object or to its being wanted; but it may also
be prescriptive and play a persuasive or commendatory role.  Sometimes one thing is meant and sometimes the other.  Depending on
what one is trying to say, on the purpose behind speech, 'good'
can have a predominantly factual meaning or it can have the evaluative force of an implicit injunction.  To state that a watch is
good may mean simply that it has certain characteristics which
make it an object of approval; or it may mean that it ought to be
approved, that it exemplifies the right way to make watches or that
it must be included in any general list of valuable things.
Sentences incorporating these distinctive usages behave quite
differently; and since neither entails the other logically, they
represent quite separate realms of discourse.  And there some contemporary philosophers, like R.M. Hare in 'The Language of Morals',
would have us leave the matter.  Once we have cleared up the confusion caused by employing the same word for two such various ends,
we can just accept that we are naturalists when we make factual
statements about useful things and that we are non-naturalists when
we make value judgments.
    If we ask for an explanation of this linguistic phenomenon,
we are very likely to be fobbed off with yet more examples proving
that 'good' really is used in these two different ways.  The method
of inquiry precludes the possibility of going behind language in
some way to discover why it takes the forms it does — just as a
logical positivist cannot account for his division of meaningful
propositions into formal tautologies and empirical hypotheses
without offending against his own classification.  And just as we
fail to see how these two types of propositions could ever combine

to give us valid knowledge unless there were some relationship
embracing both, so it seems unsatisfactory to accept any final
distinction between descriptive and prescriptive sentences.  The
idea of separate realms of discourse is not really very different
from the Kantian conception of membership in the two different
worlds of sensibility and understanding.

We inhabit both worlds:  there must be some link between them.
The theoretical world which appears in our descriptive propositions
about useful objects and our attitude toward them must bear some
relationship to the practical world in which we advise people about
the feelings they should have toward various things, commend certain
objects as being better than others and, even, state categorically
that this thing or that ought to be regarded with approval.  What
we are looking for is a connection between the utility of the
objects we call 'good' and their value.  We cannot derive the latter
from the former without committing the naturalistic fallacy.  We
cannot deduce the former from the latter without assuming an
idealism that defies our common-sense acceptance of the basic
nature of sensuous experience.  But if neither can be defined in
terms of the other, may it not be that each is a distinguishable
aspect of some comprehensive whole in which their relationship
could be understood?  Are we not, perhaps, victims of our own
analytic methods in having taken something apart and then forgotten
the nature of whatever it was we began with?

The problem of accommodating 'facts' and 'value' within the same
realm of interpretation without loss in what each essentially
means is like the problem of other sets of terms which remain
isolated, irreconcilable and ultimately inexplicable as long as
they are not seen as part of a larger whole in which they are
related as different moments of the same process.  Empiricism and
idealism, for example, have been taken as opposite poles around
which philosophers have collected like children choosing sides in
a game.  The sensing of physical reality, the empirical moment,
and the combining and re-ordering of sense impressions to formulate
propositions and draw inferences, the ideal moment, are two stages
in the total process of knowledge which is only completed with the
submission of such logical hypotheses to the test of social
practice.

A dead, static universe could be studied analytically and dis-
junctively;  but process in its sweep and in the changes which are
the measure of its development has to be seen historically and
dialectically.  If one logical system is more suitable than
another, depending on whether we are pigeon-holing a statically-
conceived reality or comprehending a reality in which there is
movement, growth and change, then the very laws of thought cannot
be said to be without content and must be recognised as in some
degree synthetic.  As will be seen, there are social circumstances
in which internal relations tend to be obscured:  the lively links
between man and nature and between man and man are distorted to
the point of seeming to have broken altogether and reality appears
to be made up of discrete objects best handled by a classificatory
logic.  The laws of thought themselves are rooted in social
experience.

ECONOMIC VALUE

The meaning of 'good' seems to split apart into a description of a
thing's suitability to satisfy human needs and an evaluation of a
thing as somehow worthy of choice.  It is this latter sense
which has proved philosophically troublesome.  If a thing satisfies a desire or serves a purpose, it can be described as 'good'
and why should that not be the end of the matter?  Why have we
developed an evaluative language at all?  Factual statements can
describe a thing's useful qualities;  emotive utterances can express degrees of personal satisfaction.  How has the terminology
for conveying the idea of a thing's worthiness ever come to be
devised?  It would be pure fetishism to suppose that we wished to
praise objects themselves for gratifying our desires;  but what
else can be meant by regarding objects as value-bearing?

The answer to this question will involve us in an historical
quest for the social origins of our value language which, because
of the internal relationships of all fields of knowledge, will be
interdisciplinary in scope — with particular reference to
economics.

Now the close similarity between the philosophical argument about
a natural or non-natural interpretation of value and a discussion
about the nature of objects belonging to a different field of study
altogether may already have been noted.  If it is said of a particular class of articles that 'they have two forms, a physical or
natural form, and a value form', and that 'value represents a non-
natural property of the object', we might suppose it was a continua-
tion of our old ethical debate about the definition of 'good'.  In
fact, these quotations are taken from Marx's analysis of a commodity
in the first chapter of 'Capital'.  And if there is an analogy
between defining 'good' and defining 'goods', if there is a connection between things qualified by our most general word of
appraisal and the articles which are exchanged in the market, it
can prove useful in an investigation of the nature of value.

Just as we found that the word 'good' combined two distinct
meanings, so we find that a commodity has two quite different
aspects — its use value or utility and its exchange value or,
simply, its value.  Every commodity has certain recognisable properties which qualify it to satisfy some human want.  This aspect
corresponds with the utilitarian, naturalistic, descriptive sense
of 'good'.  But in the act of exchange this same commodity reveals
a quantitative character by which it proves commensurable with
all other commodities.  This non-natural property of having a fixed
place in an orderly scale of goods is a consequence of the social
conditions of production and is not directly perceptible in the
isolated object itself.  This is its value, and it is this aspect
of the commodity which corresponds with the prescriptive sense of
'good' in value judgments.

One of the difficulties about defining the word 'good' is that
it can be applied to a vast variety of things which apparently
have nothing in common — not even the fact that they are all con-
tinuously wanted.  In much the same way commodities of every
different kind can be exchanged against each other in the market.
This is possible because, however various such goods may be, they

all embody measurable quantities of the same thing — the human labour that produced them.  It is in the operation of exchange that economic value reveals itself as 'a congelation of undifferentiated human labour'.  'Value is labour', Marx says;  'it is materialised labour in its general social form.'(3)  The fact that this human labour in the abstract not only creates all values but, as a power which can be rendered in units, is also the measure of all value, accounts for the equivalence obtaining among varying proportions of the most diverse commodities.  This relationship among objects which enables us to apply the same standard to the whole multifarious range of marketable articles reflects a relationship among men as mutual contributors to a fund of labour power which is their common capital in all dealings with their environment.  Since the connection between the labour of any one individual and that of the rest appears as a connection between commodities, Marx describes the relations of producers to each other as, paradoxically, 'material relations between persons and social relations between things'.

We can see why economic value is a non-natural property and remains imperceptible.  It is not an intrinsic characteristic of objects as such but represents the social history of an object in the context of all other value-bearing objects on which human effort has been expended.  The act of exchange by its very nature involves an evaluation;  and this evaluation, in effect, releases the human story of associative production which is locked up in commodities.

Can this labour theory of value, borrowed from the field of economics, help to solve a philosophical problem encountered in attempts to define the nature of 'good' as a value word?  An active, dynamic quality was noted in value judgments which distinguishes them from the passive, informational role of statements of fact and which could best be rendered as imperatives of choice.  Is this not because value judgments, like the price tags hung on commodities, refer ultimately to some purposive human activity behind those things which are judged to be good.  In a value sentence such as 'This is a good watch' are we not, in fact, commending the workmanship which went into its manufacture?  Is it not this causal connection between an object and successful human activity in the past to which attention is drawn in prescriptive judgments rather than some immediately discernible property of the object itself or some psychological effect in which the object is instrumental?

The economic value of goods does not refer directly to the immediate desires people have for them, else the prices of foodstuffs would fluctuate wildly before and after mealtimes;  and value judgments have this same objective character of not varying according to how much anyone at the moment actually wants what is called 'good' — though, of course, an article which no one could ever want at all would not have been produced to begin with.  It has already been remarked that a non-naturalistic interpretation of value seemed to depend on our having put value into the world ourselves, in much the same way as an idealistic theory of knowledge depends on our having put meaning into the world.  It now appears that we *have* put value into the world — not subjectively but in the very practical sense of physical changes wrought in our environment by our own efforts.

While an explanation of value generalised from its economic sense may seem reasonable enough in judgments like 'good watches' or 'good motor cars', it might appear odd to interpret an expression like 'good apples' in terms of past activity. And yet apples are no mere gift of nature: they represent many generations of selective cultivation, quite apart from the work of picking, packing and transport which must all enter into their being available for consumption in an optimum state. Indeed, it will be found that few things encountered in ordinary civilised existence are unmixed with human labour, 'man's universality manifesting itself practically', as Marx puts it, 'through his capacity for appropriating nature as his inorganic body.'(4)

Those things on which man has not acted at all, such as stars or oceans or mountain ranges, are not usually referred to in our ordinary speech as 'good' because we do not normally pat nature on the back for her efforts. We are more likely to call them 'sublime', 'awesome' or 'beautiful' in reference to the feelings they invoke in us. If we disagree about our responses to such phenomena, it is not possible to argue about such differences as it is possible to argue about whether a watch is good or not. As applied to things like virgin forests, deposits of minerals or the creek-bed stones of an earlier example, 'good' is evaluative in the prospective sense of what human effort can make of them. At the other extreme from entirely natural formations are those things which represent an expenditure of human labour but turn out to be useless. We might wish to commend the effort behind some contraption that failed to work, as for example 'a good perpetual motion device', meaning a good stab at such an impractical undertaking; but we would not intend 'good' to be taken as descriptive of the object itself. Most of the things met with in our day-to-day living fall within these limiting cases and, being at once useful and the result of purposeful activity, can be qualified as 'good' in both its descriptive and evaluative senses.

In Marx's words 'Value in general is a form of social labour.' Man's labour through the ages has transformed the objective world to satisfy his needs; and the sum total of changes in that world as a result of man's productive efforts, 'putting his life' into the objects around him, is the measure of value in the world.


VALUE AND THE DIVISION OF LABOUR

It is obvious why the analysis of a commodity yields the two distinct aspects of utility and value. The social fact of the division of labour implies a separation between productive effort and enjoyed satisfactions with some form of exchange providing the link between them, and this split between production and consumption is reflected in the double nature of every marketable object.

Unlike Robinson Crusoe on his island or the directly associated labour of the most primitive communities, human exertion in commodity-producing societies is not aimed immediately at satisfying desires but at creating exchange values. Utility results from the concrete labour of various workers making this or that specific article; but before such articles are actually used they appear as values on the market — that is, as quantities of abstract labour which can be measured against each other in terms of the universal commodity, money.  Only by purchase can these articles, whose essential characteristic as values is their temporary removal from the area of human use, be converted into objects of personal consumption.

Thus the same commodity can be seen at different stages as either utilisable or valuable, but not both at the same time.  We are forced to think about the matter dialectically because commodity production and exchange itself, like any process, cannot be dealt with by a purely disjunctive logic without producing philosophical puzzles.

Is it not this same social division of labour which accounts for the two different meanings we found in analysing the word 'good'? Once the effort of producing goods has become separated from their acquisition for use, there is a consequent polarisation of the concepts relative to each phase.  Ideas like the value of human effort, the necessity of working for a living and the justice of a fair return are found in connection with production, while in respect to consumption one is concerned with enjoyment, with human needs and desires and the things which can satisfy them.  Furthermore, production is social and objective in the sense that men pool their resources in the fabrication of objects embodying value, while consumption is individualistic and subjective.

Each set of concepts is valid for one moment of a process which includes both the laborious provision and the pleasurable use of goods;  but each on its own tells only half of the story.  The utilitarian, subjective aspect of 'goodness' expresses man's dependence on nature for the satisfaction of his wants:  value as an objective measure of the exertion employed in supplying our needs expresses man's dominion over nature.  It is this division between passive enjoyment and active effort which is reflected in the distinction between a descriptive and prescriptive use of the value word 'good'.

But is it reasonable to suppose that a simple economic fact like the division of labour could sink so deep into human consciousness as to determine our very use of concepts and affect our ways of thinking?  We can ask such a question because the social process by which we satisfy our needs in an indirect manner is so familiar that it seems perfectly natural;  but ordinary human beings in the early stages of commodity production must have required a long period of adjustment to get accustomed to this idea that the things they made by their own efforts were not theirs for immediate use. Even now, we can imagine how odd it might seem to anyone who had not grown up in our kind of society to see men working to produce types of goods they will never themselves be able to use in any way or moving among displayed articles of use and, in spite of the most pressing need for them, regarding all but that tiny proportion for which they have artificial counters to exchange as strictly taboo or, more horribly, to see Indians in their hundreds dying of starvation on the streets of Calcutta in 1943 in front of res-taurants within which the normal purchase and consumption of meals was going on as usual.

The interdiction of use, on which the emergence of value as

distinguishable from utility depends, must have made a tremendous
impact on the awareness of those who had first to accommodate themselves to the divorce between satisfactions and work done.  This is
attested by the whole weight of primitive myth and religion required to back up the extension of the earliest biological division
of labour within the family to the entire tribe — taboo, totemism
and the very tribal clan structure all associated with the simple
fact that our ancestors had to learn not to devour things the moment
they caught or found them.  Not only must it have conditioned their
entire mental and moral outlook but we ourselves have inherited
from that primitive advance in social organisation such splits in
our own thinking as that between a humanistic and a scientific
approach to reality, reflecting the distinction between the qualitative aspect of useful goods and the purely quantitative aspect
of those same goods as abstract value.  Moral philosophies based on
hedonism and those based on concepts of duty and obligation mirror
the same division.  Nor could the conception of time have remained
unaffected by the need to think in longer periods than the short
cycle of desire and fulfilment in pre-commodity life.  The whole
enormously increased range over which human purpose is free to act
effectively can only have developed under the influence of the
roundabout methods of production originating in the division of
labour.

But if historical economic facts like the division of labour and
the rise of commodity production can help us to understand the
nature of value in its widest sense, why have not philosophers
availed themselves of this key?  Why have they not explored the
relation between the economic and the ethical significance of value
instead of insisting on distinguishing them absolutely?

Part of the answer to this question is provided by the way the
division of labour itself may be carried to ridiculous extremes,
as in the rigid compartmentalism of various mental disciplines.
Economists deal with theories about the practical ordering of
society;  philosophers deal with the ideas and concepts about life
which men in society have;  and if there is any relationship between these two areas of study it will never be found by the pro-
fessionals on either side who remain strictly within their own
academic territory.

More profoundly, the division of labour, particularly the division
between manual and mental labour, also determines the experience of
the economic process professional philosophers in our society have.
Not directly involved in production itself, nor even for the most
part having so much as seen the inside of a factory, they are
influenced in their attitudes by their role as consumers and tend
to be more concerned with the end results of the system, the goods
made available for use, than with the activity which produced them.
Take up any recent book on ethics and consider the illustrative
examples offered.  Many will be about the act of choice involved
in buying one thing rather than another or about the way in which
we order our subjective preferences for things:  few if any will
be about the associative labour process which brought such things
into being.  The productive activity of men in their relations to
each other, to the means of production and to the objective world
not only provides the goods on which life depends but also

conditions the concepts on which valid thought depends.  A consumer's eye-view of society in slighting such basic activity is
prone to miss the full significance of concepts whose origin and
development are largely determined by the way in which commodities
are produced and exchanged.

This consumer's attitude can lead naturally to a utilitarian
bias in which 'good' is identified with whatever aspect of an object
makes it suitable for individual use, and value is either defined
in terms of such suitability or left altogether unaccounted for.
A subjective view of this kind is the obvious response of a shopper
who is not interested in how various articles have appeared on the
shelves but merely wishes to arrange in a private order of priority
the satisfactions he can afford.  These same goods would appear in
a different light to a worker involved in the manufacturing process
which made them available;  but ours is not a society in which
industrial workers get books of philosophy published.  In a
socialist country like China where in Mao Tsetung's words 'philosophy has been liberated from the confines of lecture rooms and
textbooks and has become a sharp weapon in the hands of the
masses', there would be no such subjective bias to ethical thinking.

Suppose a professional philosopher does realise that this
utilitarian account is not adequate, that it by-passes the essential
problem of value instead of solving it.  He may be aware that the
enjoyment of goods implies some kind of effort;  but if his own
experience has never included any acquaintanceship with the productive activity on which all value is ultimately grounded and if
he continues to approach the question from a consumer's point of
view, this effort is likely to appear to him, idealistically, as
the moral exertion by which a man becomes worthy of the good things
of life.  Value thus pertains to things not in respect to the actual
labour of their makers but out of regard for the spiritual aspirations of their prospective users.

In this way the non-naturalist, ignoring a thing's utility,
arrives at a view of value as so completely detached from any
context of human satisfaction that choice seems 'free' in the sense
of being purely arbitrary or else appears to be motivated in the
empty terms of duty for the sake of duty.  What has actually
happened in this derivation of the sense of value is that by
stressing, however unconsciously, that moment in a commodity's
history when it is under the interdiction of use as a mere quantification represented by its price, the non-naturalist sees value
as belonging only to the abstract idea of an object.  As simply
marketable, objects have no natural properties and are as unchanging
and timeless as Platonic archetypes.  Therefore goodness by this
account can come to be regarded as 'The Good', an ideal conception
which has lost all connection with the world of actual human effort
and can only be sought in some 'remembered' realm of pure thought.

Both kinds of mistakes about value, either explaining it away
altogether or turning it into something transcendental, are the
result of an unconscious bias rooted in the mistake of starting
from the wrong end of the production process — the consumer's
end.  As Marx says:  'If you proceed from production, you necessarily concern yourself with the real conditions of production
and the productive activity of men.  But if you proceed from

consumption ... you can afford to ignore the real living conditions
and the activity of men.'(5)   That is why Marx's definition of class
is based not on criteria of consumption like arbitrary levels of
income, the possession of status symbols or the ideas people may
have about themselves as a result of such considerations, but on
the objective social fact of a person's position in the productive
process, of his relationship to the means of production.

Naturalists in failing to grasp the dialectic of the whole process from production through distribution to consumption cannot
account for a thing's being both useful and valuable;  non-
naturalists in seeing this process, if at all, as a dialectic of
ideas tend to make value other-worldly.

Value, in fact, stamps an object as what Marx calls a 'social
hieroglyphic' and it can only be deciphered by reference to the
productive relationships of a commodity-exchanging society.  Value
is the language of men's economic intercourse with each other and
has for its subject the constructive changes effected in the world
by their associative efforts — just as factual propositions are
the language of men's scientific communications about the nature
of the world as presented.  All language is a social product and
must be accounted for ultimately in terms of the type of society
in which it functions.  The language of value has the peculiar
characteristics we have noted because in our own kind of society
it reminds us, however indirectly, that everything we call 'good'
in a prescriptive sense is the result of human activity.  It is
the means whereby tribute is paid to man's productive labour.


THE RELATION BETWEEN VALUE AND UTILITY

It has been shown how the descriptive and prescriptive senses of
'good' are an ideological reflection of the distinction within a
commodity between utility and value, a distinction resulting from
the division of labour which gives rise to commodity-exchanging
societies.  In order to show how these two senses of 'good' are
related to each other, it is necessary to trace the kind of
relationship that obtains between the commodity as an object of
use and the commodity as a value-bearing object.

The economic law of value derives the worth of commodities from
the labour incorporated in them and thus fixes their values in
terms of the relation of each to all others.  How then does this
law relate the value of these commodities to human needs?  What,
in other words, is the connecting link between things exchangeable
at determinate ratios and people who bring to the market their
personal demands for satisfaction?

Now this is to approach from the opposite direction the problem
Marx describes as confronting the possessor of capital who wishes
to make a profit from the buying and selling of commodities.  In
conditions of free competition any trade in commodities whose value
relationships are fixed by the amount of incorporated labour will
always leave him right where he started.  He is really looking for
a special kind of commodity whose usefulness consists in its being
value-creative.  Since only human labour can create value, his
requirement is met by the appearance on the market, as a commodity,

of the labour-power of free workers — free in the double sense
that they can dispose of their labour-power at will and that they
have been 'freed' of anything else to dispose of.

We are looking for a human relationship which by taking the form
of commodity exchange will reveal the connection between utility
and value, the link between what men want and the worth of their
efforts in making things.  And this relationship is, of course, that
same contract between the purchaser of labour-power and the labourer
himself who thus turns his own capacity to work into a commodity.
The value of labour-power is determined, like that of every other
commodity, by the labour time necessary for its production, which
is only to say that the value of labour-power is the value of the
means of subsistence required for the labourer to maintain and
reproduce himself.  The means of subsistence are simply commodities
whose utility sustains the labourer and his family and whose value
expresses the worth of his labour-power.  It is therefore through
the act of exchange whereby a human quality, labour-power, becomes
a commodity among commodities that the law of value establishes a
causal relationship between work done and needs which can be satisfied.  It is because so much labour-power has been sold that an
equivalent amount of goods can be acquired for use.

The appearance on the market of labour-power as a commodity is
the basic social fact of the capitalist system and the key to
understanding how, in human terms, that system works.

The historical conditions of capitalism's existence are by
no means given by the mere circulation of money and commodities.
It can spring into being only when the owner of the means of
production and subsistence meets in the market with the free
labourer selling his labour-power.  And this one historical
condition comprises a world's history.  Capital, therefore,
announces from its first appearance a new epoch in the process
of social production.(6)

The alienation of the worker's capacity to produce value so that
it can be bought by the capitalist who thereby acquires the products
the worker makes is the relationship Marx explores so penetratingly
in the 'Economic and Philosophic Manuscripts of 1844', showing how
alienated labour on the workers' side is private property on the
capitalists' side.  The worker who once owned his own tools becomes
himself a tool in the hands of the capitalist and, having fulfilled
his work contract, buys back for his own use that portion of the
product which is the accepted equivalent of the labour-power he has
sold.

While the law of value of which this transaction is an expression relates acquired satisfactions to work done, it by no means
equates human labour and the reward which might be considered its
due.  The law of value in no way prevents the dealer in labour-
power who is the dominant partner in all labour contracts through
his possession, as property, of the means of production, which is
simply past alienated labour, from exacting value-creative work
beyond the worth of the labourer's own needs.  Although an employer
only pays for labour-power, a commodity with a fixed market rate,
he acquires the use of labour itself, the creative source of all
values whatsoever.

That portion of the labourer's output produced in working beyond

the time necessary for supplying the substance of his personal
needs Marx calls surplus-value which, as a result of the labourer's
alienation of his value-creative capacity in the contract he makes
with an employer, becomes the property of the employer.  In his
definition of the value of labour-power Marx does not accept the
'iron law of wages' theory whereby this value can never rise above
a bare subsistence level.  'The number and extent of the labourer's
so-called necessary wants, as also the modes of satisfying them,
are themselves the product of historical development, and depend
therefore to a great extent on the degree of civilisation of a
country.'(7)  The law of value does not fix the precise amount of
goods a worker receives in terms of what will barely keep him
alive any more than it fixes the exact price of goods in terms of
their incorporated labour:  it establishes the area in which wages
and prices can move without breaking the relations of production
which make the capitalist system what it is.

Nor does the law of value, as we shall see, prevent such cancerous
growths in capitalist society as commodity fetishism, money idolatry
or profit as an end in itself, which are all expressions for the
way the alienated labour of the worker changes, under control of
the capitalist, into a hostile thing standing over against its
original creator.  For our present purpose, the law of value simply
provides a clue by means of rough equivalents to the way alienated
labour, or value, passes through various transformations in
commodity-exchanging societies from production through distribution
to consumption, thus serving as a link between the socially sundered
operations of making things and enjoying them.  The value form
commodities assume as 'congealed abstract labour' can be compared
to a kind of deep freeze into which all utilisable goods pass,
with the guarantee that what the members of a commodity-producing
society take out bears a socially determined, but by no means
necessarily equitable, relationship to what they respectively put in.

It has been shown that the difference between naturalistic and
non-naturalistic interpretations of a value word like 'good', the
distinction between 'good' as a description of usefulness and 'good'
as a prescriptive evaluation, is rooted in the material conditions
of life in a society based on a market economy and reflects the
social division of labour which gives rise to such societies.  We
are now in a position to see how the economic law of value which
governs exchanges in societies of this type can help us to understand
the nature of value judgments in general.

If this law has the economic function of relating the utility
of commodities to their value, and if the two different senses of
'good' are grounded in the double nature of commodities, then it is
reasonable to argue that value judgments have the logical role of
indicating the connection between the descriptive and prescriptive uses of value words.  By referring to the labour of adapting
things for use and also to the enjoyment of using these things, such
judgments enable us to weigh the objective cost in human effort of
our subjective preferences.  They give us in highly abridged form
the history in human terms of any object presented for our appreciation.

Value judgments, in effect, restore us momentarily to a pre-
commodity situation in which the active labour of making or

acquiring something and the passively-felt desire for it are still united in a single comprehensive reflex. 'This is a good watch' thus means not only that it has certain qualities such as accuracy and compactness which can make anyone requiring a time-piece regard it favourably, but also that a person ought to admire its craftsmanship, to respect the knowledge, implicit in its manufacture and to imagine retrospectively the human effort and skill it represents — all in selecting it or recommending it to others as an object of choice.

It may seem strange that value judgments could perform such a task without our being altogether aware of it each time we attribute 'goodness' to something; but then the economic law of value itself, operating as a characteristic of objects, as an exchange ratio of commodities, appears to men not as the rule of their own isolated acts but as an external necessity inherent in the nature of things. This same false consciousness engendered by commodity exchange which transforms social relations into relations between things both creates the logical need for value judgments and obscures their true function. In a social order where, as a result of the alienation of human labour, things arrogate to themselves the kind of relationships which can only really pertain to persons we need to be reminded, however obliquely, of the connection between useful objects and the human effort embodied in them. This value judgments do, thus making the act of choice, in the highly complicated circumstances of commodity-exchanging society, rational.

Economic value can only be understood in terms of the buying and selling of labour-power. Value judgments in general must also be considered in conjunction with the way work is performed and paid for in society, since every evaluative use of a word like 'good' is ultimately an appreciation of someone's labour or skill.

In the context of class-divided society the economic law of value, by revealing a huge discrepancy between contributed labour and distributed satisfactions, lays bare the fact of surplus-value. This is the levy the class in control of the means of production, which are simply the objectified form in the present of labour-power purchased in the past, exacts from the class owning nothing but its capacity to work.

Once the true function of value judgments is grasped, it may be seen that they, too, are not silent on the scandal of this exploitation which hides behind commodity operations. Indeed, some philosophers, in glossing over this sort of depredation by the class which having also bought their mental labours on the market they feel subservient to and in resenting the verbal tribute they pay to the class of workers whenever they make a value judgment, may be suspected of a certain disingenuousness in cloaking the whole subject of value in a pall of obscurantism.

## OBJECTIONS TO THE LABOUR THEORY OF VALUE

As corroboration of the argument that value judgments are closely related in function to the economic law of value, it can be pointed out that the attempts of certain philosophers to empty the concept

of 'value' of any real meaning and the attempts of certain political economists to refute the 'labour theory of value' follow
precisely similar lines.  It can hardly be a coincidence that in the
same place and at the same time the Viennese Circle of logical
positivists and the Austrian marginal utility school of economists
were endeavouring to explain away value in either an ethical or an
economic sense.  This intellectual task seemed socially necessary
because any realistic account of value risked calling attention to
surplus-value and the way in which it was disposed.  The task was
carried out by deducing from the tendency toward atomisation in
capitalist society, of which these intellectuals are both masters
and victims, a philosophy of extreme individualism and then using
this assumption of discrete, individualistic egoism to deny objectivity to a social product like value.  Since knowledge itself is a
social product, it, too, was robbed of objectivity by the same mental
process;  but that was not considered an excessive price to pay for
sterilising value by making it purely subjective.

In general, attacks  by the apologists of capitalism on the labour
theory of value as developed by Marx have taken the form of mis-
representing him in order to refute him.  By pretending that Marx
refined and developed the theory in order to account for individual
prices instead of, as was actually the case, using it to explain
the fundamental dynamism of the whole economic process of capitalism, they can claim to have caught Marx out when, later on, as a
detail in the overall structure, he gives a price of production
analysis its due place.  And this price of production itself is
based on the original formulation of the theory of value since the
element of profit depends on the difference between the value of
labour-power and the value of finished commodities, involving, of
course, the appropriation of surplus-value.

The analysis of a particular mode of production in 'Capital' sets
before us a working model of a whole society with all its inter-
locking relationships.  In constructing this model abstracted from
reality, Marx begins with a world in which there are goods which
have been adapted or created for human use.  All these goods represent the labour and ingenuity which men have expended in transforming their natural environment into a better-stocked and more
suitable home for themselves and their descendants.  Value is the
measure of this effort and serves the economic purpose of enabling
us in a commodity-producing society to trade very different things
against each other in terms of the human effort they incorporate;
and, generally speaking, the prices of these things are proportional
to the amount of labour-time required at a particular stage of
social development to produce and distribute them.  The very distortions resulting from natural or man-made scarcities imply a
basic standard from which prices can temporarily depart.  Value
also serves the ethical purpose of reminding us, each time we judge
some article useful and worth acquiring, of what we owe to the
activity and skill of fellow human beings.

But the equivalence which value establishes among different
things in terms of incorporated labour and between these things
collectively and the claims on them those who created them are
entitled to make also reveals the social fact that another class
of people, whose ownership or control of the means of production

enables them to traffic in labour-power, enjoy material wealth and political power far beyond any contribution in energy or skill which they have made to the production of goods.

This broad picture of capitalist society with all its ethical implications is not challenged by pointing out limitations on the labour theory of value as a means of predicting what a feather boa will cost in three months' time.  Objections usually take the form of setting forth difficulties in computing labour-time as an exact measurement, involving such problems as distinguishing between productive and non-productive or skilled and unskilled labour, as differentiating between hours actually spent on a job and socially necessary labour-time, or as separating labour expended over a given period from the value given up in the same period by capital goods in which labour has been embodied in the past.  All these difficulties arise in connection with misapplying the theory to try to determine the price of a specific article instead of using it to provide an explanation of the approximate price-relationships over the whole range of goods — relationships which may fluctuate with changes in productivity but can only be accounted for in any given period by the labour theory of value operating with the social norms of productive work relevant to that time.

Critics of Marx's objective theory of value may bring an enormous subtlety to bear on questions of consumption;  but by practically ignoring production except as an investment possibility, they can profess to find no need for any principle which links the two together and accounts for the eventual distribution of goods in terms of the values they acquire in being produced.  Marxists would not object to the use of a marginal utility calculus as an adjunct to planning, in societies where planning is in fact possible;  but they would rightly deny that any mere description of propensities to consume could obviate the need for a theory of value.  The tendency of latter day economists in the capitalist world to combine a cunning analysis of the superficial aspect of things with an obstinate, or perhaps terrified, refusal to look beneath the surface may be compared with the philosophy of phenomenalism.  Just as phenomenalists ultimately reduce the whole science of reality to certain pointer readings, so the marginal utility school finds the only significance of the economic process in price movements.  The only reforms which could be envisaged on such a superficial reading of social organisation would be very minor schemes of redistribution.

Ideological motivation in terms of class interest is often no more conscious than the rationalisations of behaviour offered by a patient on a couch;  but this is not always the case.  In the early stages of the attack on the classical school of political economy from which Marx had taken and further developed certain basic concepts, writers on economics like Boehm-Bawerk were quite open in admitting that they were inspired to denounce the labour theory of value by their dislike of socialism.  Philosophers approaching the question of value in general have occasionally been as frank.  W.D. Lamont, for example, in 'The Value Judgement' appreciates the relevance of economic analysis to the whole problem of value but in accepting the utility theory of the supply-and-demand school he can only give a superficial account of the

value judgment as forward-looking, not backward-looking, and as
therefore having nothing to do with past effort but only with
future utility.   This we can now recognise as an expression of the
consumption bias of those who assume unquestioningly an automatic
flow of commodities on which they can confer 'value' simply by
deigning to consume them.


VALUE AND THE MARXIST THEORY OF KNOWLEDGE

We have already noted that theories of value and theories of knowledge do not belong to separate mental compartments and that
adopting any particular form of the one has implications for the
other.   The problem of the relationship between prescriptive and
descriptive sentences proves in fact to be a question of the
epistemological accommodation of value judgments.   We have seen
that empiricism in general finds it impossible to account for
evaluation without either explaining it away or committing the
naturalistic fallacy.   The various schools of idealism, on the
other hand, appear to do more justice to concepts like 'value' but
at the expense of an acceptably simple explanation of factual
knowledge.   How does the Marxist theory of value fare in respect to
its own theory of knowledge?
    As has been shown Marxism maintains an objective theory of
value which, somewhat like the intuitionists, takes certain non-
natural qualities of a thing as the subject of value judgments
while, at the same time, its materialist approach to the problem
of knowledge seems closer to the empiricists.   How is this logically
possible?   It will be remembered that in Marx's analysis of a
commodity he shows that it has both utility and value but that these
two aspects are mutually exclusive and can only qualify an article
successively.   This characteristic of commodities is grounded in
the dialectical nature of change in general and of the productive
process in particular.   Marxist epistemology, being grounded in
these material conditions, is itself dialectical and can therefore
accommodate both prescriptive and descriptive sentences which are
related to each other in much the same way as the value and
utility of a commodity.
    Indeed the production of valid knowledge exactly reflects in its
phases the production and distribution of valuable goods.   The
making of a thing within the natural limitations imposed by the
qualities of the raw material and the skill of the maker is like
physical perception;   the stripping of the object of its particu-
larity to appear on the market as a mere quantification of value is
like the process of thinking in abstract terms whereby new relationships are discovered;   and the re-acquisition of the commodity
to satisfy human needs is like putting ideas and theories arrived
at abstractly back into the world to be tested and proved right or
wrong in social practice.
    Statements may be distinguished according to which of the three
moments in the process of knowledge they belong to.   Those belonging
to the first phase correspond to the natural environment they
immediately reflect;   those in the second, abstracted from the
first, cohere logically among themselves;   and the whole process

is finally verified by virtue of the fact that the third phase
simply is the practical reapplication of duly deliberated sense
impressions.  Lenin makes the point that idealism is one phase of
the process of knowledge and only becomes absurd as a movement of
thought out of this context.

Philosophical idealism is only nonsense from the standpoint of
crude, simple, metaphysical materialism.  From the standpoint
of dialectical materialism, on the other hand, philosophical
idealism is a one-sided, exaggerated development of one of the
features, aspects, facets of knowledge into an absolute,
divorced from matter, from nature, apotheosised.(8)

And Mao Tsetung in 'On Practice' sets out the whole process with
his usual clarity:

The first step in the process of knowledge is contact with the
things of the external world;  this belongs to the stage of
perception.  The second step is a synthesis of the data of perception by making a rearrangement or a reconstruction;  this
belongs to the stage of conception, judgment and inference....
But the process of knowledge does not end here.... The third
step is the practical application of theoretic conclusions.(9)

The mass line, 'from the people, to the people', which we will have
occasion to refer to often is simply this same Marxist theory of
knowledge applied to social practice.

Take the ideas of the masses (scattered and unsystematic ideas)
and concentrate them (through study turn them into concentrated
and systematic ideas) then go to the masses and propagate and
explain these ideas until the masses embrace them as their own,
hold fast to them and translate them into action, and test the
correctness of these ideas in action.(10)

Statements belonging to different moments in the process of
knowledge cannot simply be resolved into each other — any more
than a plant, say, can be at once seed, flower and fruit;  but
though distinguishable these various types of statement are yet
related to each other in the total act of knowledge.  Empirical
propositions are based on sense impressions;  but reasoning cannot
work with these particular impressions as such.  It requires concepts
which are abstracted from the facts of sensuous experience:  even
to compare two objects it needs universals like 'roundness' or
'hardness' which are not mere passive reflections of anything in
nature.  The great act of human abstraction by which men projected
value in the form of a circulating currency about the fifth
century B.C. in Greece, India and China stimulated a vast upsurge
of philosophical thinking in those places, beginning with the proto-
scientific search for a substance which could be the ultimate source
of all natural objects on the analogy of money which can manifest
itself in the form of all man-made objects and then going on to a
proto-sociological concern with the relations of men in society
prompted by the effects of the disruption of old tribal forms of
organisation by new class distinctions.  And after the combination
of abstract ideas in inferential judgments which remain arbitrary
constructs till tested comes verification in social practice,
theories and hypotheses validated by new sense impressions which
they lead us to expect.

Descriptive sentences, in which 'good' appears as an adjective qualifying either the object to be enjoyed or the psychological state of the enjoying subject, are perceptual propositions belonging to the first moment of thought.  Prescriptive sentences, in which 'good' has an evaluative force, draw upon insights from the second or speculative moment to become injunctions belonging to the third or practical moment.  In this dialectical account theory and practice are not separated and therefore the link between theoretical propositions of suitability and the practical imperatives implicit in value judgments is always there to be discovered by peering beneath the superficial phenomena of commodity exchange.

## HUMAN VALUE AND CAPITALIST DISVALUE

Value of course is not only the measure of physical effort resulting in the production of objective goods, though that is its most patent form.  The mental effort which produces a new type of tool or a useful scientific formula is also measurable in terms of values of an intellectual order.  Those forms of human activity which have become more and more detached from the actual productive process — song, dance and music, the graphic arts and ultimately literature — are all extensions of the basic equivalence between human effort and valuable goods.  The very mental and spiritual climate we breathe is as rich an atmosphere of man's imaginative creations as the cities in which we dwell are vast memorials of his physical labours.  Ours is a world full of value, material, mental and spiritual, which our fellow men, past and present, have put there by their exertion over the whole field of human endeavour.

The recognition and appreciation of value and the desire to contribute to that store of value in the world are the characteristics of civilised human beings.  That is why in socialist countries like China and Albania all young people are expected to labour at hard physical tasks in factory and field, so that they can learn through sweat and tired muscles that fundamental equation between work done and goods produced in which all values are grounded.  That is why those citizens whose service takes them into offices, lecture halls, laboratories or libraries also spend one month a year at manual tasks to reaffirm the basic physical comradeship of all who labour together with their hands for the general good.

With this attitude can be contrasted the early efforts to enforce the division of labour and to defend the institution of slavery by regarding all physical labour as utterly contemptible and those who performed it so depraved as to deserve no better fate.  It must have required the same sort of continuous pressure over a considerable time to win people over to this view of manual work as had been required to make them observe interdictions of use on consumable goods so that they could appear in the market for exchange.  Plato puts a taboo on all such labour as far as free men are concerned and strongly admonishes any citizen who should stray from the path of virtue by soiling his hands in hard work. Platonic values are completely detached from anything so degraded as physical effort and become the abstract universals with which the mind works in the second phase of the process of knowledge where, for Plato, all understanding is arrested in eternal con-

templation of the ideal.  A priorism is the philosophical device
for justifying the division of labour by showing that some men are
naturally endowed with the intellectual qualities to control and
direct while others are born to be society's slaves — a kind of
service performed for the ruling class today by such 'thinkers' as
the Eysencks and Jensens and in the past by those like Carlyle
whom Marx explicitly condemned for treating historically-created
class differences as eternally ordained natural differences people
were supposed to 'recognise and revere by bowing before the wise
and noble ones in a cult of genius.'  In socialist China an ideological campaign has been waged by the people against this kind of
vicious idealism by attacking the reactionary views of Confucius,
Plato's approximate contemporary, who also supported a caste
society based on slavery and was opposed by relatively progressive
'legalists' who, like the 'sophists', have usually been presented in
a bad light because of the influence down the ages Plato and Confucius have enjoyed as useful to successive ruling classes.

In commodity-exchanging societies, of which capitalist countries
are the final and most extreme cases, mental and spiritual values,
productions of the intellect and creative imagination, are themselves commodities.  Designers, inventors and artists sell their
skill in exactly the same way as workers sell their labour-power,
and in the same way what they produce is determined by what is
profitable to the purchaser of their talent, not by what might be
useful and inspiring to the public.  Even such a value as justice,
created out of the struggle and sacrifice of countless martyrs in
the past, is a commodity which has to be bought and paid for.

To appreciate what has happened to value and our understanding
of it in present-day capitalist society we have to look at the
basic presuppositions of capitalism as a mode of production influencing the whole way of life of a vast, though fortunately
shrinking, proportion of the world's population.  The 'ethics' of
capitalism have been succinctly stated by Adam Smith when he writes:

> It is not from the benevolence of the butcher, the brewer or
> the baker that we expect our dinner, but from their regard to
> their own interest.  We address ourselves not to their humanity
> but to their self-love, and never talk to them of our own
> necessities but of their advantage.(11)

Individual self-interest is, then, the key to the motivation of the
system.  It can be compared with the popular exhortation of the
socialist proletarian cultural revolution in China:  'Fight self-
interest.  Proceed in all cases from the interests of the people
and not from one's self-interest or from the interests of a small
group.'

In theory the principle of bourgeois morality, individual selfishness, was supposed to work in such a way that all the individual
wills selfishly competing with each other would cancel out for the
general good.  In theory the capitalists in the course of seeking
their own private profit would incidentally feed, clothe and house
all those who worked for them and in this way an acceptable relationship between values produced and goods consumed would be maintained without interfering with reasonable exploitation.  In fact
the idea that the capitalist system could dispense with morality
and that its more or less equitable functioning could be a by-product

of a profit-motivated market economy is a colossal and tragic
example of the naturalistic fallacy on a world-wide scale.

It was the same presupposition in the Soviet Union after 1953
that the further development of socialist man could be the automatic by-product of a system dispensing with morality and increasingly depending on material incentives which led to the collapse
of socialism and the restoration of capitalism.  Revisionism which
is simply bourgeois economics and social attitudes disguised as
Marxism incorporated the same fallacy of a de-valued 'ethics'.  The
fight against self-interest and revisionism is the form class
struggle has to take during the whole transitional period of
socialism.

Not only is it impossible to reconcile the profit-seeking of the
few with the general good of the many, it is not even possible to
reconcile it with a moderately orderly economy having a reasonably
constant rate of growth.  The contradictions generated by the clash
of interests between the wealthy few and the propertyless millions,
whether in the under-industrialised countries or in the very heart-
lands of economic imperialism, have become more violently disrup-
tive, and the passing of whole areas out of the capitalist orbit
altogether has enormously exacerbated those conflicts.  Without
considering such contradictions in any detail it can be said that
they manifest themselves as distortions due to erratic and uneven
development which prevent the law of value from functioning effectively in maintaining a balance either between different kinds of
production, like consumer goods and goods to promote the further
growth of production, or between the employment of value-creative
labour at its market price and the effective market demand for goods
which have been produced.  This results in a disastrous decline in
the economy as a whole till it has sunk to a more primitive level
at which the law of value can come into proper play again.  Much
heralded non-Marxist solutions to these contradictions, like the
Keynesian answer to the problem of under-consumption by deficit
financing, pump-priming and so forth, have merely led to other
contradictions even more intractable, like world-wide inflation —
not but that a considerable degree of inflation, depreciating wages
in the worker's pocket and appreciating the capitalist's property,
suits the ruling class very well.

Since 'value' as having both an economic and an ethical meaning
serves as a middle term relating the material base of society to its
ideas of morality, we can describe this malfunctioning of the law of
value in moral language.  The critical economic dislocations to
which capitalism is prone amount, ethically speaking, to a growing
disjunction between the efforts of those whose work is value-
creative and the goods they can expect or even the respect they
enjoy.  Honest toil and skilled craftsmanship lose their value in
the quite practical sense that they are inadequately rewarded and
may well be denied any opportunity for employment at all.  In a
society where this disjunction has occurred there is, to begin
with, a diminishing correlation between social merit and economic
recompense;  and, eventually, at a more advanced stage of deterioration, there is even a negative correlation.  Not only does
genuinely constructive work in any particular field cease to
receive its due acknowledgment but a monetary premium is placed on

the most anti-social forms of activity.  The dignity of human
labour is mocked when it is so obviously the parasitical and
destructive elements which flourish under a system increasingly
characterised by waste and speculation and activated by appeals to
people's basest motives.

Even if it were possible for the capitalist system to function in
such a manner that there was a fairer share-out of goods among those
whose efforts are value-creative, it would not meet the real point
of the Marxist social critique.  It is not simply distribution which
is defective but production itself — the very process by which men
objectify themselves in commodities that do not belong to them,
that are directly determined neither in quantity nor quality by
men's real needs, that stand over against their creators as an
alien world of things obeying laws of profit which are utterly
irrelevant to the well-being of those who actually made them.
Instead of profit serving as a stimulus to the production of the
things society needs, it becomes openly what it always was in
intention — an end in itself on which human beings are perpetually
sacrificed.  Instead of prices serving as guides to economic
decision, price maintenance becomes an absolute to be achieved by
ruthlessly destroying crops in a world where half the population is
undernourished.

The split between duty and pleasure, between work and enjoyment
which is itself a consequence of commoditisation has the effect of
freeing desires from any natural context to be played upon by
advertising and sales campaigns so that demands can be artificially
created for goods which are profitable.  Unable to absorb the
values it is technically capable of producing capitalism finds it
profitable to divert human effort into the production of shoddy,
ephemeral and harmful objects, thus wasting man's natural heritage
to fill the world with things to which the name 'goods' can only be
applied in irony — the production not of value but disvalue.
Criminal waste of this kind cannot but be reflected in a moral
crisis as grave as the economic.  All those implicated in preserving such a system inevitably tend, in Oscar Wilde's phrase, to
know the price of everything and the value of nothing.  The ultimate example of this perversion of man's productive ability was the
search by the major imperialist power after the Second World War for
a commodity whose only utility would be the massive destruction
of human life while leaving property intact.

The full development of commodity exchange under capitalism by
which human relationships become more and more a function of things,
leads in time to the dehumanisation of whole societies.  In no other
way can we account for the cruel barbarities of those capitalist
countries most industrially advanced.  A system which begins with
the robbery of surplus-value, cloaked behind a deal in commoditised
labour, goes on to loot and massacre on a world-wide scale, often
hiding such crimes behind movements in world prices.  Have so many
hundreds of thousands of people died of starvation in this or that
part of the world which depends on the sale of raw materials?  The
terms of trade have moved against them, that is all.  It is like
being able to commit mass murder by pushing a button rather than
having to hack people to pieces with a sword.  Piles of human hair
in extermination centres, preserved for some possible economic use,

are the final monument of a system which turns people into commodities to profit from them.

It is in connection with value and its distortion and degradation under capitalism that the basic impulse to overthrow the
system is born — whether it is a question of the personal and
particular injustices suffered by a man and his fellows or of the
general demoralisation and corruption over the whole contemporary
scene.  Any professed love of humanity which is not accompanied
by a hatred in one's very bowels of this vicious, dehumanising
system is pure humbug.

# Chapter 2

# RIGHTS-THE MEANING OF NORMATIVE JUDGMENTS

INTRODUCTION

As was demonstrated in the previous chapter the meaning of 'good'
as it appears in value judgments is ultimately derived from an
analysis of the specific goods men produce.  This meaning, bound
up as it is with certain relations of production, can only be
understood in the context of definite forms of social existence;
but since the production of goods for exchange is as old as, and
not unconnected with, the keeping of written records, the word
'good' with approximately the same intention has a very wide
historical extension.

   In the present section we shall be considering the meaning of
'right' as it appears in such normative judgments as 'It is right
to keep one's word' or 'He has a right to it because he paid for
it'.  This meaning, too, has to be deduced from specific rights
which are grounded in the material conditions of life in this or
that type of society.  As a completely abstract term which applied
everywhere at all times 'right', like other ethical expressions,
would prove in fact to apply nowhere and at no time.  It could
only maintain the absolute purity of so universal a nature by never
suffering the violation of getting involved in any concrete situation.  Morality, on this interpretation of its terms, instead of
being practical would become a matter of ideal contemplation, a
Platonic obsession with universal forms.  And yet if concepts like
'right' were not to some extent abstractions, thought could make
no use of them.  Therefore, in the course of investigating what
'right' means we shall also try to discover how such a concept
could have arisen as a relatively detached idea.

   Rights represent claims and they can take the form of claims on
other people or claims to things.  Whenever we say that it is 'right'
to do this or that, we are recognising the legitimacy of some claim
on us.  'It is right to help a friend in need' implies a respect
for a claim he has on us by virtue of that relationship.  'It is
right to return a lost article to its owner' implies a respect for
his claim to possession.  This respect for claims, this respect for
their legitimacy is our acknowledgment of the element of universality in the concept of 'right' by which every admitted claim

involves certain things it is right for people to do, not ex-
cluding ourselves.  Expressions like 'might is right' or 'possession is what counts' describe a situation in which the idea of
respect for claims is missing.  Mere descriptions of what people
do cannot be universalised into what they ought to do;  and in
themselves they invest the concept of 'right' with no ethical
significance.

RIGHTS AS CLAIMS ON OTHER PEOPLE

Recognised claims on others are based on certain social relationships linking people together in a particular type of society.
There are considerations which children owe to parents and parents
to children which must be taken into account in assessing the
actions they respectively perform;  the marriage tie and the bond
of friendship carry with them the idea of mutual claims whose
recognition is the real meaning of such relations;  and membership
in a community involves a whole complex of reciprocal rights.
    If these relationships were eternal and unchanging, the concept
of 'right' as deduced from them would have the universal quality
sometimes ascribed to it.  In fact, looked at historically or,
for that matter, geographically, such relationships are seen to
vary considerably at different times and places.  Recognised
claims of parents on children and on each other can hardly be the
same in patriarchal as in matriarchal communities which owe their
difference originally to whether the provision of food is predominantly a wide-ranging pursuit like hunting or keeping cattle
or a more home-based activity like primitive agriculture.  The
bonds of friendship which in a feudal context can involve loyalty
unto death may only imply a special concern for promise-keeping
in a contractual society like ours.  Robbery under certain circumstances, like 'lifting' another tribe's cattle, may be considered
a social duty while in another type of society it is a crime to
steal a loaf of bread to feed starving children.  And even
according to the same legal code, gambling on the street for
pennies may be an indictable offence while gambling in commodities
for millions is highly respectable.  And the whole range of social
relationships may be quite rapidly transformed by the changes in
circumstances which accompany a change in class relations like the
English revolution which paved the way for the development of
modern Britain.
    Since generally conceded claims depend on social relationships
and since these relationships are determined by the material conditions of life in various societies, 'rights' as what people are
entitled to expect from each other are ultimately grounded on the
economic base which supports this or that form of social organisation.  We cannot say that there is some essential and unchanging
meaning of 'rightness' to which all particular expressions of it in
concrete circumstances are irrelevant.  It simply does not make
ethical sense to say:  'You must do what is right, and it does not
make any difference what it may be right for you to do.'  In fact,
where 'right' had no specific content, non-ethical considerations
like 'might is right', would inevitably fill the vacuum.

It might be thought that family relationships which are bound up with the reproduction of human beings common to all society would be distinguishable from those relationships which are involved in the production of goods for human use.  Actually, variations in the forms of inheritance and the status of women, to say nothing of the nature of family life in conditions of slavery, show that family relationships are only a special instance of the general quality of social intercourse which echoes a particular mode of production.

From our original thesis that  the social existence of men determines their consciousness, we can deduce the fact that religious and philosophical ideas also reflect the basic economic structure of society;  and social relationships and the rights implicit in them are then accounted for in terms of these ideas. This ideological supervention can obscure the connection between such relationships and the material conditions of life which gave rise to them.

As Marx puts it in 'The German Ideology':

Men are the producers of their conceptions, ideas (expressed in the language of politics, laws, morality, religion, meta-physics of a people) — real, active men, as they are conditioned by a definite development of their productive forces and of the intercourse corresponding to these, up to its furthest forms. Consciousness can never be anything else than conscious existence and the existence of men is their actual life process.  If in all ideology men and their circumstances appear upside down as in a 'camera obscura', this phenomenon arises just as much from their historical life-process as the inversion of objects on the retina does from their physical life-process.... As soon as this active life-process is described, history ceases to be a collection of dead facts as it is with the empiricists (facts themselves still abstract), or an imagined activity of imagined subjects, as with the idealists.(1)

In our historical studies we often see the influence of economic considerations on the conduct of some social group when its members were quite unaware of it at the time.  To the question 'Why is it right to bear arms in the service of my lord?' a vassal in the Middle Ages would have answered:  'Because God commands me to honour and obey my liege.'  We realise of course that such service was inherent in a social organisation based on a particular system of land tenure when land was the only form of wealth — though we may not always realise that the same applies to our explanations of our own actions.

These social relationships usually reveal their economic origin by finding their most practical expression in some form of the disposition of property — rights of inheritance, succession to titles and so forth.  Rules of conduct in different societies are much concerned with such questions as what recompense in goods a man can expect for some injury to him or what rights a man has in the possessions of relatives or how a man must set about acquiring a wife where women themselves are regarded as property.  An analysis of property can therefore help us to appreciate the derivation and meaning of the concept of 'right'.

RIGHTS AS CLAIMS TO THINGS

We have seen how the concept of 'value' arises in connection with
the production of goods for human use.  The concept of 'right', in
so far as it is grounded in a respect for other people's proprietary interests, arises in connection with the distribution of
those goods.  All value is the result of the expenditure of human
effort.  That effort, at the same time that it creates valuable
things, also establishes rights in them.  As Locke puts it:
'Whatever a man removes from the state of nature and mixes his
labour with, thus joining it to something that is his own, thereby
becomes his property.'(2)
    This simple formula seems obvious enough in the case of an
individual working on his own to satisfy his personal needs and
those of his family.  It could be extended to cover a self-
sufficient tribal group which provides for the immediate wants
of its members on a communal basis by directly-associated labour.
But in such cases there is no problem about the ownership of
property and therefore the question of 'rights' in the abstract
could hardly arise.  It is only at a socially advanced stage of
the division of labour that property rights become a distinguishable aspect of human relationships, since, as Marx explains:
    The various stages of development in the division of labour are
    just so many different forms of property;  and the stage reached
    in the division of labour also determines the relations of
    individuals to one another with respect to the materials,
    instruments and products of labour.(3)
The attempt to find some development in the material conditions of
life which could account for the precipitation of the idea of
property rights as a relatively detached abstraction leads us to
consider that stage of the division of labour when there are the
beginnings of a market economy.
    The law of value only makes its appearance as a distinguishable
relationship when the separation between production and consumption
has been confirmed in commodity exchange.  Similarly, the concept
of 'right' as a recognised claim to the possession of things only
takes the form of an abstract principle when all property has begun
to assume the character of commodities.  As we have already noted,
prior to the development of commodity production, rights in things
can be defined in terms of obvious social relationships, like those
obtaining between members of a family or tribe or, even, between
masters and slaves or lords and serfs.  The customary rules regulating the disposition of property within social organisations in
which relations of productions are recognisably human relations are
quite simple and transparent as compared with the distribution of
goods in the complex market economy which attains its fullest
development under capitalism.  Such pre-commodity rules cannot
themselves give rise to an abstract bourgeois conception of 'right'
as an eternal principle obtaining at all times and places because
those rules are too closely tied to specific human relationships
in societies still founded upon 'the immature development of
man individually, who has not yet severed the umbilical cord that
unites him with his fellow men in a primitive tribal community or
upon direct relations of subjection.'(4)  But once the domination

of one class of men by another ceases to appear as naked subjection and becomes the law of private property by which the position of the dominant class is established through ownership of the means of production, once the transaction between the hirer and the provider of labour-power takes a purely economic form as a commodity deal, there is a change from possession of things dominated by human relationships to human relationships dominated by possession of things and 'right' itself, losing its exclusive reference to claims between man and man, becomes more and more objectified as a stake in commodities, the golden calf to which all must bow. Just as relations between producers mutually engaged in creative work take the form of an equivalence between things themselves, so other social relationships express themselves through rights to things — from the international speculator who exerts a completely careless and arbitrary control over the lives of millions through his control of things to the ordinary householder who once a year sums up all his close relationships by the relative price of the gift he estimates each is worth.

In the early stages of commodity exchange, when direct human relationships reflecting the material conditions of simpler types of society are in the process of being transformed into functions of a market economy, rules of conduct may still be borrowed from previous forms of social organisation to regulate trading operations. Hybrid notions like the 'just price' or arbitrary injunctions against usury or profiteering are characteristic of this phase of social development. But once commodity production has attained its fullest growth and exchange relationships have extended into every sphere of society, the economic system appears to be self-regulating and to require no correction nor guidance from normative principles formulated in pre-commodity terms. Instead of invoking ideas of human relations derived from membership in earlier societies as a check on market deals, those very relations are conceived solely on the basis of men's encounters with each other in the market place as buyers or sellers of goods and as buyers or sellers of the capacity to produce goods.

This freeing of the concept of 'right' from any immediate reference to interpersonal ties to reappear as proprietary relationships to things makes it sufficiently abstract to be codified in civil laws which seem to have an impartial universality for whole societies and even for mankind in general. When such legalised rights come into conflict with rights which are still bound up with more direct relationships, as when mother and son go to court over a will, husband and wife fall out over the question of their joint property or a man sues a friend for non-payment of debt, the human quality of the relationship is utterly irrelevant to what is regarded as a purely contractual problem.

Since sellers of labour-power and owners of the means of production are assumed to meet freely in the market place to strike a bargain whose terms are largely determined by an impersonal law of value, the agreement between them can be generalised abstractly as exemplifying one of the basic rights of man, the prerogative of every member of society to exchange his goods or his capacity for producing them on an equitable footing. The very translation of human bonds into terms of that commodity of commodities, money, so that no one need acknowledge any other master, can seem, by comparison with various forms of direct subjugation, to be a kind of individual liberation, like a slave buying his own freedom — as long as we do not look at the real social relations behind the veil of commodity deals.

In much the same way as low wages paid to workers can be 'justified' as the result of 'impersonal' considerations like supply and demand in the labour market so, as we have remarked before, the consistent exploitation of primary producing countries by highly industrialised capitalist countries which dominate world markets can be made to appear as a 'natural' movement in commodity prices with no evident human intervention.

The idea that all men are equal is itself a correlate of the equalisation of 'human labour in general' as the source and measure of value;  and, conversely, the notion of human equality had to acquire 'the fixity of a popular prejudice' before the real nature of value could be properly appreciated.

To the extent that the legal expression of property rights and freedom of contract can be universalised for all commodity-producing societies, they come to be regarded as natural law, inevitable rules of human intercourse inherent in the nature of things and therefore beyond the reach of criticism or objection. Just as the law of value appears to be a providential arrangement whereby economic order is maintained in spite of the anarchic actions of individual producers and traders, so legalised property rights seem to be the practical expression of a purely abstract justice.  In the guise of eternal principles of equity which ought to be respected at all times and places they are invoked as the ultimate justification of existing social relations instead of being recognised simply as the consequence of such relations given a spurious universality through the mediation of things.

But if the actions and attitudes of men in a commodity-exchanging society are to be regarded as an expression of abstract ethical principles, it is necessary to account for the fact that so many men come to the market with nothing to exchange but their labour-power while a few enjoy a commanding position through their control of the only means by which that labour-power can be employed.  The search for a moral starting point for the supposedly self-regulating system of a market economy leads to a mythical interpretation of primitive accumulation.  It is assumed that in the past 'there were two sorts of people;  one, the diligent, intelligent and above all, frugal elite;  the other, lazy rascals, spending their substance, and more, in riotous living.'(5)  Marx goes on to compare 'the legend of theological original sin' by which 'man came to be condemned to eat his bread in the sweat of his brow' with 'the history of economic original sin which reveals to us that there are people to whom this is by no means essential'!  Such an economic fiction by which the primitive accumulation of capital is invested with virtue serves to conceal the naked forms of exploitation — the ruthless creation of a working class at home by stripping men of every possession and the violent conquest and looting of peoples abroad which together laid the foundations for capitalism.  This myth serves to justify contemporary capitalists in their wealth and privileges as the notion of Karma enables comfortably off Indians to regard their good fortune as the result of virtuous actions performed in a previous life.

From this idea of personal thriftiness as the origin of working capital is derived the notion that the continuing abstemiousness of those who control the means of production accounts for any unconsumed product on which further expansion of the economy depends rather than on the amount of unpaid-for labour extracted from workers as surplus-value.  Such a notion relies on the extremely dubious thesis that those who dominate society through their ownership of property are remarkable for their frugality and the totally unwarranted proposition that abstention itself is value-creative.  As the law of value formulates the relationship between man as producer and man as consumer, the law of property which establishes rights in any surplus and unconsumed product expresses the relationship between man as owner of the means of production and man as owner of nothing but his capacity to work.

The concealment of exploitation behind transactions of the market place in bourgeois society having given rise to generalised 'rights' which appear to apply with the same indiscriminate impartiality as the price of bread, those 'rights' prove most useful in providing a justification for the system while at the same time hiding other aspects of exploitation.  What the right to a free press really means is that anyone whosoever, be he a coal miner or a wealthy city merchant, who has some millions of pounds at his disposal and credit facilities to raise as much again is at liberty to launch a newspaper.  Similarly, any charwoman or dustman has the right to pursue a case against the most powerful corporation in the land up to the highest court — if he or she also happens to be in a position to meet legal costs of some tens of thousand pounds. Or the even-handedness of such 'rights' may take the form that it is completely open to rich and poor alike, as long as they do not cause an obstruction, to sell matches on the street corner.

Such bogus 'rights' whose negotiability depends on an unstated membership of a privileged class, can be compared with the equally seeming impartiality of the functioning of the law of supply and demand;  but quite apart from the many ways in which monopolists can bend the law, only effective demands really count.  People with demands like, for example, enough to eat or a roof over their heads which they cannot afford to pay for do not even enter into calculations about the amount of production required to fulfil society's needs.

Rights precipitated out of property relations are inevitably illusory for the propertyless; and, by and large, all workers in even the most advanced industrial societies are never more than a month away from a poverty-stricken propertylessness.  That is why to a worker, in the words of the Communist Manifesto, 'Law, morality, religion, are so many bourgeois prejudices, behind which lurk in ambush just so many bourgeois interests.'(6)

Owning nothing but their capacity to work,the only right it was possible for the working class to assert against bourgeois right was the right to withdraw one's labour and to organise with fellow workers for this purpose.  This right had to be established in the teeth of ruling class opposition.  Once it had been established, the ruling bourgeois class took it over and tried to incorporate it

among their own list of bogus rights.  The 'right to strike'
became one of the boasted liberties of the so-called 'free
world';  but there has never yet been an actual strike in any
capitalist country which was not either at the wrong time, the
wrong place or called for the wrong reason and which, therefore,
could qualify as a 'proper' exercise of that 'right'.

## COMMODITY PRODUCTION AND ETHICAL INTERPRETATIONS OF RIGHT

We have seen how an analysis of commodities yields two distinct
meanings for a value word like 'good'— a descriptive sense which
refers to an object's usefulness and a prescriptive sense which
honours the human labour incorporated in it.  This analysis also
reveals a discrepancy between the value of the social product
which human labour has created and the value of the goods
actually enjoyed by those who produced them which equals the difference between the total of what labour has made and the total
labour-power paid for.  This surplus-value which, in fact, represents the saving of the working community is appropriated as the
private property of those controlling the means of production.
    We have further seen how rights as claims to goods are derived
from social relationships as determined by the material conditions
of life in a particular economic ordering of society.  As these
relationships are 'dehumanised' by commodity exchange and transformed into relations between things, there is a tendency for
claims on other people to take the form of legalised rights in
things.  The social fact of surplus-value no longer appears as the
exploitation of one class by another but as the 'rational' consequence of the laws of property.
    This rationalisation could only have arisen in the course of
development of a system of production in which human effort is not
directed to the satisfaction of wants but to the creation of value
in the form of marketable goods.  The division of labour which is
the prior condition for such a development is also, as Marx points
out, the institution of private property:  'in the one the same
thing is affirmed with reference to activity as is affirmed in the
other with reference to the product of activity.'(7)
    Over the whole period of commodity exchange, which may be con-
veniently dated from the appearance of a recognised currency in
circulation to its fullest development under capitalism, the split
between the production of value and the consumption of goods, the
appropriation of value as naked or legalised exploitation and
attempts to justify such exploitation have all profoundly influenced
men's ethical attitudes toward their actions.
    From the time when craftsmen made articles not for their own
use but to barter for other things, they had begun, in a sense, to
divide themselves into two beings.  Man as maker and man as
enjoyer had become distinguishable within each person and there
was a tendency for them to pull in opposite directions.  The gap
between purposeful effort and its due reward had the effect of
driving apart reason which looked ahead to future satisfaction and
feelings which made their demands in the present.  This potential
split in each man's integrity was inevitably deepened as the

sundered functions of useful work and desirable gratifications
became more and more identified with distinct classes — those who,
on the whole, laboured without enjoyment and those who enjoyed
without working.  The same kind of socio-economic schizophrenia
which characterised individuals in commodity-producing societies
affected the entire community.  The distinction between duty and
pleasure which was to be such a marked feature of ethical thinking
can therefore be seen as a reflection on the moral plane of both
the split personality of the individual and the irreconcilability
of class interests.

The ideological consequences of this distinction can be traced
in the extreme positions various philosophers have taken on the
issue of whether duty or pleasure is the ultimate motivating force
in human conduct — from the opposite views of the Socratic and
Cyrenaic Schools or of Stoicism and Epicureanism right down to
similar oppositions in our own times.

In Kantian morality the division between reason and duty on the
one hand and feeling and pleasure on the other takes so final a
form that they inhabit entirely different worlds.  The rightness of
an act is considered to be vitiated by any motivation which does
not stem directly from a purely rational regard for completely
universalised maxims of behaviour;  and this regard must never be
confused with personal emotions of any kind — not even the most
altruistic feelings of benevolence.

At the opposite extreme are those thorough-going hedonists like
Hobbes who argue that no actions are disinterested and that the
pursuit of pleasure and avoidance of pain provide the sole impulse
to all conduct.  Reason is held to play a secondary role in merely
suggesting how this overriding purpose may best be served.
While utilitarians like Bentham and Mill subscribe to such a view
of man's nature, they do not altogether deny themselves the language
of duty when they attempt to move from this postulated fact of
egoistic hedonism to the advocacy of acting for the greatest happiness of the greatest number.  This transition from descriptive
statements to normative or evaluative judgments is, as we have seen,
illegitimate;  but the naturalistic fallacy is an illogical expression of the perfectly reasonable belief that there should be some
connection between what it is in a person's interest to do and what
it is right for him to do.

The dissociation of a self-interested concern with pleasure
from a dutiful respect for the claims of others in regard to human
actions, like the distinction between utility and value in regard
to goods, is ultimately rooted in the separation of consumption
from production which originates in the division of labour.  The
division of labour is also the division of private from social
property and the realisation of individuality, of egoistic as
opposed to group interests which is tied up with the projection
of a man's selfish nature as a consumer in objects which belong
exclusively to him.  At that stage of the division of labour when
relationships between people have been largely transformed into
exchange relationships and the 'rules of human conduct increasingly take the form of the economic laws of a supposedly self-
regulating social system, the idea of 'right' may practically disappear from the language philosophers use to account for behaviour.

They may speak of actions purely in terms of self-interest as
when Adam Smith, both moral philosopher and political economist,
speaks unambiguously of men acting not from benevolence 'but from
their regard to their own interest' and counsels us to address
ourselves 'not to their humanity but to their self-love'.  Other
philosophers and psychologists look upon man as simply moved by
mechanical responses of pleasure-seeking, pain-avoidance, like a
machine for which moral considerations are totally irrelevant.

But still other philosophers, aware that the functioning of the
economic system is only apparently automatic and that the production and distribution of goods reflect a bargain struck between
capitalists and workers, feel the need to speak in two voices to
classes with opposed interests and include contradictory elements
in what is essentially a utilitarian account of ethics.  Promise-
keeping is vital to a contractual society like our own.  The
crucial relationship in an exchange economy is the purchase of
labour-power;  and the contract between capitalist and worker
requires a moral sanction over and above mere market fluctuations.  A writer on ethics like W. David Ross, mainly utilitarian
in outlook, makes a special place in his theory for a deonto-
logical treatment of the obligation to abide by contracts.  The
idea of a 'free' contract between employer and employee as the
justification of economic relationships may be compared with the
idea of the social contract as underlying political relationships.
Of course this general attitude toward contractual agreements does
not leave unaffected other social relationships like marriage.

Over the whole period of commodity exchange we find that philosophers can be grouped according to whether they emphasise self-
interest or respect for the claims of others, hedonism or a sense
of duty as the key to understanding human actions.  But which of
these two general attitudes toward morality may be chosen is
neither an accident nor a matter of personal preference.

Moralists who identify themselves with a class which has
enjoyed power and is threatened from below have an understandable
tendency to stress duty and obedience as of primary ethical
significance, particularly for the inferior classes;  and their
naturally conservative attitude makes them resist change which
they describe as illusory anyway, referring all expectations of
happier circumstances to some ideal existence other than this
present life.  Moralists associated with a rising class have as
natural a tendency to stress the satisfactions which will accrue
to all once that class is firmly in a position of control.  The
very struggle for ascendancy gives a practical materialist cast
to their thought and the promise of a better ordering of society
makes them the friends of change.

On the other hand, a decadent ruling class may adopt for itself
an eat, drink and be merry philosophy of lavish hedonism while a
new bourgeois class in the period of primitive accumulation may
express a propensity to save presently for future wealth and power
in attitudes of extreme puritanism.

The distinction between an appeal to the principle of happiness
in this world or to duty sanctioned by other-worldly considerations
is thus closely bound up with the social movements of a particular
time.  This constant counterposition of duty and pleasure could

only be resolved in a more comprehensive morality associated with
a social movement holding within it the possibility of transcending
commodity production and its divisive effect on our being and
thinking.

Of course it is not to be thought that the kind of explanation
we have been considering for the adoption of this ethical attitude
or that is consciously part of anyone's motivation. A spokesman
for a particular class may quite genuinely think he is speaking for
society as a whole without qualification as to time or place —
indeed, his usefulness as an ideologist very likely depends on his
thinking it. And even when he is aware of some class allegiance,
he may, with the best will in the world, be as unreliable a guide
to the real rather than the professed interests of that class as
an individual often is in respect to his own motives.

The very development of an individualistic outlook bound up with
the institution of private property and achieving its extreme
expression in bourgeois society is bound to obscure for those individuals the fundamental role of classes in society. Property is
like a wall a man tries to erect between himself and society till
he can think of himself as completely independent; and yet property
itself is a social product and merely confirms his social being —
but in a lifeless, estranged and distorted form.

The unselfconscious and spontaneous social being of primitive
communism prior to the formation of classes, recalled in all
legends of a golden age when man's hand was not raised against man,
is eventually superseded as class divisions shatter social unity
by a self-regarding, self-interested egoism — the rugged indivi-
dualiam of man under capitalism. Milton writing at a crucial
revolutionary stage of this development could not but create the
epic of bourgeois man. Satan's rebellion is a poetic evocation
of middle-class revolt in the name of individual liberty against
the hierarchical structure of feudalism. England transformed by
the metallurgical industries is the hell he would rather rule in
than serve in heaven. The departmentalism among his daemon
henchmen reflects the specialisation in a society where the division
of labour breaks down all communal effort. There is also
colonialism, the vicious exploitation of the primitive communist
society of Eden by the introduction among its innocent natives of
sin and death in the course of their subjugation. Indeed the whole
history of capitalism is to be found in this magnificent work from
the progressive phase of the Civil War through its period of
ascendancy and subsequent degeneration right down to the hissing,
insinuating beastliness we see all around us today.


SOCIOLOGY OF KNOWLEDGE AND MARXIST ANALYSIS

General reflections on the relationship between the ethical views
of a philosopher and the social forces around him have enjoyed
a certain vogue in academic circles as studies in the 'sociology
of knowledge'; but these ideas are usually handled in such a way
as to defuse them carefully to avoid any danger of exploding present
class myths. Marxist analysis, if the task were thought worth-
while, would reveal why, in relation to the social forces around

them at this particular stage, academics should take refuge in just these intellectual games.

But let us make a little clearer this question of the way what appear to be the most abstract philosophical ideas and principles are demonstrably rooted in the social movements of a particular time and place.  Let us consider two thinkers, Plato and Aristotle, contemporary with each other and living and teaching in the same city, in order to understand why they should differ with each other so fundamentally on moral issues and why, with such varying relative influence down the intervening centuries, they should still have something to say to us today.  Let us do this not as an academic exercise but to understand our own society better because only in understanding our own society better can we change it.

Athens in the fourth century B.C. was the scene of considerable social ferment;  and this was reflected in the speeches and prose writings of the time as it had already been poetically expressed several generations before in the works of the great dramatists. Plato leaves us in no doubt that, in the welter of sectional interests, he speaks for a landed aristocracy whose rule had been challenged by a rising class of merchants and their political allies.  His remedy for this subversion of a traditional order, as set forth in 'The Laws' and 'The Republic', is to freeze into a static caste system the division of labour on which a civilised society must be founded and to prevent any social mobility by the strictest control on trade and the severest penalties for amassing wealth beyond one's station.  The caste system envisaged is as much like that successfully established in India as neo-Platonic thought is like Indian idealistic philosophy.

Because the social movement of the period was unfavourable to the interests of the class he belonged to by birth and position, the same class his teacher Socrates would have liked to be identified with, Plato wanted society to turn back to a pre-mercantile stage.  His ideal state is, in fact, an imaginative reconstruction of the past but with this major difference from the real past:  it has been carefully restructured in such a way that this time it will not generate the present.  In this imaginary Platonic state land is allocated to a certain number of founding families whose rights to it are secured by a political settlement strengthened by religious sanctions.  The land is worked by slaves who also perform all household chores.  What little trade is permitted in this enclosed natural economy is in the hands of foreigners whose corruption by commerce is a matter of no concern. Their activities are under the strict control of market commissioners whose regulations are drafted in the interest of consumers — the founding families of course.

From this ideal state are to be excluded all who might prove in any way disturbing to its stability — poets, not because a man of Plato's sensibility lacked a taste for the arts but because poetry in the hands of dramatists like Aeschylus or Euripides had extolled the more democratic institutions of Athens or questioned traditional beliefs;  Ionian scientists, because they also cast doubt on the superstitions required to prop up this rigid social system and because the very growth of physical knowledge was closely associated with the expansion of trade which Plato deplored;

and sophists, because as the teachers of the Athenian middle class
they put at the disposal of free citizens, in exchange for a fee,
the sort of education in philosophy and rhetoric which had been
the prerogative of noble youths.  What made the sophists particularly objectionable from Plato's point of view was their criticism of the conventional discrimination between Hellenes and bar-
barians, noblemen and commoners, free men and slaves on the grounds
that such distinctions were not based on natural differences but on
man-made rules.

With all menial work performed by slaves and all trade in the
hands of a closely supervised foreign community, the free-born
citizens of the  Republic have no occupation but purifying their
own souls and keeping inferior persons to their proper tasks.
This is not expressed as a privilege but as a duty;  and if any
free citizen should stray from the pursuit of abstract goodness
into some trade or craft, the urban commissioners are required to
correct him by reproach and degradation until he be brought back
into the right course.  The institution of slavery on which this
whole strictly-stratified society rests is justified on the basis
of the natural inferiority of those who are forced to do all the
work.

And why do you think that mechanical work and work with one's
hands are matters of reproach?  Is it not because in some
people the element of the best is naturally weak and unable to
rule the monsters within them?.... Well, then, is it not in
order ... that we say they must be the slaves of that best
man in whom the divine dwells?(8)

This is the moral version of the argument which has been used
countless times:  'Because he is inferior let him work at some
back-breaking task.'  And how is it known that he is inferior?
'Because he works at a back-breaking task.'

Since labour is the function of contemptible beings who deserve
their slave status, we would hardly expect Plato to accord its
products any value.  And the goods produced by such unworthy
means are not, in fact, to be highly regarded.  'Which class of
things do you think has greater participation in pure being, the
class containing bread and drink and meat and food generally, or
the class containing true belief and knowledge and mind and, in
short, all virtue?'(9)  This contempt for the material goods
provided by servile effort leads to a certain strain of asceticism
in Plato's thought;  but just as true belief cannot of itself
sustain life, so virtue is not simply its own reward.  What is
given away with one hand in an act of disdainful renunciation is
hastily grabbed back again with the other.  'Can there now be any
harm in our going further and restoring to justice and the rest
of virtue the rewards ... which it renders to the soul at the hands
of gods and men, both in a man's lifetime and after he is dead?'(10)

It is on the basis of these socially determined prejudices of
Plato's that we begin to account for his ethical ideas and even
his metaphysical theories.  The attempt to use the ideal not to
shape reality but to replace it is usually a sign of class frustration — like the daydreams in which an individual may indulge
when the normal outlets for his ambitions are checked.  The
flowering of idealistic system-building in nineteenth-century

Germany was partly the ideological reflex of a thwarted bourgeoisie,
cheated by the absence of any bourgeois revolution of playing their
full role in the development of capitalism.  So reality's progressive rejection of the class Plato favoured meant that reality
itself must be rejected.

To this must be added the natural tendency of a leisured class
to see the normal sequence of events in the productive process in
the reverse order.  Instead of satisfactions being necessarily
preceded by an expenditure of effort involving direct contact with
the physical environment, the desire itself is sufficient to command
the results of the labour of others.  This makes it appear that the
idea of the required object actually determined its existence.
Furthermore, as Plato shows so clearly, the class contempt for those
who do the work of society gets transferred in a sense to the very
things they make.  Ignorant shepherds, weavers and street-traders
may have made a white cloak available in the market place;  but such
a cloak will become soiled in time and wear out.  Only a man of
superior intellect can abstract from it the pure idea of whiteness,
eternal and changeless, residing in a world beyond the reach of the
ordinary senses which one unhappily shares with rude mechanics and
merchants.  It is not actual goods which have worth but the ideal
conception of their goodness — just as though the mental effort
of conceptualisation could be substituted for the sweat and toil of
creative labour as the true measure of value.

Of course, the freeing of concepts from their immediate circumstances is a necessary condition for logical thought which, as we
have noted, is one part of the process of knowledge.  The division
between mental and manual labour provides a social background
favouring the development of abstract thought as a correlate to the
pure value form commodities take under the interdiction of use;  but
the rupture between theory and practice which can result from this
same division of labour leads to conceptual thought becoming so
cut off from the actual world in which it originates and to which
it must return for verification that it assumes a fantastic and
arbitrary independence.  It is the prolongation of this arrested
moment in the acquisition of true knowledge, as though commodities
should be frozen forever in their value form and never consumed,
the indefinite extension of this moment when concepts are 'free'
of the restraints imposed by reality which makes it seem plausible
to deduce nature from the idea instead of the proper way about.
These same freely floating concepts, detached from the real world,
are the source from which idealistic ethics derives its notion of
a limitless but essentially meaningless moral liberty.

The most obvious difficulty with Plato's ascription of value to
universal ideas simply by virtue of their purity and immutability
is that evil and pain are just as much universal ideas as goodness;
filthiness is as abstract and changeless a concept as whiteness.
Such a point can only be overlooked by a member of a class
enjoying a sheltered existence in which filth, hunger and pain are
far less prominent than cleanliness, satiety and health.

This postulating of the Idea of Good as the supreme value from
which all other values are derived is one of the aspects of Platonic
philosophy which Aristotle most severely criticised.  Since such
hypostatised 'goodness' cannot be brought into being by human

effort, it must remain irrelevant to man's practical aspirations; and it is with just such practical interests and activities that Aristotle is primarily concerned.

Though he was much influenced by Platonism during the years he studied at the Academy, yet, as the son of a physician at the Macedonian court, his social background was different from that of his aristocratic tutor.  In his youth he must have learned something of the Hippocratic science and throughout his life his writings reflect a practical turn of mind and an unfailing curiosity about the objective world.

His concern with human activity prompts him to remark:  'All people value most what has cost them much labour in the production; for instance, people who have themselves made their money are fonder of it than those who have inherited it.'(11)  This is at least a step in the direction of recognising human effort as the source of value.  His interest in the real problems of contemporary Athenian society keeps his 'Politics' practical rather than utopian.  It is in this book that he makes a lasting contribution to the study of economics when he explains that:  'The uses of every possession are two, both dependent on the thing itself, but not in the same manner, the one supposing an inseparable connection with it, the other not;  as a shoe, for instance, which may be either worn or exchanged for something else.'(12)

This is perhaps the earliest recognition of that distinction between utility and exchange value which has not only remained valid for economic thought right up to the present day but has also profoundly influenced our ideas about ethics.  In his theory of money as the measure of value in exchange Aristotle realises that the problem of economic value is a question of equivalence, even if he is unable to press his analysis to the point of saying exactly what value is.  As Marx observes:

> There was an important fact which prevented Aristotle from
> seeing that, to attribute value to commodities, is merely a
> mode of expressing all labour as equal human labour and con-
> sequently as labour of equal quality.  Greek society was
> founded upon slavery, and had, therefore, for its natural basis,
> the inequality of men and of their labour-powers.(13)

The importance of the issue of slavery for any philosopher living at that particular time is shown by the fact that Aristotle devotes a large part of the very first book of the 'Politics' to its justification — as if no state could conceivably exist till this foundation for it had been firmly established.  He takes a middle course between the Platonic view that the authority of the slave-owner is derived from his superior virtue and the Sophist view that not nature but the human product, law, makes one man free and another a slave.  Aristotle argues that some men are, in fact, slaves by nature and it is only fitting that they should live in abject subjugation;  but their ranks ought not to include those captured in an unjust war and certainly not Hellenes!

This middle position on the question of slavery is not unconnected with his attitude toward an Athenian middle or professional class with whom he identified himself.  His prescription for a happy community is one in which the citizens of middle station preponderate and have in their hands the reins of government.

From this idea of the middle class of men holding the balance in a properly-ordered society between extremes of wealth or poverty Aristotle draws his definition of virtue.

It is a middle state between two faulty ones, in the way of excess on one side and of defect on the other: and it is so moreover, because the faulty states on one side fall short of, and those on the other exceed, what is right, both in the case of the feelings and the actions; but virtue finds, and found adopts, the mean.(14)

In a society rent by class divisions with the continuous threat of further civil strife, a philosopher, particularly if his own class enjoys a temporary ascendancy, is very likely to stress the virtue of measure, an abatement of the war of opposites, as the remedy for social ills and, therefore, as the basis of ethics. The idea of 'measure' would have been precipitated anyway as an abstract concept by the commodity exchange of an early mercantile society in which the measuring out of goods according to their incorporated value would be a daily experience.

But 'measure' means something quite different to Plato and to Aristotle. For Plato identifying himself with a class already superseded it is not something which exists on earth in any actual society. It is the harmony which would exist if men of various classes had been perdurably fixed in them and could never even think of trying to move out of them, so that the music of the spheres would be the heavenly echo of a social order on earth in which men faithfully kept through the ages to the circle assigned them. Rightness is thus conceived in terms of the purely abstract and intellectually satisfying demonstrations of geometry, and logic is so idealistic that its divine conclusions must never be contaminated by contact with reality.

For Aristotle this same 'measure' is the mean between extremes as realised in an actual community of men, a middle class which holds the balance in the opposition of classes at either end of the social scale. Aristotle rejects the Platonic harmony as a mere abstraction, something over and above society which cannot be brought within the range of practical interests.

[Plato] says that the legislator ought to make all the citizens happy; but it is impossible that the whole city can be happy, without all, or the greater, or some part of it be happy. For happiness is not like that numerical equality which arises from certain numbers when added together, although neither of them may separately contain it; for happiness cannot be thus added together, but must exist in every individual, as some properties belong to every integral; and if the military [in Plato's ideal Republic] are not happy, who else are so? for the artisans are not, nor the multitude of those who are employed in inferior offices.(15)

Plato wants to freeze society as, in his imagination, it used to be. Aristotle, identifying himself with a class that has arrived in the sense of enjoying a preponderating influence and of temporarily holding the balance between extremes of wealth and poverty, wants to freeze society as it actually is. Both philosophers are opposed to social change and development; but Plato's changelessness is other-worldly, an abstract realm of idealised

forms transcending reality and only accessible to mind, while
Aristotle's acceptance of society as it is, with its actual social
classes co-existing as separate compartments in a fixed relationship, can be associated with his 'pigeon-hole' logic — a logic
suited to classifying things and assigning them to their proper
place but incapable of dealing with motion, change and process
without generating philosophical puzzles and anomalies.

In their respective attitudes toward right conduct these two
philosophers lend support to a suggestion made before that, on
the whole, a thinker who defends a threatened social order or one
in the process of being overthrown tends to invoke duty sanctioned
by considerations external to society as the standard of ethical
conduct, while a thinker whose interests lie with an established
or rising class tends to appeal to the utilitarian principle of
happiness in this world as a sufficient explanation of behaviour.
In spite of their contemporaneity and close association in the same
Athenian school, Plato and Aristotle give quite different accounts
of normative judgments.  Plato would argue that such judgments
borrow their validity from an ideal world of pure concepts which
our exile in this imperfect world of the senses, dimly reflecting
that ideal 'reality', does not altogether keep us from knowing and
certainly does not relieve us of obeying.  Aristotle would find the
justification of these judgments in practical considerations of what
makes for a happy, useful life in the world we perceive around us.

Because they put forward these very different views in the
general language of value and because they expose the roots of even
the most abstract ideas, like the very rules of thought, in social
circumstances, primarily the relation of classes, they continue
to have something to say on ethical questions as long as commodity
exchange and class divisions are with us.  At the same time their
common concern with the specific source of a surplus in the Athens
of their day, the institution of slavery, firmly roots them in
their own period and locale.  Philosophers will not always be so
frank in their rationalisation and justification of the particular
forms of exploitation on which the power and privileges of the
classes they identify themselves with are based.


HISTORICAL MATERIALISM AND ETHICAL IDEAS

We have been considering how ideas about what is right in terms of
human conduct are rooted in the fundamental economic structure of
society and therefore change with changes in that basic social
structure.  This understanding of the way ethical attitudes and,
indeed, the way we think about ourselves and our relationships
generally are profoundly influenced by the form the production of
goods and their distribution in society takes is historical
materialism.

Using this historical materialist approach it is worth considering changes in the ethical attitude toward trading operations
since the growth of commodity exchange is such an important social
development for understanding the moral relations between human
beings.

The social roots of barter are to be found ultimately in the most primitive form of the division of labour — clan specialisation inside the tribe with respect to gathering a particular edible plant or animal, a practice reflected in totemism. Taboo, as we have already noted, originating as a prohibition against eating a certain kind of food where and when it was found in order to effect subsequently a proper interclan distribution, can be seen as the earliest instance of the interdiction of use which is an essential precondition for the simplest commodity exchange.

Further specialisation in agriculture and in the making of such objects as pots or weapons effects a greater production of certain things than the tribal community needs, leading to intertribal barter in which local chiefs exchange their surplus products for the surplus products of other communities. This traffic in goods results in a transformation of all social relationships. Artisans

cease to be workers for the community and become workers for
themselves ... the chiefs cease to represent the separate
interests of their clans. They are becoming a landed aristocracy united against the poorer clansmen by a common interest
of class against class. The artisans on their part organise
themselves in guilds formed on the pattern of the clan; but,
so long as the economy remains agrarian, they are not in a
position to dispute the supremacy of the landowners.(16)

The process in ancient Greece described by George Thomson by which tribal settlements, based on the equal sharing of goods by lot, were converted into city states 'governed by a landed nobility and surrounded by a poverty-stricken peasantry in dependent villages' would apply generally to human communities at a similar stage of development. As he goes on to say:

The new unit [the city state] was the expression of a new
division of labour, agrarian and industrial, which, once
established, promoted further divisions of labour and thereby
raised human life to new levels of complexity on a slave
basis.... The later its date, the more pronounced was its
class character.... During the Sixth Century B.C. the development of commodity production precipitated, in all the advanced
city states, a further revolution — the overthrow of the landed
aristocracy by the merchant class.

This background helps us to understand the very different attitudes toward trade of Plato and Aristotle. As one who identified himself with the landed aristocracy Plato considered the whole business of exchange so reprehensible that in his ideal Republic it was to be kept to a minimum and only carried on by a despised group of foreigners whose activities were regulated by the strictest rules of 'fair practice'. Aristotle, taking a much more sympathetic interest in mercantilism, distinguished between money-making as a necessary aspect of sound house-keeping, from which the word 'economics' comes, and money-making as an end in itself. The former was natural and commendable while the latter was to be censured 'for it has not its origin in nature, but by it men gain from each other; for usury is most reasonably detested, as it is increasing our fortune by money itself, and not by employing it for the purpose it was originally intended, namely, exchange.'(17)

At the beginning of the Middle Ages, following on the collapse of the Roman Empire in the West and, later, on the shutting of the Mediterranean to European trade by Islamic expansion, most of Western Europe was split up into self-sufficient manorial units fairly closely approximating the Platonic ideal of a natural economy dominated by a land-owning aristocracy; and the philosophy of Plato, with its contempt for commerce and its otherworldly values was itself suited to influence early Christian ideas about the morality of trade.  Saint Augustine's description of value as purely subjective is characteristic of a point of view determined primarily by the interests of consumers; and his doctrine that no Christian ought to be a merchant accorded well enough with the conditions that were to prevail for some time.

With the revival of trade following on the Crusades, Aristotle was rediscovered, often through the medium of Arabic scholarship. In the writings of Saint Thomas Aquinas, whom he so greatly influenced, a crude form of the labour theory of value can be found side by side with a subjective theory; and the economic incentive of private property is defended on the basis of the Aristotelian argument that not the institution of property itself but the way it is used determines whether it is good or evil.

In the earlier period all commercial activity, natural in Aristotle's sense or not, was regarded as a distraction from a man's true business of purifying his own soul and contemplating eternal 'values'; and the abusive word 'usury' was applied to almost any profitable transaction.  In the later period profiteering or the charging of excessive interest on money was condemned, but there was considered to be such a thing as legitimate trading whose limits were fixed by ethical notions like a 'fair return' or a 'just price'.  In both cases the attitude was moral; but while one form of morality required men to turn away from the things of this world, the other attempted to order their activities here and now on an ethical basis.

Further change in these moral attitudes was bound to be brought about by the growth of towns and the expansion of trade with the European revival of mercantilism.  The views of a landed nobility whose interests were largely those of consumers were being challenged by the views of a rising merchant class; and this clash of views was the reflection of the beginnings of a class struggle which was eventually, in one part of the world after another, to overthrow feudalism altogether.

The Church itself was gradually forced to retreat from its original position on the ethics of trading and to accept various qualifications of the idea of the 'just price'.  By the fifteenth century Saint Antonino, while still insisting on the general notion of 'fair dealing', is prepared to recognise the 'impersonal forces of the market' with his admission that 'there was a debatable ground within which prices might move without involving sin.'(18) Similar qualifications were accepted in respect to usury by conceding that lenders might be re-imbursed for losses incurred or for delays in repayment and even for the chances of gain which had been missed.

Not only does the temporal sequence of events show that a quickening of commercial life was the occasion for a transformation

of ethical attitudes;  but also the very locale of these changes in
attitude emphasises the relationship between economic base and
ideas of morality.  The impetus to trade by the discovery of the
New World (which did not, of course, know that it was lost) would
lead us to expect a rethinking of the ethics of mercantilism to
appear in Spain;  and in the School of Salamanca, for example,
churchmen do begin, early on, to modify their views of usury by
distinguishing between divergence in place and divergence in time
in order to justify the exchange bills which had become a feature
of trade fairs.

But although theologians might make concessions to the economic needs
of  the  time,  the Church could never wholly abandon its prerogative
of drawing the precepts for human behaviour from the realm of the
ideal.  As the gulf between precept and economic practice widened,
the ideal foundation on which the precepts rested could only be
saved by giving up the claim that they were directly relevant to the
conduct of practical affairs here and now, referring instead to an
idealised existence in some other time and place.  In spite of the
secularisation of trading practices as the Church surrendered its
right to legislate morally for the market place, religion still had
a social function to perform.  In class-divided societies some way
has to be found of preserving the idea of an integrated social life
to counter the centrifugal tendencies of directly-opposed class
interest.  Religion means literally a renewed 'link' or 'bond'
between man and god where god, in one form or many, represents the
spirit of a social organisation.  It does not try to put an end to
class divisions but to bind society together and make some sort of
communal life possible in spite of economic exploitation.  By
recalling the past when tribal communities were not yet divided into
exploiters and exploited and by supposing that such brotherhood can
exist ideally in the present, even though the actual material conditions rule it out, or by projecting this conception of fraternal
harmony into a life after death, religion offers hope to the dispossessed while leaving everything as it is.

From the point of view of the ruling class, religion serves to
distract the masses from active steps to improve their lot, to
inculcate the social laws which subservient classes have to obey if
the system is to continue and to provide a means whereby they themselves can enjoy easy consciences without surrendering any privileges.  From the point of view of the ruled, religion is a source of
consolation prior to the time when political struggle to relieve
their distress is feasible.  Marx likens it to flowers entwined in
the chains of the toiling masses which hide their bonds from sight.
It is no help to pluck away the flowers:  the chains must be broken.
'The abolition of religion, as the illusory happiness of men, is a
demand for their real happiness.  The call to abandon their illusions about their condition is a call to abandon a condition which
demands illusions.'(19)  Religion, then, provides a spurious recon-
ciliation of divided societies whereby Dives and Lazarus can kneel
down together in the same communion, the one content in his earthly
possessions, the other anticipating a reversal of fortunes in a
hypothetical life to come.

It is possible for religion to perform this function in divided
societies because man himself is divided.  The dualism of commodities

as useful and valuable reflects and is reflected by the dualistic nature of those who make them — as having both a physical and non-natural character.  Men work to satisfy their material needs but the value of their work is incorporated in things that do not belong to them.  Value thus appears to them as something inhabiting a different world from this one of sweat and toil, something only to be enjoyed in another life than this one.  Some additional effort on the moral plane seems required to possess what they themselves have made.  This aspiration growing out of the negation of physical satisfactions takes a spiritual form;  and it is to this aspect of man, the producer whose products slip through his hands to appear on the market as abstract values often beyond his means, that religion speaks — the louder, of course, where deprivation is greatest.

In the historical development of ideas about the ethics of exchange, once we reach the stage of a full-blown, freely-competitive market economy in which overcharging for goods or for the use of money seems to be penalised automatically, injunctions against usury in any form tend to become a thing of the past.  In the same way that human relationships in the productive process are transformed from personal ties into commodity deals, so the ethics of commerce is translated into a purely descriptive science of market operations.  Freed from any obvious role in regulating the great issues of the creation and distribution of the goods by which society lives, morality in capitalist countries suffers a progressive trivialisation by which it becomes primarily concerned with personal areas of life apparently impervious to commodity exchange — like sexual relationships.  It must not be thought, however, that even these personal aspects of life are left untouched by changes in the mode of production.  Marx mentions the fate of Don Quixote as a pathetic example of what happens to anyone who thinks that a particular code of conduct is compatible with all economic forms of society.

This translation of the ethics of commerce into a descriptive science, 'the end of ideology' referred to by superficial observers, does not mean that the functioning of the economy has ceased to have moral implications — only that they have temporarily sunk out of sight and are no longer debated as such.  It remains for political opposition to the system as a whole to bring these implications once more into the open where they can be reconsidered in normative judgments.

Now through all these changes in ideas about trading relationships which reflect material changes in the basic mode of production it is still possible for the spokesmen of different periods to speak to each other across the centuries.  Plato and Aristotle may differ from each other about the ethics of exchange and their views on this subject may be at even greater variance with the attitudes of philosophers writing since their time;  but they all still seem to speak in a general philosophical language in which their differences can be expressed.  Marxists do not explain this in terms of an essential human nature which stays the same through all social vicissitudes.  Human nature, like the consciousness peculiar to human beings, is determined by social existence.  Therefore similarities in ways of thought must be accounted for by common features

in the way societies at various times have been organised in
respect to the material maintenance of life.

In spite of the revolutionary disjunctions in any story of
social development stretching from the slave-based communities of
ancient city states through various forms of feudalism right up to
contemporary capitalism, all these modes of production have something in common — the division of labour, with the division between
ruled and rulers, exploited and exploiters as one of its main consequences, and the production of commodities evidenced by the
existence of some form of currency. At each of these periods
society was divided into classes, the mode of production simply
being the form class exploitation took, and in all these periods
there was production for the market. Since we have found that these
two aspects of the material conditions of life are fundamental for
the deduction of our most general ethical concepts, their presence
over the whole historical period provides the basis for a common
moral language.

A key concept in this language is value. Value, as we have
seen, by virtue of being a concept common to both economics and
ethics serves as the middle term enabling us to move logically from
one realm of discourse to the other. Just as the law of value is
the economic formula for reuniting the activities of making and
enjoying which have been sundered by the division of labour, so
the general idea of value is the philosophical formula for comprehending the connection between material social base and the broad
cultural superstructure raised upon it. Economic value operates
across the division of labour to relate man as enjoyer to man as
maker: value in its broadest sense operates across class divisions
to relate man as thinker and ideologist to man as the creator of
material goods.

This connection has been obscured for us by the separation between intellectual and manual tasks, which has divorced thinking
from doing, theory from practice; and it is by reminding ourselves
that the source of all value is human effort that the connection
can be recovered. Since value has this peculiar importance in
commodity-exchanging societies of containing within itself the clue
to the real social relationships concealed behind deals in things,
the views about value which philosophers profess at any time, even
when they represent failures in comprehension or deliberate
attempts to mislead, are themselves revealing in terms of trying
to understand that particular age.

But if attitudes toward value in general give us the moral framework within which men reflect on matters of conduct, it is the form
surplus-value takes which largely determines what specific ethical
details shall be filled in. The idea that certain actions are
'right' holds for all societies since all societies have certain
common basic features; but in any particular society the actual
type of conduct advocated as 'right' and the reasons adduced for its
'rightness' depend on how the surplus product in that society is
created and appropriated.

In a tribal economy which has advanced beyond the mere subsistence level but in which the means of production like land are held
in common, all right is group right and the morality of the tribe
consists of group loyalty. Every member of the tribe is a brother;

everyone outside the tribe is a potential enemy.  There is no
question of individual rights because there is no such thing as
personal property.  Ceremonies and rituals serve to ratify the
bonds holding the tribe together and the threat of ostracism  —
of being excluded from the life of the tribe, which means moral if
not physical death — is a sufficient sanction for ensuring compliance with traditional practice.

Once tribal expansion and conquest lay a foundation based on
slavery for a greater surplus product appropriated by a landed
aristocracy, loyalty to the group as a whole is superseded by
class loyalty.  Thinkers who belong to or identify themselves with
that aristocracy, whose name begs the question of their right to
rule, are concerned, as we saw in the case of fourth-century B.C.
Athenian philosophers and as was to be the case with eighteenth-
century English divines, with defending and justifying the institution of slavery because slave-worked mines were the most obvious
source of a surplus for the one and the slave-trade a major source
of primitive accumulation for the other.  Discussions about the
actual numbers of slaves in ancient Athens or the exact proportion
of primitive accumulation netted by trade in slaves in pre-
industrial England are not entirely relevant to this issue.  What
counts is whether a particular area of the economy is one where
exploitation is most intense and in yielding the greatest surplus
deserves the largest effort in justification.

Under feudalism there is a hierarchy of obligations, corresponding to a mode of production in which serfs tied to the fields
they till are constrained to fulfil by services or dues the economic
demands of an overlord, and overlords owe fealty to that king or
conqueror who is the source of assigned rights in the land.  This
social organisation is reflected in such metaphysical ideas as a
scale of beings from man, up through various ranks of angels to god
himself, the grand seigneur — each creature with his duly allotted
place which establishes his relations with those above and below
him.  Production is more for use within natural feudal units than
for exchange and this explains the relative permanence of this
economic mode.  As Epicurus says, natural wants are limited by
nature while idle imaginings stretch to infinity.  The commodity,
money, as the equivalent of all created values, gives such idle
imaginings a concrete form and, where it circulates freely with a
quickening of commercial activity, carries a propensity to greed
with it.  Marx expresses the same idea when he points out that in
societies where not the exchange value but the utility of the product predominates, surplus-labour is limited by a given set of
wants and there is no boundless thirst for additional surplus-
labour arising from the nature of production itself.

It is this absence of the drive for maximising surplus-value on
the part of overlords which gives feudalism its stability and
resistance to change.  Conquerors come and go;  overlords fight
among themselves to engross more land and the labour attached to it;
but the economic units of feudal society, self-contained and more or
less self-perpetuating communities ruled by tradition and custom,
remain largely untouched — till mercantilism introduces the
universal solvent, money.

Under capitalism and the full growth of commodity production,

which transforms human ties into economic relationships and appears
to liberate men from having to acknowledge any master but money,
individual rights, in theory, attain their maximum expression.
But actually the creation of a surplus depends on the exploitation
of workers through the purchase of their labour-power, and the
unequal contract between employer and employee sets the tone of
an ethical system based on promise-keeping and contractual agreements — and the fundamental dishonesty of the pretence that these
deals in the worker's capacity to create value are fairly struck.
It is this fraud at the heart of capitalism that makes it the least
stable and shortest lived of all modes of production.

It is at the capitalist stage that classes reveal themselves as
what they always were, stripped now of all status-trappings, birth
rights and claims to natural superiority — simply the relationship
social groupings in an antagonistic exploitative situation bear to
the means of production. Ownership of the means of production is
the basis of exploiting the non-owners, the dispossessed. Where
the means of production is still mainly the individual's brute
force, this possessive power takes the form of ownership of the man
himself — slavery. Where the means of production is mainly land,
it is rights in land which define the ruling class and give them
power over those who work it. Where the means of production are
capital goods, it is the possession of capital which gives the
dominant class its rights in the labour of other men and what that
labour produces. Slavery, serfdom and wage labour are the keys to
an understanding of what the different modes of production, ancient
conquest-based, feudal and capitalist, are in essence and also keys
to understanding changes in moral attitudes with these changes in
material circumstances.

> If the moral consciousness of the mass declares an economic fact
> to be unjust, as it has done in the case of slavery or serf-
> labour, that is a proof that the fact itself has been outlived,
> that other economic facts have made their appearance, owing to
> which the former has become unbearable and untenable.(20)

There is no logical reason within morality itself why attitudes
toward slavery, for example, should change so radically or why the
opprobrium attached to making a profit at one period should have
turned into approval at another. Therefore the ground of the change
must be the material circumstances which underlie all thinking
about ethics.

Few serious writers on the history of human thought deny that
there is at least some connection between what men are thinking at
any particular time and the socio-economic conditions in which they
find themselves. But granting the connection, there can still be
differences about which of the related terms is the dominant factor.
Max Weber's view that the spirit of a particular mode of production like capitalism must precede the development of capitalist
institutions is of a piece with the bourgeois idealistic thought
of Germany. R.H. Tawney's compromise, that sometimes the ideal,
sometimes the material, takes precedence, is characteristic of
British empiricism which itself is the way of thought of a class
so successful that it feels it can afford to dispense with theory
and 'muddle through' pragmatically. Marx's historical materialism
which places the emphasis on economic considerations, such as the

forces of production and the class relationships determining the
distribution of the product while recognising the part ideological
considerations play once they have developed, is the ideology of
the working class — materialistic because workers cannot doubt
the reality of the natural world with which they mix their labour
in useful work;  historical because the fact of profound social
changes in the past validates the working-class's mission of also
bringing about revolutionary change, liberating themselves from
wage-labour and mankind generally from exploitation;  dialectical
because the experience of class struggle teaches the working class
that on the physical, social and mental levels, all interrelated,
reality is not static but a unity of opposites in which process is
continuous and change, even mind-directed change, is possible.  'The
philosophers have only interpreted the world in different ways;  the
point is to change it.'(21)

The view that only economic considerations in the narrowest
sense determine in a unilateral relationship our philosophical ideas
would rule out any possibility that those ideas, abstracted from
material conditions, could react on the circumstances which gave
rise to them and make thought practical.  This kind of deterministic
economism is mechanical materialism and must not be confused with
dialectical materialism.  Isaiah Berlin, in a series of lectures on
Historical Inevitability in 1953, seemed to think that in demolish-
ing a determinist, mechanical interpretation of history he had
finally polished off Marx, to say nothing of Hegel, Condorcet,
Spengler and others.  As far as Marxism is concerned he never came
to grips with the subject at all.  F.H. Bradley's refutation of
mechanical materialism in which he argues that if a series of mental
states are assumed simply to mirror a series of events causally
related, each particular mental state may be considered passive in
respect to the event of which it is the image but nevertheless must
be admitted to be active in respect to a successive event, since it
is one element in its total cause,(22) far from raising any problems for Marxism is a proof of the dialectical relationship of
matter and mind.

We can only decide which assumption about the relationship
between socio-economic ground and human consciousness, between
material base and ideological superstructure is more nearly true
by considering whether holding one or the other yields the more
fruitful consequences — not on the opportunistic, pragmatic
grounds that what works is true but on the genuinely practical
assurance that what is true works and can be proved workable in
social practice.  Which assumption, for example, has proved the
sounder in respect to the advance of our physical knowledge of the
universe — the view that nature is merely the phenomenal aspect
of mind and can be known deductively, in an a priori way, from the
logical categories of thought, or the view that nature is the
objective context in which minds have developed with laws of its
own, discoverable precisely because it provided the original ground
of the birth of human consciousness?

Similarly, the proof of historical materialism is whether it
gives us a better understanding than any alternative hypothesis of
human relationships and the conditions of social change, thereby
enabling us to control our future as men working and living

together — much as an understanding of physical laws has given us our control over nature.  And almost as a by-product of this effort to understand the world in order to change it, historical material- ism also explains why those who disagree with it have come to think as they do.


## CLASS DIVISION AND ETHICAL RELATIVISM

'The history of all hitherto existing society is the history of class struggle.'(23)  We have been considering changes in ethical attitudes as a result of changes in modes of production which are different forms of the relationship between exploiting and exploited classes.  These revolutionary changes, which are critical stages in the class conflict characterising all class-divided society, revolutionise ethics itself.

These successive differences in class ethical attitudes appear at any one particular time as the opposed ethical attitudes of contempory classes in their opposition to each other within the same society.  These differences are fundamental but because only the ethical attitudes of the exploiting or ruling class tend to be published and propagated as the attitudes of society as a whole, the character of these differences has to be grasped by appreciating the basic nature of classes themselves.

This task is, however, made easier by a distinctive feature of our own epoch which first made it possible to define exactly what classes are — a simplification of class antagonisms under capitalism.

> Society as a whole is more and more splitting up into two
> great hostile camps, into two great classes directly facing
> each other:  Bourgeoisie and Proletariat.  The bourgeoisie has
> stripped of its halo every occupation hitherto honoured and
> looked up to with reverent awe.  It has converted the physician,
> the lawyer, the priest, the poet, the man pf science, into its
> paid wage-labourers ... has pitilessly torn asunder the motley
> feudal ties that bound man to his 'natural superiors', and has
> left remaining no other nexus between man and man than naked
> self-interest, than callous 'cash-payment' ... in one word,
> for exploitation, veiled by religious and political illusions,
> it has substituted naked, shameless, direct, brutal exploita-
> tion.(24)

Thus, in the oldest capitalist country, Britain, this process has reached a point where it can now be said that there are only two classes:  capitalists and workers.

This polarisation of classes is of course the social manifesta- tion of the law of contradiction in things, the law of the unity of opposites which is the basic law of materialist dialectics.  'Dia- lectics in the proper sense', Lenin writes, 'is the study of contradiction in the very essence of objects.'  It is on this con- ception of the essential contradictoriness at the heart of every- thing from the atom, which is a unity of negatively and positively charged elements, right up to the most complicated social structure, which is a unity of the class opposition of exploiters and exploited, that the Marxist understanding of development and change is based.

There is internal contradiction in every single thing, hence
its motion and development.  Contradictoriness within a thing is
the fundamental cause of its development, while its interrelations and interactions with other things are secondary causes....
Changes in nature are due chiefly to the development of the
internal contradictions in nature.  Changes in society are due
chiefly to the development of the internal contradictions in
society, that is, the contradiction between the productive
forces and the relations of production, the contradiction
between classes....(25)

Materialist dialectics does not exclude external causes — 'external
causes are the condition of change and internal causes are the basis
of change, and the external causes become operative through internal
causes', which is the dynamic of revolutionary change as opposed
to the 'metaphysical' conception of change as mere decrease,
increase or repetition of isolates whether idealistically or
materialistically conceived.

Because reality is dialectical, valid thinking must be dialectical and the rules of thought reflect the laws of contradiction in
all things.  One of Mao Tsetung's contributions to the formulation
of the dialectical materialist rules of thought is his emphasising
that in the process of development of any complex thing there is
necessarily a principal contradiction which reveals the essential
quality of the thing, a main contradiction 'whose existence and
development determine or influence the existence and development
of other contradictions.  For instance, in capitalist society the
two forces in contradiction, the proletariat and the bourgeoisie,
form the principal contradiction' and give us the essential character of such a society.  This rule of dialectical thought, look for
the major contradiction in any subject under study, has helped make
dialectical materialism a useful tool for peasants and workers in
solving production problems and a sharp weapon for the working
class in its struggles.  It further frees the materialist dialectic
from such idealistic Hegelian expressions as the 'negation of
negation' which does not help anyone see how the dialectic is
actually to be used rather than merely understood.  This is also the
difficulty with Althusser's 'over-determination' in which the
plurality of contradictions is stressed in a way that makes the
dialectic useful for studying history but not for making it.

We have already noted the tendency, though at no time so clearly
marked as under capitalism, for the development of the division of
labour in society to result in two broad classes — those primarily
concerned with the laborious production of goods and those whose
interest is centred in the possession and enjoyment of them.  The
basic moral sensibilities of these two groups are distinguishable
because production and consumption with which they are respectively
associated became separated under the system of commodity exchange
developing out of the division of labour.  These broad moral sensibilities with their implications in terms of ideas about what is
right are part of the whole conception of value once it has been
differentiated according to the respective experience had of value-
bearing goods by those who make them and by those who, by and
large, possess and enjoy them.

Production is social in the obvious sense that men must enter into close relationships with each other in the creation of useful things, and indeed language itself originated in the cries and signals of associated labour.  Consumption is private and individualistic since no one else can satisfy our physical needs for us.  Production involves workers in a direct causal relationship with the material environment by which satisfactory goods are recognised for what they are, the result of practical human effort.  Consumption in itself, as we have so frequently noted, can give rise to the notion that the provision of goods is merely preceded by the desire for them.  These goods represent for their producers certain specific amounts of expended energy;  but to consumers they appear simply as abstract quantities of money, itself an abstraction.  The surplus product which is alienated from those whose labour created it takes the form of a profitable increment to those who acquire it through their control of the means of production.

From these familiar observations can be deduced quite different basic ethical inclinations characteristic of these two broad classes — a practical, down-to-earth, socialistic morality in which there is a strong sense of alienation on the one hand, and a reflective, abstract, acquisitive, individualistic morality in which there is a strong note of self-justification on the other.

All moral theories have been hitherto the product, in the last analysis, of the economic conditions of society obtaining at the time.  And as society has hitherto moved in class antagonisms, morality has always been class morality;  it has either justified the domination and interest of the ruling class, or, ever since the oppressed class became powerful enough, it has represented its indignation against this domination and the future interests of the oppressed.(26)

The distinction between manual and mental labour which is one aspect of class differences explains why class relationships in the broadest sense correspond in general with phases of the Marxist theory of knowledge.  A class intimately concerned with the physical world in the practical task of making things corresponds with the perceptual stage of understanding.  A class at one remove from material reality through not being under the compulsion of manual labour, a class for whom that reality and indeed relationships generally are mediated by money, corresponds with the stage of abstract thought and inferential judgment.  Both tend to be arrested at a particular phase of the total act of knowledge by the partiality of their experience and to fall short in different respects of the full understanding which requires all three moments — sensuous contact with the external world, conceptualisation and rearrangement of sense impressions in drawing logical conclusions and the application and verification of these hypothetical conclusions in social practice.

This class correspondence draws attention, through the Marxist theory of knowledge, to the two kinds of human knowledge there are, which Mao Tsetung describes as follows:

Ever since class society came into being the world has had only two kinds of knowledge, knowledge of the struggle for production and knowledge of the class struggle.  Natural science and social science are the crystallisations of these two kinds of knowledge,

and philosophy is the generalisation and summation of the
knowledge of nature and the knowledge of society (27) —
or, as we shall have occasion to consider them subsequently, the
knowledge of the forces of production and the knowledge of the
relations of production.  Knowledge of the struggle for production
through the development of the physical sciences is the ground of
all truth about the world we live in.  Knowledge of class struggle
through the development of the social sciences, including as its
most consistent, comprehensive and compelling expression, Marxism,
scientific socialism, is the ground of all truth about our relations
with each other in society including the relation of morality.

A social development which has altered the rough correspondence
between manual workers and the perceptual stage of knowledge on the
one hand and mental workers and the conceptual stage of knowledge on
the other is capitalism's requirement, with the advance of technology, for educated workers, industrial workers who are fully
equipped to think through the most abstruse problems of production.
At the same time the tendency of capitalism to simplify class
structure by proletarianising the intelligentsia, teachers,
designers, artists, managerial staff and all others who by living on
their wages have the same relation to the means of production as
industrial workers, has meant a swelling of the ranks of workers with
a capacity for both manual and mental tasks and has brought the
working class as a whole more nearly into line with all three
phases of the Marxist theory of knowledge.  Capitalism in creating
the working class 'produces its own grave-diggers'.  In producing
a literate, educated working class it makes sure that the grave
will be nicely squared off and efficiently dug.

Only the moral attitudes of the class with a possession and
consumption bias are likely to be expressed in published writings,
expounded from platforms and taught in schools.  As Marx reminds
us:  'The ideas of the ruling class are, in every age, the ruling
ideas', since 'the class which has the means of material production at its disposal, has control at the same time over the means
of mental production.'(28)  Control of the means of production
inevitably yields political control: without political oppression or the threat of it there can be no exploitation.

Marx goes on to say that
the division of labour ... manifests itself also in the ruling
class ... so that within this class one part appears as the
thinkers of the class (its active conceptualising ideologists,
who make it their chief source of livelihood to develop and
perfect the illusions of the class about itself), while the
others have a more passive and receptive attitude to these
ideas and illusions, because they are in reality the active
members of this class and have less time to make up ideas and
illusions about themselves.  This cleavage within the ruling
class may even develop into a certain opposition and hostility
between the two parts, but in the event of a practical collision
in which the class itself is endangered, it disappears of its
own accord and with it also the illusion that the ruling ideas
were not the ideas of the ruling class and had a power distinct
from the power of this class.
It is like, and just as inconsequential as, the apparent conflicts

that develop in Britain, say, between industrialists and the ideologists of capitalism in the government, whether Labour or Conservative, since the state, whoever nominally heads it, is 'an organ of class, an organ for the oppression of one class by another' and can never have any real differences with the ruling capitalist class of which it is the 'executive committee'.

Critics of Marxism often make the charge that identifying certain views with class interests is an attack on the integrity of reason itself and that pointing out the class character of ethical attitudes has the effect of introducing a moral relativism destructive of morality.  But class bias is not something Marx either invents or advocates:  it is a social fact to be recognised if we are serious about wanting to know how society works.  Such recognition provides a critique of reason which not only shows what its limitations are in class-divided societies but also what relative degrees of validity it can achieve within those circum- stances and how by a change in those circumstances distortions can be progressively eliminated.  Knowing why we think as we do is a necessary step in affirming or correcting our ideas.  Similarly, we shall have to show that the understanding that ethical stan- dards change with changes in the economic base of society or with changes of class perspective within the same society does not turn morality into a mechanical response to a particular social situa- tion nor does it cynically brush aside all ethical considerations to clear the way for the operation of naked self-interest.

Marxism's first contribution to the problem of relativism is to bring some order into this chaos of conflicting moral standards by showing that at all periods since the disruption of primitive communistic tribal units different classes have had their distinc- tive norms of conduct;  and, further, that at any particular period the pattern of socially-recommended behaviour has reflected the mode of production prevailing at that time.  Since these modes of production are historically limited in number and fairly determinate in form, general patterns of behaviour derived from them are similarly limited and recognisable.  And before the time when one of these modes of production, capitalism, developed to the point at which the obvious polarisation of society into exploiting capitalists and exploited workers made possible the Marxist analysis of thinking and morality themselves as thoroughly class-influenced, thinking and morality were not freer from class subjectivism:  people were simply ignorant of the class nature of ideology, that is all.

But let us look more closely at this question of the class subjectivism of ideology.  If the history of all hitherto existing society, at least the written history, since primitive communism is preliterate, is the history of class struggles, if at any time we dip into history we find that the whole character of the period is being shaped by class forces contending for economic and poli- tical domination, then the only way thinking at any time can inter- vene effectively is in a class form.  Only in its character as class ideology can thinking be practical.  As 'objective' in the sense of being above or outside the class contention which is making that historical epoch what it is, thinking would not be somehow 'purer';  it would simply be irrelevant.

Not that for Marxists it is a matter of indifference, from the point of view of relative truth, which class one is identified with.  According to the Marxist theory of knowledge truth is the result of the social practice of production.  It is not to be found in the minds of certain exceptional individuals.  Its source is the productive experience of the broad mass of the working people everywhere, renewing and enriching itself from generation to generation — the source socialism taps in unleashing the energies, skills and knowledge of the whole people.  The test of this truth is the enormous expansion down the ages of man's productive forces, limited only by the relations of production which are the particular form class exploitation takes in any given period.

Working-class ideology, in so far as it is the democratic expression in terms of knowledge of the vast practical experience of working people, really is truer than any ideology more partially based.  Marxism's identification with and development of this ideology is not the result of some kind of sympathy for the underdog but of a concern for truth in the most complete form it can take in our era.  The political expression of this claim made for working-class ideology is that 'the proletarian movement is the self-conscious, independent movement of the immense majority, in the interest of the immense majority', while 'all previous historical movements were movements of minorities, or in the interest of minorities.'(29)  Or as Marx makes the same point in terms of successive forms of class rule:

Every new class, therefore, achieves its hegemony only on a broader basis than that of the class ruling previously, in return for which the opposition of the non-ruling class against the new ruling class develops all the more sharply and profoundly.  Both these things determine the fact that the struggle to be waged against the new ruling class, in its turn, aims at a more decided and radical negation of the previous conditions of society than could all the previous classes which sought to rule.(30)

Furthermore, with the growing contradictions within bourgeois society there is a degeneration in the ruling class's regard for truth and bourgeois ideology becomes increasingly a false ideology.  Marx writes in 'The German Ideology':

The more the established form of intercourse in society, and thus the conditions of the ruling class, come into conflict with the developed productive forces, and the greater therefore is the dissension within the ruling class itself and between it and the subject class, the less viridical naturally becomes the consciousness which originates from and expresses this form of intercourse; i.e. it ceases to express it.  The earlier conceptions of these relations of intercourse, in which the real individual interests were asserted as general interests, decline into mere idealising phrases, conscious illusions and deliberate deceits.  But the more they are condemned as falsehoods, and the less they satisfy the understanding, the more dogmatically they are asserted and the more deceitful, moralising and spiritual becomes the language of established society.

The truth of Marxism itself, which both philosophically and politically is the most cogent expression of working-class ideology, can only be tested and proved, according to its own theory of knowledge, in social practice — in the October Revolution, and also in the understanding of how it was possible for it to be betrayed, in the Proletarian Cultural Revolution in China, in the Vietnamese people's heroic defeat of the mightiest imperialist aggressors of all time, in tiny Albania's successful building of socialism in the teeth of almost global hostility.

Critics of Marxism like Eugene Kamenka complain that it confuses 'absolute truth' in the sense of total knowledge to which our actual knowledge must be relative with 'absolute truth' in the sense of 'conveying an unambiguous issue, of being either true or false and not both.'(31)  This is deliberately to ignore that for Marxist materialism, as explained by Lenin in 'Materialism and Empirio-Criticism':

> the limits of approximation of our knowledge to objective, absolute truth are historically conditional, but the existence of such truth is unconditional, and the fact that we are approaching nearer to it is also unconditional.  The contours of the picture are historically conditional, but the fact that the picture depicts an objectively existing model is unconditional.

When and under what circumstances we reach, in our knowledge of the essential nature of things, the discovery of, say, electrons in the atom is historically conditional;  but that every such discovery is an advance of 'absolute objective knowledge' is unconditional.  Truth in relation to the whole and the truth of a particular aspect of the whole can be distinguished but they cannot be separated.  The dialectic of process and change is absolute but statements made about a changing reality are, at any given instant, both true and false, for the whole itself is not some static hypostatised super reality beyond experience to which truth approaches as a postulant to a shrine.  These critics would either dissolve all truth into general relativism or else they still hanker after discrete absolute truths handed down from on high on tablets of stone.  For Marxists truth whether of physical nature or human relationships is grounded in social practice. As Marx puts it in the Second Thesis on Feuerbach:

> The question whether objective truth can be attributed to human thinking is not a question of theory but a practical question.  In practice man must prove the truth, i.e. the reality and the power, the 'this-sidedness' of his thinking. The dispute over the reality or non-reality of thinking which is isolated from practice is a purely scholastic question.

The reality of the objective world as the pre-existent context of human thought and action prevents this practical vindication of truth which is the concluding stage of the dialectic of knowledge from degenerating into a subjective pragmatism.

Just as the recognition that thinking is inevitably influenced by considerations of class does not represent an attack on reason as such but a critique of reason based on the realisation of how it is anchored in reality, so recognition of class influence on ethical attitudes does not represent an attack on morality as such

but an explanation of its real nature and practical limitations.
Thinking about ethics and acting in a moral way take place in the
context of an existing society with a certain mode of production
and a certain relationship of classes, and normative judgments
are relatively valid to the extent that they express the real
purposes implicit in that mode of production or the real interests
of the classes whose relationship as exploiters and exploited is
implied by that particular mode of production.  In the same way
that there has been a progression in the clarity with which class
relationships have revealed themselves, so that with the final
commoditisation of labour-power itself in the capitalist mode of
production it became possible to define exactly what classes are,
there has also been a progression in the openness of declarations
of real class interests in contrast to all the mystical, religious
or pseudo-political banners under which social movements have
marched and fought in the past.

This recognition of the way ethical beliefs and practices
cannot but be the expression in terms of class relationships of
life in a particular society leads Marx to say:  'Right (in the
ethical sense) can never be higher than the economic structure of
society and its cultural development conditioned thereby.'(32)
It would be quite pointless to expect people to behave in ways that
were uncharacteristic of the 'cultural development' of a particular
society.

> Communists preach no morality at all.... They do not put to
> people the moral demand:  Love one another, be not egoists,
> because they know very well that egoism is under certain condi-
> tions the necessary form of the individual's struggle for
> survival.(33)

The morality Marx rejects here is the kind of abstract, universal
morality based on no understanding of the nature of society or the
classes that make it up which has always been the form of religious teaching.  It is like the 'philosophy' Marx rejects when
he says:

> where speculation ends — in real life — there real,
> positive science begins;  the representation of the practical
> activity, of the practical process of the development of men.
> Empty talk about consciousness ceases, and real knowledge has
> to take its place.  When reality is depicted, philosophy as
> an independent branch of activity loses its medium of
> existence.(34)

Philosophy as a separate branch of study carried out by 'gifted
individuals' is what Marx is attacking, not to put an end to
philosophy but to free it to play its proper role.  As Mao Tsetung
puts it:  'Liberate philosophy from the confines of the philosophers' lecture rooms and textbooks and turn it into a sharp
weapon in the hands of the masses.'(35)  In the same way 'morality'
must be freed from the professional moralists who cannot or will
not recognise its social character so that its proper role in
terms of the aspirations of oppressed masses can be understood.

Since the exploitation of man by man is the basis of class
divisions in society and since all thinking in class-divided
society inevitably has a class bias, the struggle to eliminate
exploitation is also a struggle to free thought from class

subjectivism.  If the working masses liberate themselves from wage-slavery, the final form that exploitation of class by class takes, they also free ideology from its character as special pleading on behalf of some partial interest to become the objective thought of socialist man.  The ideology of the working class which was already truer than any other by virtue of its more democratic base becomes the even truer and more extensive knowledge of men who no longer exploit each other but only nature in their united co-operative interest.  'This whole semblance, that the rule of a certain class is only the rule of certain ideas, comes to a natural end, of course, as soon as it is no longer necessary to represent a particular interest as a general interest or "the general interest" as ruling.'(36)

The transition from class-divided to classless society requires a change in the economic basis of society to a socialist mode of production.  Class relationships, as we have seen, are ultimately determined by the relations of different sections of the community to the means of production and when the means of production belong to society as a whole, that is the beginning of the abolition of classes.  This change is only different from other fundamental alterations in the social base which have occurred in that, while previous changes concerned which class was to exploit workers, the working class itself exploits no one and in emancipating itself it liberates all society from the exploitation of man by man.

Moral systems in the past, arising within class-divided societies, have 'represented either a dominant class's sanction to rule or an exploited class's consolation in suffering' as two aspects of the same antagonistic social situation.  Even so obviously an ethic of consolation for the oppressed as primitive Christianity could also be turned into an ideological instrument for the prosecution of the most ruthless class rule.  Any attempts of these systems to reconcile conflicting class interests have been spurious because no practical programme for changing the basic social conditions out of which class conflict arises were ever proposed.  Since society was to go on being divided, any resolution of class antagonism had to wait on the advent of utopias where either there was such an abundance of goods that with no necessity for work no one need go without or where beings with no material bodies to sustain did not need goods anyway.  And these earthly or heavenly paradises of the future could be used by those who might be highly sceptical themselves of any such eschatological happy ending to persuade the working masses to moderate their claims for goods here and now, so that the very hope of a classless society of human brotherhood and plenty was turned into a class weapon in the hands of the exploiters.

In a world like ours where class differences not only divide capitalist exploiters from the workers in their own countries whose lives are at the disposal of their bosses but also from the toiling masses of the colonial and semi-colonial world where millions upon millions live on the verge of starvation, to talk in terms of vague expressions of general good will and universal brotherhood is meaningless.  The principle of humanism cannot bridge such a gulf without becoming stretched so thin that it is without content.  Expressions of 'loving one's fellow man' in such a situation are not just hypocritical or impractical:  they are obscene — like urging the Vietnamese people, when the USA aggressors were raining down on them the most vicious and diabolical weapons ever devised, 'to turn the other cheek'.  As Mao Tsetung has said:

as for the so-called love of humanity, there has been no such all-inclusive love since humanity was divided into classes.  All the ruling classes of the past were fond of advocating it, and so were many so-called sages and wise men, but nobody has ever really practised it, because it is impossible in class society.(37)

Therefore Marxism preaches no morality of brotherly love in general in material circumstances rendering it impossible.  Instead it considers how those circumstances themselves can be changed by studying the means whereby the foundations for a classless social order can be laid.  Now in the context of moral systems based on various forms of class division, a theoretical and practical collective effort directed toward altering that very basis of all past morality is not merely relative to those other moral systems: it is absolute in the only sense in which we can ever know absolutes — as a conflict of opposites in which one aspect so completely overcomes the other that the whole situation is completely altered and entirely new considerations come into play.

Marxism is thus a completely radical approach to the question of morality because it envisages a fundamental change in the very conditions under which thinking about morality takes place.  In the process of changing those conditions people also change themselves.  What Marxism ultimately says in normative terms is simply this:  if you are serious about wanting a world in which all men can work together in harmony, helping one another to realise the full human potential in each, then there is a certain kind of social organisation you must struggle to achieve.  And, further, it says:  since 'mankind only takes up such problems as it can solve because the problem itself arises only when the material conditions for its solution already exist or are at least in the process of formation',(38) this moral challenge to transform society only sounds when the means for its realisation are at hand.


CONSCIENCE AND CLASS CONSCIOUSNESS

Everyone is born in a particular social environment and is subjected from his earliest days to a number of influences which guide his conduct and shape his very ideas about how he ought to behave.  These conditioned responses become so habitual as to seem almost instinctive.  They develop into an inner regulator of behaviour that would continue to function for some time even if the social pressures by which it was originally determined were suddenly altered or removed.  This internal censor governs conduct much as any memorised set of rules, the highway code or parliamentary procedure, regulates specific forms of activity like driving a car or organising a meeting;  but while such activities as these are optional, everyone has to live in society and therefore socially acceptable patterns of behaviour as represented in the individual conscience have a much more compulsive force.  This guidance from

within is practically automatic except when some occasion arises
for acting against its dictates, whereupon one becomes acutely
aware of it through a sense of uneasiness, a foreboding of im-
pending disaster, a feeling of guilt.  Since conscience is the
individual's built-in compendium of social rules, to defy its
injunctions is to act out in some degree the old tragedy of
breaking a taboo and finding oneself ostracised from the tribal
group.

Because all who grow up in society acquire a conscience and
because all social groupings have certain human relationships more
or less in common, it is often assumed that the moral contents of
everyone's conscience must be the same.  The kind of sanction
invoked in a particular society to give social rules a greater
force will also be used to explain the origin of the individual
conscience:  if such rules are taken to be prescriptions handed
down from on high by some supernal being, then conscience is
described as the god-given faculty enabling the individual to
appreciate the relevance of those rules to his daily life;  if
rules of social behaviour are deduced from an eternal and universal
reason, then conscience is the individual's innate rationality by
which he can recognise the validity of such ideal principles.
Whatever the form of these sanctions they all rely for their
authority on the assumption that they apply to all men under all
circumstances.

But, in fact, conscientious behaviour reveals the same variety
as the patterns of social mores which have characterised different
societies or different classes within the same society.  In the
latter connection it is hardly surprising to find that members of
the working class are most conscientious about solidarity with
fellow workers, particularly those in the same trade or industry,
and 'sending someone to Coventry' for an infringement of that
solidarity as the result of a sentence by what the bourgeoisie call
a 'kangaroo court' is the proletarian equivalent of tribal ostracism.  The bourgeoisie, on the other hand, are most conscientious
about money matters and contractual agreements, and the whole
system of their kangaroo courts exists largely to accommodate
litigation over these questions.  Even in respect to those relationships which all would seem to have in common, like attitudes
toward sex and marriage and toward parental and filial obligations, the classes diverge in what they naturally consider proper
conduct.

Differences in norms of behaviour as rooted in the consciences
of people with different social experiences become crucial for the
moral philosopher when confronted with the problem that men who it
may be widely agreed have perpetrated the vilest acts in history
often seem to have been perfectly sincere in believing that they
were behaving conscientiously — and, furthermore, have been able
to persuade others under the same morbid social conditions that
they were doing right.  This has even led some writers on ethical
questions to enter a plea for a life of personal indulgence as
opposed to one of high moral endeavour on the ground that if the
former achieves nothing to the benefit of mankind it at least,
unlike the latter, avoids the risk of doing any great harm either.
But, of course, what is really wanted is a critique of the individual

conscience, implying thereby a critique of the social order conscience reflects.

In relatively stable societies, like the village communities of Asian feudalism in which life may have gone on virtually un-changed for centuries, the implanted consciences of individual members are in harmony with society's moral requirements and the whole ethical pattern of life is a more or less unconscious repe-tition of well-established customs. But in a situation of social mobility where individuals may be altering their class position or where classes themselves may be experiencing a change in their relationship to each other, people find that their consciences conservatively refer to a social context which no longer exists for them.  This inevitably involves the individual in a moral crisis;  and conscience can offer no guidance since its irrelevance to present circumstances is the very source of the trouble.  Such a crisis in which the fundamental principles of conduct no longer seem to apply can, in times of rapid social change, afflict whole societies with a general malaise and the various neuroses which psychiatrists attempt to treat in terms of complexes rooted in a personal past are often individual instances of this wide-spread discrepancy between private consciences and altered social conditions.

The therapeutic treatment implied by a Marxist diagnosis of the problem is not unlike the effort to restore a patient to mental health by uncovering deep-seated disturbances and bringing to light unsuspected impulses — except that the cure has to be con-ceived in social rather than individualistic terms.  The private conscience must be raised to the level of awareness where its moral content can be studied and criticised:  it must be seen for what it really is — unconscious group allegiance.  Seeing it for what it is transforms the private conscience into class conscious-ness.  Once it is realised that conscience is the uncritical and spontaneous form of one's sense of belonging to a particular class, it is possible to affirm those social ties consciously in purposeful activity or, if they do not seem to be in one's real interests or do not appear to conform to one's real class circum-stances, to break them in order to adopt social ties that do.

The problem of a conscience at odds with real class interest is particularly characteristic of an exploited class.  The fact we have already noted that 'the ideas of the ruling class are, in every age, the ruling ideas' and therefore the only ideas to circu-late freely contributes to the problem.  The ruling class has every interest in foisting its own ideology on those it oppresses in order to exploit.  The capitalist system produces a working class whether its members realise it or not, a class-in-itself;  but when its members are fully conscious of being workers and examine their ideology to make sure that it really is their own and not in some other class's interest, then it becomes a class-for-itself.

In its knowledge of capitalist society, the proletariat was only in the perceptual stage of cognition in the first period of its practice, the period of machine-smashing and spontaneous struggle;  it knew only some of the aspects and the external relations of the phenomena of capitalism.  The proletariat was then still a 'class-in-itself'.  But when it reached the second

period of its practice, the period of conscious and organised
economic and political struggles, the proletariat was able to
comprehend the essence of capitalist society, the relations of
exploitation between social classes and its own historical
task;  and it was able to do so because of its experience of
prolonged struggle, which Marx and Engels scientifically summed
up in all its variety to create the theory of Marxism for the
education of the proletariat.  It was then that the proletariat
became a 'class-for-itself'.(39)

Only as a class-for-itself does the working class become a
revolutionary force, hence the concern of the bourgeoisie that the
working class should not know itself for what it really is —
particularly in terms of its historic mission as the liberator of
mankind.  Full conscious membership in this liberation force, the
working class, is an act of deliberate choice over and above the
mere fact of having a certain relationship to the means of production —  a choice which in so far as it is made on the basis of
one's own long-term interests is rational and, in so far as it
commits one to the ethical standards of a class-for-itself, is
moral.  The choice, whether it is actually put into words or
merely expresses itself in the quality of behaviour, is quite
fundamental since it amounts to a decision about what system of
ethical principles one intends all future actions to be judged by.

Marxist morality consists of an identification in struggle with
the oppressed and exploited against the oppressors and exploiters.
By such a commitment one has chosen not only that class morality
which is to be the standard of one's present actions but also that
course of social conduct which will eventually resolve conflicting
moralities into one embracing ethic reflecting the aspirations of
all men in an undivided society from which oppression and exploitation have been eliminated.

As Lenin expresses it in answer to the question of whether there
is a Marxist ethics:

Of course there is such a thing as communist ethics.... But we
repudiate all morality derived from non-human and non-class
concepts.... We say that our morality is entirely subordinated
to the interests of the class struggle of the proletariat....
Our morality serves the purpose of helping human society to
rise to a higher level and to get rid of the exploitation of
labour.(40)

The whole of working-class ethics is implicit in class struggle.
In the idea of 'class' is all fellow feeling, comradeship, sympathy
and concern for others — not a profession of regard in general
for oppressors and oppressed alike which in embracing everyone
actually clasps no one, nor comes to grips with anyone either;  but
a real, mutual, practical working relationship with all those
sharing the same great historic task of ending the exploitation
of man by man.  In the idea of 'struggle' is the realisation
that it is not a question of simply understanding the world but of
changing it and of changing oneself in the process.  It is the
conviction that human nature can be changed — not by private conversion but by social revolution, by overthrowing a system where
exploitation and inhumanity pay and establishing a system built on
cooperative work and a general sharing of the good things of life.

These are the ideas, drawn from the historical experience of the working people of the world and elaborated as the Marxist theory of revolutionary change, which taken back to the working masses grip them and become 'a material force which changes society and changes the world'. Or as Enver Hoxha has expressed it:

Marxism-Leninism is not a privilege and monopoly of certain able-minded people who can understand it. It is the scientific ideology of the working class and only when its ideas are mastered by the working class does it cease to be something abstract and become a great material force for the revolutionary transformation of the world.(41)

The working masses recognise these ideas, as concentrated in revolutionary theory, because they came from them to begin with and 'have the mark of the people on them'. This is the meaning of the mass line — from the masses to the masses, taking the ideas of the masses, scattered and unsystematic, concentrating and systema-tising them and then going to the masses and propagating and explaining these ideas 'until the masses embrace them as their own, hold fast to them and translate them into action, and test the correctness of these ideas in action.'(42) Because, of course, the gripping of the masses by ideas which thus become a material force is simply the third stage of the process of knowledge — the social practice without which the act of knowledge remains incom-plete and there is no proper relationship between theory and practice. 'Theory becomes purposeless if it is not connected with revolutionary practice, just as practice gropes in the dark if its path is not illumined by revolutionary theory.'(43)

Once the unexamined conscience, as a result of self-realisation in a struggle situation alongside one's fellows, appears as what it really is — class consciousness, then morality can appear as what it really is — the morale of a class force conscious of the justice of its struggle. Marxism lays great stress on the impor-tance of morale which is the ethical aspect of ideas becoming a material force. In people's war, for example, which is the colonial form of class war, waged by the working masses against the vastly superior and infinitely better-armed professional armies of invaders, morale is the decisive factor. It enables the people of a small or industrially backward country to defeat and repel the aggressive forces of powerful imperialist countries — as the people of China, Indochina or Albania, under communist leadership, were able to smash and roll back the massively-armed forces of Japan, the USA or fascist Italy and nazi Germany. Mehmet Shehu who was one of the partisan leaders in Albania's war of liberation describes this advantage of morale:

In fighting on the plains as well as in the mountains man is the decisive factor that determines the fate of the war regard-less of armaments. A small army can defeat a bigger one, superior in numbers and means, if it wages a just war and if it is made up of men who are politically enlightened on the just nature of the war they are waging....(44)

The fighting morale of the Vietnamese people, under the leadership of Ho Chi Minh, sustained them through thirty-five years of con-tinuous war during which they successively and decisively defeated the imperialist forces of Japan, France and the USA.

Morale is, in the same way, the ethical realisation of politically enlightened workers, class conscious workers, that their class war to end oppression and exploitation is itself a just war.  This keeps the working class in good heart for the great liberation battles they have to wage, reminding them that they have class brothers in struggle the world over and that, in Mao Tsetung's inspiring words: 'Countless revolutionary martyrs have laid down their lives in the interests of the people, and our hearts are filled with pain as we the living think of them — can there be any personal interest, then, that we would not sacrifice or any error that we would not discard?'(45)

In the act of commitment to this class struggle one has not only taken a decision about one's own ethical conduct, one has also expressed a concern for the ethical conduct of those yet unborn by working for a form of society in which — because it is characterised by shared abundance rather than selfishly manipulated scarcities, because it is based on co-operation rather than competition — 'being good' in the fullest human sense will not only be the right but also the natural thing to do.  This attitude can be contrasted with the moral athleticism of those thinkers who, usually in the comfort of their studies, are prepared to accept social injustice and human suffering as a sort of ethical challenge by which men test and prove themselves.  Of such 'moral heroism' one could say with Brecht 'happy the land which has no need of heroes'.  Marxists summon us to action thus: Let us end the infamy of starvation in a world capable of plenty and the waste through unemployment or misemployment of the creative talents of millions upon millions of people;  let us smash once and for all a system which values things but not the people who make them and rests on the bodies of babies condemned to death, rejection or misuse at birth;  and let the future use its ingenuity to find its own moral causes when all completely unnecessary suffering has been eliminated!

They say this because such a moral response is simply part of what it is to be a class-conscious worker, conscious of one's ties with working people everywhere and a Marxist because Marxism is the ideology of the working class.  'When a communist', by which Marx means a worker whose political enlightenment has placed him in the vanguard of his class, 'stands in front of a crowd of scrofulous, overworked and consumptive starvelings he sees the necessity and at the same time the condition of a transformation both of industry and of the social structure.'(46)  The Marxist-Leninist Party which is the political vanguard of the working class, in concentrating and elucidating the political consciousness of the working class, is its moral conscience also.

In making a point of the consciousness of this fundamental moral choice, which is simply an affirmation of working-class allegiance in full understanding of all its implications, it is interesting to note that it is a privilege of the historical time we live in to choose with greater awareness than ever before of just what that choice entails.  Past transformations of society resulting from the conflicts of classes have either taken place over so long a time scale that individuals at any particular period would have been unaware of the change, or else they have assumed obscure

ideological forms like religious or dynastic wars so that people
could not always recognise the nature of the economic interests at
stake.  The beginnings of feudal societies are never distinct
enough to assign even approximate dates to their origin.  The
change from feudalism to capitalism was marked by certain precise
engagements in this country or that;  but these struggles often
failed in definitiveness and, because they usually involved the
recruitment of class forces not intended to benefit from the
change, were fought out under a confusing multiplicity of banners.
There has thus been a progression in history by which each succeed-
ing transformation has been a more distinct event in time and a
more consciously-orientated social change than the one preceding.
Lenin makes this point when he says that in the bourgeois revolution the new economic organisation 'gradually matured in the womb
of feudalism'(47) while the socialist revolution is faced with
the problem of creating all its institutions on a foundation swept
clear of previous formations, which implies both that revolutionary theory plays a more dynamic role in this most decisive of
all social transformations and that the real nature of the class
interests involved reveal themselves more clearly than in past
transitions.

So now in the capitalist world we are confronted with the most
distinctive, the most sharply-defined change of all history — the
change from bourgeois rule to working-class rule as the transitional
stage of the change from class-divided to classless society.  There
are only the two sides now, the exploiters and the exploited,
those who want to keep things as they are and those who want
this great revolutionary change.  There are no neutrals.  Not to
choose at all is to opt for the side with every interest in maintaining things as they are.  Few can pretend that they do not know
what the issues are and can therefore be absolved of the responsibility of choosing what is socially right.


THE ETHICS OF REVOLUTIONARY CHANGE

The economic base of capitalist society will not be altered
because men arbitrarily decide that the cultural and ethical superstructure which might be raised on some other social base would be
preferable.  Cracks have to appear in that capitalist base,
internal contradictions must reach a critical point before the
utilitarian amorality in which economic rules usurp the role of
moral standards breaks down.  As long as the economic system appears
to operate automatically and continues to hold out at least the
promise of expanding material benefits for the majority, it will not
be challenged.  A protracted crisis in such a system, however, precipitates morality out of its solution with economic rules to
resume its place as a distinguishable, though never unrelated realm
of discourse.  The basic ordering of society, having failed to
achieve what people had a right to expect, becomes once more a
subject for normative speculation.  An unresolved crisis in the
capitalist mode of production must lead in time to its supersession
by another, which simply means that the capitalist ruling class in
whose interest society was basically organised is no longer able

to maintain its rule and is supplanted by another whose very class
nature involves an entirely different ordering of the economic base.

During the period of inevitably violent transition, since no
class in history has ever voluntarily abdicated from class supremacy,
the ethical implications of these conflicting forms of social organisation confront each other in fierce debate.  Then with the establishment of a new material foundation,

> the entire immense superstructure is more or less rapidly
> transformed.  In considering such transformations a distinction
> should always be made between the material transformation of
> the economic conditions of production, which can be determined
> with the precision of natural science, and the legal, political,
> religious, esthetic or philosophic — in short, ideological
> forms in which men become conscious of this conflict and fight
> it out.(48)

Not only must a distinction be made between the material transformation of the base and the ideology of the new class to assume
economic and political power, but unless that new ideology is
purged of the elements of the ideology of the overthrown class in
a moral revolution as sweeping as the economic transformation, the
base will be subverted by that unreconstructed ideology and there
will be a more or less rapid reversion to something like the old
corrupt system — as happened in the Soviet Union after Stalin's
death.

Marx goes on to say in the same quotation:

> Just as our opinion of an individual is not based on what he
> thinks of himself, so can we not judge of such a period of
> transformation by its own consciousness;  on the contrary, this
> consciousness must be explained from the contradictions of
> material life, from the existing conflict between the social
> productive forces and the relations of production.

We have noted some of these religious and philosophical forms of
special pleading in which class conflict in past periods of transformation has been fought out, and we are familiar in the present
with the attacks on Marxism, that is, on working-class ideology,
as godless, immoral, subversive of eternal truth, scientifically
unsound and in every way vicious and reprehensible.  But Marxism
itself, as shown in the quotation from Marx, is capable of characterising the very way in which interested participants may fail to do
justice to the actual contradictions of material life and of expressing the working class's own consciousness of the real nature
of the conflict between the forces and the relations of production
which can only be resolved by a revolutionary change in those
relations.

Present-day capitalism is in a state of crisis as a result of
the exacerbation of its internal contradictions, these contradictions being just so many economic forms of class struggle.  This
has been so throughout the history of class-divided society.  If
there were no slave revolts, no peasant uprisings, no organised
working-class resistance to exploitation, there would be no contradictions in the relations of production, no economic problems and
there would never have been any revolutionary changes in society.
Fully developed commodity production depends on a free market for
ordering the outlay of capital among the various kinds of goods to

be made;  but the falling rate of profit under free competition, which is partly due to organised defence by workers of their standard of living, requires capitalists to try to gain control of the market in respect to the goods they themselves produce.  The resulting monopolisation interferes with the free market and upsets the mechanism which preserves the balance between investment in means of production and investment in consumable goods.  Any attempt to increase profits by rises in productivity while real wages are frozen or cut is obviously self-contradictory since it increases output at the same time that it restricts effective demand.  Attempts by capitalists to evade these dilemmas at home force them to seek markets abroad, which brings them into conflict with capitalists from other industrialised countries seeking the same remedy.  The formation of cartels, like the growth of monopoly in a single country, merely reproduces on an international scale the domestic effects of tampering with the freedom of the market while not replacing it with a rational scheme of production and exchange.  And also the export of capital abroad where labour may be cheaper and profits higher deprives domestic industry of investment and erodes the production of value at home on which an economic empire must ultimately be based.  The phase of finance capitalism, of commodity speculation increasingly dissociated from the creation of value in the actual making of things, is like the second purely idealist and sterilely speculative phase of the acquisition of knowledge once it is cut off from any base in the real world where nature is transformed and theory is vindicated in practice.

Growing organisation of the working class at home to defend themselves against the capitalists' onslaughts and growing resistance abroad to imperialist depradation intensify all these contradictions which can no longer be glossed over by geographical expansion into uncapitalised parts of the globe.  Vast areas like China are closed completely to the operations of monopoly capitalism and the rest of the world is like a bear pit of frantically competing super and middle powers.

What this all means is simply that an anarchic system of production for profit, rather than a rational system of production geared to people's needs, cannot indefinitely survive the class antagonism it engenders.  Capitalism will be destroyed by its internal contradictions, the essence of all these contradictions being that between exploiters and exploited, the class struggle. Revolution triumphs in Lenin's words when 'the lower classes do not want the old way, and when the upper classes cannot carry on in the old way.'  What is essential for revolution is,

first, that a majority of the workers (or at least a majority
of the class conscious, thinking, politically active workers)
should fully understand that revolution is necessary and be
ready to sacrifice their lives for it;  secondly, that the
ruling class should be passing through a governmental crisis,
which draws even the most backward masses into politics.(49)

The working-class revolution in the relations of production puts an end to production for profit by destroying its base in property rights.  Since production is social, ownership of the product cannot equitably be based on the private ownership of

property.  This is not to suggest that justice would consist in
disentangling for the purpose of fair payment the contribution of
each separate individual to social production.  Once capitalist
private property has been established by divorcing the peasant from
the land and the craftsman from his tools, it is not feasible to
return to Locke's simple formula of deducing rights in specific
things from the individual labour that produced them.  Instead
property itself must be socialised by common collective ownership of
all the means of production, whereby a social right in things is
fairly established on the basis of the co-operative efforts of all
who are associated in the productive process.  Under capitalism,
particularly in its final and most corrupt phase, neither an individual nor a social relationship properly exists between productive
effort and appropriation, and there is thus no ground for an ethical
deduction of 'rights' in general, which means there is no longer any
basis for capitalist morality.

Even if it were possible for the capitalist system to function in
such a manner that there was a fairer sharing of goods among those
whose efforts are value-creative, as reformist social democrats
never tire of proposing as an alternative to revolution, it would not
meet the real objection to the system.  It is an example of that consumers' bias which vitiates all such petty bourgeois schemes of
pleading with capitalism to be nicer.  Alienation of the product is
not the only nor even the gravest crime of capitalism against the
working class.  More serious is the alienation of the workers'
creative ability in the act of production, so that the very source
of value, that which makes him a human being, is prostituted to
profiteering and brings forth articles of dubious quality in which
he can take no pride because he had no say in their production.
This is not free labour but wage-slave labour.

In the succession of modes of production there is no gradual
advance from lower to higher.  Progress depends on shifts in the
unity of opposites, which is the basic nature of everything, including societies, till one aspect of the major contradiction determining the character of a thing suppresses the other and a new
unity of opposites, that is to say, a new thing is born.  This
process of change cannot but be discontinuous, revolutionary rather
than evolutionary.

Each of the modes of production must find conditions right for
its inception, grow to its full extent and exhaust all its possibilities before giving way to a successive mode.  But progress may
also be discontinuous in the sense that a society which experiences the earliest and fullest development of a particular mode of
production, while generating the ideas which will help shape the
next stage, may have become so encumbered with a bureaucratic and
military apparatus, so encrusted with all the forms and institutions
of an outworn ideology that it will not itself be the immediate
locus of revolutionary change.  Such change will begin on the
periphery of the unevenly developed system where its organisation is
weakest and where the forms of an even earlier mode of production
still exist but are in process of rapidly collapsing — as in the
case of Russia, and to an even greater extent as far as the very
primitive development of capitalist institutions is concerned,
China and Albania.

Critics of Marx have tried to make capital out of his alleged mistake of prophesying that the working-class revolution ought to begin in one of the older industrialised countries. At various times in the shifting historical perspective of nineteenth-century Europe Marx thought various countries might be the scene of the first successful proletarian revolution, including Russia which might proceed directly to a successful 'socialist revolution without the intervention of a developed bourgeois stage'. But all he actually predicted on the basis of his scientific analysis of capitalism was working-class revolution at some point within the capitalist system which by 1917 encompassed the whole world. That is precisely what happened where the system was weakest and it has had and is continuing to have a profound effect on the working class movements in the older industrialised countries themselves.

There is a kind of glee with which critics pounce on the alleged errors of Marx — almost as though they hold it against him personally that the revolution they so fear and hate has not yet taken place in their own country. One of the forms of this criticism is to take what Marx described as tendencies and treat them as mechanical laws disproved by the slightest variation. Think of all the arguments against the falling rate of profit when the whole impulse of monopolisation and investment abroad is a tribute to it. Or that other tendency which has aroused such controversy — the pauperisation of the working class. With the uneven development of capitalism it has been possible at particular times and places, during transitory periods of prosperity, for a well-organised working class to wrest some economic and political concessions from the employing class; but never to the point of altering basically the relative positions of a tiny capitalist minority owning and controlling a huge proportion of the wealth of a country and the vast working majority never, at the best of times, more than a couple of weeks away from penury. And at all times a poverty-stricken 'reserve army' of unemployed was available to drive down the market value of labour-power and keep wages from rising above the subsistence level characteristic of that particular society.

What has been made most of in this context is the greater degree of oppression and misery of workers in colonial territories compared with workers in metropolitan countries and the effects this is supposed to have had on the revolutionary élan of these latter workers. Naturally the ruling class in the metropolitan countries would like to associate the working class ideologically, but not of course economically, in their colonial depradations. Certainly the Fabians and other social democrats based their case for social reforms on the argument that only a well-fed, well-educated working class could man a world-wide economic empire. But since there is no more material basis for workers in the metropolitan country to think of themselves as sharing in the exploitation of workers in the underdeveloped world than for a skilled worker in a factory to think that his higher rate of pay means he has joined the ranks of management in exploiting his work mates, the illusion of 'sharing in the crumbs' of the imperialist feast could take no firm hold on workers' minds. Only thinkers of the so-called 'left' have fallen for the line of treating imperialist exploitation as

some new kind of conflict, between rich and poor countries or even
between whites and other races, which made capitalists and workers
in the metropolitan country partners in crime.  For them the working class of the older industrialised countries has become so fat
and corrupt with good living that emancipation can only be conceived of in terms of a liberative force of poor workers and peasants from the colonial world arriving on the shores of the metropolitan country to free it.

Trotskyites also divide the working class of the imperialist
countries from the workers and peasants of the colonial world but
by mechanically applying a class analysis to liberation movements
and pronouncing them non-revolutionary because they are not led by
a large urban proletariat and are likely to be distorted by
industrial backwardness.  If according to the former the older
industrialised countries are too rich to have a socialist revolution, according to the Trotskyites all other countries are too
poor to have one.

Of course the reason why Trotskyites, more intellectual
descendants of Bakunin than of Marx anyway, are the darlings of
the bourgeoisie is that they always try to turn every conflict
between workers and employers into one between different sections
within the working class — as when they attempt to set unskilled
against skilled workers, unorganised against organised, rank and
file against stewards or officials, ostensibly because the worst
off are supposed to be the more revolutionary, actually because
they are thought to be easier dupes of these would-be leaders.  If
there were an automatic relationship between degrees of oppression
and degrees of revolutionary fervour, every real revolutionary
would be primarily concerned with making the working class as
miserable as possible.

To these enemies of working-class unity must be added all those
agents of the bourgeoisie who try to divide up workers academi-
cally — sociologists who want to compartmentalise them on the
basis of income differentials, status symbols, accent or what not
and thus serve the same overriding interest of the ruling capitalist class whose policy toward workers at home or abroad is always
'divide and rule' — just as the policy of the working class must
always be 'unite and liberate'.

Workers can only fight where they are and the best service the
workers of a metropolitan country can do for their embattled class
brothers overseas is to make a revolution in their own land —
just as immigrant workers themselves can only be mobilised for
revolutionary struggle within the organised ranks of their working
class brothers in the adopted land where they are being exploited.
At various times the class struggle may be more intense within the
major capitalist countries or between imperialists and the working
masses of the semi-colonial territories;  but these struggles are
always complementary, being waged against the same class enemy,
and taken together they confirm 'the main trend in the world today
as revolutionary'.

Another attempt to split workers by a critic of Marx is that of
Dahrendorf who insists that the working class is becoming more
diversified in spite of the evidence in Britain that so-called
'white collar' workers including even government employees not

only recognise themselves as belonging to the working class but are increasingly adopting the same methods of struggle as industrial workers. He also makes much of the diversification in the ruling class itself between owners and controllers as though this invalidated somehow the revolutionary prescription of expropriating the owners of the means of production. But Marx had made the distinction himself in his discussion of joint-stock companies and had realised it was a distinction without a class difference and certainly did not, as some of these critics maintain, change capitalism into some different mode of production.

Most of these apologists for capitalism are victims of their own propaganda. They adduce as reasons for rejecting the Marxist analysis 'changes' in the nature of capitalism which are only capitalism's superficial attempts to pretend to be something else in order to avoid the consequences of that very Marxist analysis. If they really did think that redefinition of classes or changing capitalism's name had made revolution impossible, they would probably not go on making it their life's work to show why revolutions cannot happen. Perhaps they are only trying to reassure their employers or, even, to disarm them as a contribution to a less violent transition!

The moral crisis of capitalism is a reflection of the economic crisis — not just a periodic depression but the chronic underemployment or misuse of human skills and productive capacity. Just as a particular ordering of the material basis of society and its characteristic relations of production give rise to a productive potential on which those relations begin to act as a limitation, so it also gives rise to moral ideas which cannot be realised within its confines. Implicit in the development of capitalism was the promise to free man from subservience to others and abolish the relationship of subjection. What it actually did, as we have seen, was to conceal the fact of exploitation behind a commodity deal — and in its external relationships with technologically less developed regions it dispensed with any mask at all. 'The colonies secured a market for the budding manufacturers, and, through the monopoly of the market, an increased accumulation. The treasures captured outside Europe by undisguised looting, enslavement, and murder, floated back to the mother-country and were there turned into capital.'(50)

From the law of value, as the fundamental principle of commodity exchange, was deduced by way of the equalisation of human labour the idea of the equality of man; and this same principle both recalls the primitive formula that what a person has mixed his labour with ought to belong to him and points ahead to a rational and moral order in which the values produced socially will belong to the whole society. But the fact of surplus-value, as a levy the class controlling the means of production exacts from the class possessing only its own labour-power, negates these ethical ideas of past and future. Colonialism is only the most blatant and brutal form of the scramble for surplus-value. Marx describes it as 'the strange god' who perched himself on the altar cheek by jowl with the old Gods of Europe, and one fine day with a shove and a kick chucked them all of a heap. It proclaimed surplus-value making as the sole end and aim of humanity.'(51)

To the very extent that capitalism fails to justify the economic
and ethical hopes which were the ideological motive force of its
conquest of feudalism it is preparing the way for its own supersession.   The same process which perverts and exploits human
labour in setting up profits for a small capitalist class as the
sole aim toward which the entire energy of society is directed also
produces the agents of its own transformation — a propertyless
proletariat with little stake in the present order and sound reasons
for wishing to see it replaced.

Not that it is simply the induced misery of a labouring class
which leads to the overthrow of a particular form of exploitation:
people have lived at a bare subsistence level for long periods without revolting against their condition.   There must also be the
awareness that some other form of social organisation is possible;
and this depends in part on the productive forces having attained
such a level that further expansion is seen to be thwarted not
by the limits of man's ability but by arbitrary restrictions imposed
in the interest of profit.   Workers who know that products which
are the fruits of their labour could be made to last by using
better materials or that good materials, the fruits of other
workers' efforts, should not be wasted on gimcrack products;   farm
workers who know that land considered 'uneconomic' for tilling
could produce much needed food;   inventors who see their ideas
bought up simply to be suppressed;   social scientists who are
employed to use their understanding of human motivation to intensify exploitation;   research workers whose facilities for experiment
depend on a government's military aggressiveness in policing
overseas investments — all of these may be brought to a realisation that there ought to be some social system which would free
their talents and skills for the unhampered creation of values that
all men could share in peace.   This 'ought' crystallises the moral
impulse which cannot find its proper expression in the existing
system.   It can only be realised in a revolutionary transformation
in the material conditions of life by which the commodity form
of articles disappears and production is directly related to human
needs.

In the classless society of the future, once all exploitation
has been eliminated and all the habits, customs and ways of thought
characteristic of an acquisitive society have been purged, men
will be engaged in a co-operative social effort giving everyone
full scope for self-expression in creative work and at the same
time providing the fund of goods from which everyone draws at need.
The whole process of production and consumption will have become
united once more, as in the case of a peasant family or a primitive
communist tribe — but with the difference that it will represent,
through the enormous increase in knowledge of productive technique
during the commodity period, a direct sharing of wealth instead of
poverty.

The law of value, relieved of the task of relating the disparate
acts of men working blindly in an atomised society, will vanish;
and goods themselves will no longer pass through a phase in which
their relative pricing marks them as abstract values in contra-
distinction to their usefulness.   Labour and satisfaction will
cease to be separated from each other, healing the breach between

duty and pleasure, reason and feeling.  The distinguishable elements
of value and utility which we found within the very meaning of a
word like 'good' will coalesce;  and anything whatever which is
conducive to the realisation of the human potential in all of us,
by way of creation or recreation, will be designated as good in a
completely integrated sense.  The conception of labour as 'dis-
utility', something painful and unpleasant by its very nature,
partly because of the actual conditions of work where labour is
exploited and partly because of attitudes toward physical effort
by an intelligentsia, will disappear.

As Marx describes it:

In a higher phase of communist society, after the enslaving
subordination of the individual to the division of labour,
and with it also the antithesis between mental and physical
labour, has vanished;  after labour has beoome not only a means
of life but itself life's prime want;  after the productive
forces have also increased with the all-round development of
the individual, and all the springs of co-operative wealth
flow more abundantly — only then can the narrow horizon of
bourgeois right be crossed in its entirety and society
inscribe on its banners:  From each according to his ability,
to each according to his needs!(52)

This must have seemed very utopian when it was written in 1875.
We are more fortunate than Marx's contemporaries in that we have
examples we can study, not yet of course of communist society, but
of the period of the revolutionary transformation of capitalist
into communist society, the period when the working class has
assumed state power and is in the process of liquidating exploitation and also thereby of liquidating itself as an exploited class,
the period in which the state can be nothing but 'the revolutionary
dictatorship of the proletariat'(53) — a period when the fund of
goods is distributed not yet simply on the basis of need but
already, fairly and justly, on the basis of work done.

In those countries where there has been a proletarian revolution one can see ample evidence of that unleashing of people's
skills and talents, that tapping on the widest scale of the source
of all knowledge stored in the broad mass of the people through
their social practice of production down the ages, what Lenin
calls 'the vivid creativeness of the masses, the fundamental factor
of the new social life'.

In twenty years the Soviet Union, from a position of economic
ruin, was able to construct an industrial base which enabled the
Soviet people to meet on the battlefield and destroy the most
powerful invading army ever assembled up to that time.  And even
now that Russia has reverted to state capitalism and in a system of
restored exploitation no longer draws in the same way on the free
creativity of the people, the economic base established under
socialism still supports one of the world's most industrially
advanced nations.

The two huge Asian countries, China and India, emerged from the
Second World War facing very much the same problems of large,
under-fed populations the victims of both natural and man-made
disasters and an economy based on primitive agriculture with no
developed industry, though India was probably the more industrialised

of the two.  China had liberated itself from Japanese occupation and following on a revolutionary civil war to rid the country of class oppressors was engaged in laying the foundations of a socialist society by her own efforts.  India after a popular and on the whole peaceful struggle against imperialism was granted nominal independence by a relatively weak Britain to preserve its investments and embarked on the 'free enterprise' way of creating an industrial base assisted by aid from the big capitalist countries.  Thus began the Great Asian Steeplechase with apologists for capitalism and exponents of socialism cheering on the countries they respectively backed, a race which was reasonably good-humoured to begin with but soon became very grim for the loser.

Today China can feed, clothe and house all her eight hundred million people and is one of the truly great nations of the world. In India over half the population is undernourished, famine is still common, for millions upon millions housing is practically non-existent and extreme poverty appears even more appalling in contrast with a thoroughly corrupt wealthy upper class.  All there is to show for aid from abroad is vast debt with the whole country in pawn to imperialist powers.  So concerned was the Indian bourgeoisie with China's example of socialist success and its effect on India's starving millions that a war was provoked with China over land in dispute, a war India lost disastrously  though it did have the effect of doubling American 'aid'.  The Chinese having driven the Indian army out of the disputed territory halted their advance though nothing stood between them and India's heartland, released the prisoners taken and returned to India all arms and vehicles captured, even first repairing any which had been damaged in the fighting.  This most magnanimous treatment of a conquered foe ever recorded in history is an example of socialist morality in relations between states.

At the opposite end of the geographical scale from China in point of size, Albania, at the beginning of the Second World War the most backward country in Europe without a single university and with 80 per cent of the people illiterate, also liberated itself by its own efforts from Italian and German occupation and turned its fight for freedom into a revolutionary war barring the return of the old regime of exploiters.  In spite of the hostility of Britain and the USA, the conspiracy against Albanian independence by Yugoslavia and the threats and economic boycott of the Soviet Union after its betrayal of socialism, Albania, a country of some two million people about the size of Wales, has maintained year by year the highest economic growth rate of any country in the world and secures for the working people a steady rise in their standard of living with no unemployment, no taxes, no inflation.

The Vietnamese people have defeated and driven out the USA imperialist forces as a culmination of thirty-five years of fighting for the right to build socialism in their own land.  Although one American general boasted of bombing Vietnam 'back into the stone age', it is the barbarous American capitalist system which looks archaic by comparison with the advanced socialist institutions in North Vietnam and in the liberated South.

In these socialist societies there are already changes in ethical attitudes toward property and property relationships as a result of all but personal possessions belonging to the people generally and production being geared not to profit but to people's needs.  Public property belonging to all is respected for the value of the human effort incorporated in it.  The kind of vandalism endemic in the capitalist West, a reaction of alienation character- istic of propertyless people in a society based on property owner- ship, is unheard of in these socialist countries.  This alienation begins with a hostile attitude toward things as always belonging to those others enjoying wealth and power;  but since things in capitalist society stand for social relationships this hostility extends to people as well in wanton violence.  Such conduct would seem utterly strange in these socialist countries where the basis for it has been destroyed.  The care for public property, the cleanliness of the towns, the pride in all that they have con- structed and constructed well are all characteristic of the citizens in these lands where they are masters of their own destiny.

There are many ways in socialist society by which the lesson is learned that things are not enjoyed at the expense of others but with their help.  In all these countries there is a great deal of voluntary work in which individuals without any immediately observable gain to themselves give their time and effort for the general good.  In Albania, for example, the state supplies building materials and the people in their spare time, old age pensioners, children on holiday, supply the labour voluntarily for building blocks of flats which others will inhabit.

This regard for public property which belongs to all extends as well to private belongings which also come into the individual's possession on a co-operative rather than a competitive basis.  The absolute probity in this respect, so that travellers in China have found it impossible to get rid of anything because someone is always punctiliously returning it wherever found, is the result of associating all goods with the co-operative social effort which produced them for general or personal use rather than with indi- vidual acquisitiveness on the consumption side which manages to snatch certain goods away from others for private satisfaction like some primitive savage growling over a bone.

What this comes to in ethical terms is that social production creates social rights in goods, and in socialist society the appropriation of these goods, whether the general ownership of public property or the personal possession of consumer goods all earned by work both as a social and individual activity, is rea- sonably and morally appropriate.  It is this superiority of socialist society in respect to the quality of motivation and to the rational deduction of rights from the co-operative process of production which creates an 'ought' attitude on the part of the working class toward the making of social revolution.

Chapter 3

# OBLIGATIONS – THE MEANING
# OF OUGHT SENTENCES

INTRODUCTION

In the previous section we saw how normative judgments expressing
the idea of 'rights' or 'the right' are grounded in certain specific
claims and their recognition inherent in a particular mode of production and in the exploitative class relationships characteristic
of that mode.  When one is confronted with alternative modes of
production in periods of social transition, the need arises to
judge normatively between two different systems of normative judgments.  Which of two contrasting moralities is closer to the
realities of social production, thus providing a sounder basis for
the exercise of human purpose, or which of them seems to guarantee
a fuller, richer life for the vast majority of people, thus
broadening the base of human creativity for the general good,
these are considerations which transcend the conditions of ethical
thinking identified with a class concerned with preserving its
own interests by defending an existing exploitative situation.
   Having stated the circumstances under which judgments of this
'transcendent' type became incumbent and having indicated the
ethical superiority of socialism over capitalism as an ordering
of human affairs, we ended the last section with the obligation of
commitment in the social struggle to bring the superior system
into being.  This is the moral aspect of Marx's famous dictum:
'The philosophers have only interpreted the world, in various ways;
the point, however, is to change it.'(1)  This statement, by
postulating the unity of theory and practice, draws attention to
the link which, we have argued, must be found between the descriptive and prescriptive aspects distinguishable within our
ethical concepts.  We have dealt with the question of how the same
philosophical language can accommodate both facts and value and
also explain the relationship between them.  Now we shall be concerned with what is basically the same problem but taking the form
of how, on the one hand, there can be scientific socialism, or
knowledge of the laws of social change permitting valid predictions about the future and how, on the other, there can be enough
freedom of choice for it to make sense to urge on people the injunction to change society and to change themselves in the process.

83

Of course, as we have seen already, such a choice is not made in a vacuum. Marx has said of human activity in general: 'Men make their own history. But they do not make it just as they please; they do not make it under circumstances chosen by themselves, but under circumstances directly encountered, given and transmitted from the past.'(2) Men make their own choices, but they do not at the same time choose the conditions under which that choice is made, nor even, generally speaking, do they choose the class influence through which, for them, historical conditions will be filtered, profoundly colouring the moral attitudes which are the basis of choice. The question of the extent to which men acting under the compulsion of class interests can reasonably be applauded or condemned for their actions according to standards of conduct based on more comprehensive human interests is a bit like the question of the moral culpability of soldiers carrying out orders in time of war. What we have to consider is whether these historical and social qualifications of individual choice leave any freedom at all; and if so, just what is meant by such freedom.

We have dealt with the whole question of value by analysing the concept of 'good'; we have dealt with the question of claims on people and things by analysing the concept of 'right'; and now the question of the limits and scope of freedom of choice and action requires us to analyse the concept of 'ought'. When we say that a person ought to do a certain thing, we normally mean both that he has some kind of obligation to do it and that he can do it. We would not say that a person ought to do something he could not conceivably accomplish. Nor would we be likely to say that he ought to do something he cannot possibly help doing. This ordinary usage indicates some element of freedom in the very meaning of 'ought'. Many philosophers have elaborated accounts of human action in which there was no such element; but the very logical difficulty of urging, on the basis of such accounts, that people ought not to use sentences with 'ought' in them draws attention to some of the peculiarities about this aspect of morality. We must try to discover what this element of freedom is and how Marxism with its account of the springs of human action accommodates it, thus allowing Marxists their legitimate expressions of political urgency implying moral imperatives which can only be advanced in 'ought' sentences.


MOTIVES AND EFFECTS

In the first section it was pointed out that one use of the word 'good' is for the purpose of commendation. A thing can be designated as good because it is something which ought to be approved. This use of 'good' as the ought-to-be-approved cannot be a mere description of what the thing actually is, for commending it implies that it need not have been what it is, that it could have been something else of an inferior nature. Descriptive statements about a thing's utilisable qualities are limited to the present; but the prescriptive meaning of 'goodness', as expressed in the injunction that it ought to be liked or approved, refers us back

in time to the purpose for which the thing was originally made
and the constructive efforts of the maker.  In other words, value
judgments, by linking an object's observable properties which
satisfy a human need here and now with the purposive effort which
went into its fabrication at some time in the past, give us the
history of that object in human terms.  Such judgments thus combine, in making appraisal possible, the presently existing object
with a reminder of its non-existence in a previous period when it
was as yet only an unrealised intention, this combination of exis-
tent thing with the idea of its non-existence in order to appreciate it properly being the practical application of the purely
idealistic synthesis between Being and Non-being which sets the
Hegelian dialectic in motion.

Similarly, any moral judgment that an action is what ought to
have been done and therefore one of which we ought to approve,
includes not only a description of that act in terms of its
immediate consequences but also a reference back to the motives
of the actor before it was ever performed and to the moral exertion
its performance required.  According to whether the present results
of an act or the past decision to perform it is emphasised, we get
quite different theories of morality.  If the descriptive aspect
of an act is stressed, our moral judgments can be translated into
factual propositions about the objective changes which the act
has effected;  if more importance is given to the original choice
of performing that particular act rather than some other, then we
must concern ourselves with such subjective considerations as the
nature of the impulse which led to its performance, whether, on the
information available, the most reasonable means to a proposed end
was selected and also, going more deeply into the matter, just how
free that original choice was and what such 'freedom' means.

To say that a particular effect of some action is good or bad
irrespective of how or why it was brought about, thereby divorcing
the idea of morality from the motive for producing that effect,
would make all action a complete ethical gamble with no possibility
of knowing till after a thing was done and its results observed
whether it had been right or not.  In placing the onus of moral
judgment on the act as objectively described we are saying that
the act itself has the character of ought-to-be-doneness, which
makes obligation a function of the act's performance.  We have
already noted that part of the meaning of 'ought', the very part
we are interested in as the source of some degree of freedom, is
bound up with the possibility of an enjoined act's not being done;
and this possibility can characterise the one who acts or does not
act but not the act itself.  Assertions containing the terms
'ought' or 'ought not' attribute a certain character not to a
certain activity but to a certain man.  In any attempt to explain
the morality of actions in terms of their objective results alone,
we are either denying ourselves the use of a moral language altogether and cannot even say that a particular result of action is
good or bad in any ethical sense, or else we are committing the
naturalistic fallacy of employing moral terms which cannot legitimately be deduced from the mechanical materialist theory of
human actions we have adopted.

But if we attempt to attach moral significance solely to the

motives from which an act is performed, the difficulties are just
as serious.  For one thing, motives are seldom simple and, taken
on their own, we can hardly ever say even in the case of actions
we perform ourselves to what extent they are to be accounted for
in terms of doing our duty, serving the interests of others,
wishing to be thought well of or any number of other considerations, some admirable, some not.  And, of course, in the case of
actions performed by others the problem of judging motives is
still more complicated.  Furthermore, while at any particular
moment we can decide to do a certain thing, we cannot decide then
and there to have certain motives for doing it.  Our motives seem
to be part of a given situation in which the decision to act
occurs;  and if 'ought' sentences are about them, we are no closer
with this idealist approach to finding the element of freedom
which is part of the meaning of 'ought'.

Objections to either the view that we are obliged to produce
certain results or that we are obliged to act from certain motives
have led some philosophers, as W. David Ross notes, to argue that
morality consists in the setting of ourselves to produce certain
results.(3)  It is thus the intention in an act, including to
some extent both motive and result, which makes it right or wrong.
By partially relating motive and result this view meets some of
the objections raised before.  If the setting of ourselves to
achieve a particular result is what we are obliged to do, we
would not have to know in advance all the effects of our act nor
even if it is going to prove possible to carry out our intention.
And it may be that, within limits, we can set ourselves to act
from one motive rather than another.  However, if it is psychologically possible for our intentions at the moment of choice to
be distinguished from our motives to the extent of being able to
select among them for the right one, such intentions, divorced
from any very compelling force to act, are likely to remain idle;
and if it is not possible, then we have not really avoided the
difficulties of a purely subjective account of obligation.

Now these two aspects of any action subjected to moral analysis,
the objective results it brings about and the subjective motives
which led to its performance, cannot be explained separately nor
can the relationship between them be found by fixing our eyes
steadily on the individual action itself — any more than we
could account earlier for the two aspects of a commodity, its
utility and its value, simply by staring hard at any particular
commodity.  'Turn and examine a single commodity, by itself, as
we will, yet in so far as it remains an object of value, it seems
impossible to grasp it.'(4)  Study an isolated act as we may, we
do not discover what it is about the act or its performance that
gives it moral significance.  We only succeeded in accounting for
the value of commodities by considering their history as extended
in time and by understanding the social relationships encapsulated
in them.  It is only by looking at actions in the same manner that
we can hope to explain the nature of their morality and understand
the extent of our own freedom to perform them.  Looked at in this
way we can see that motive and effect are inseparably related
aspects of human action in the world.  As Mao Tsetung expresses
this:

How can we tell the good from the bad — by the motive (the
subjective intention) or by the effect (social practice)?
Idealists stress motive and ignore effect, while mechanical
materialists stress effect and ignore motive.  In contradis-
tinction, we dialectical materialists insist on the unity of
motive and effect.... The criterion for judging subjective
intention or motive is social practice and its effect.(5)

So that the test for the moral nature of an action is the same as
the test for the validity of an act of knowledge — social practice,
without which we are like 'a doctor who merely writes prescriptions
but does not care how many patients die of them.'


OURSELVES AND OTHERS

Once we have put actions back into the social context in which they
actually occur, the distinction between objective results and
subjective motivation can appear to us as a distinction between
the actions of others and our own acts.  In the case of our own
acts we are primarily aware of what we intended to do;  but as far
as other people's actions are concerned, we tend to describe them
solely in terms of their observable effects.  Since ought-to-be-
doneness cannot be a characteristic of actions themselves and since
the moral conduct of others has to be inferred from the actions we
observe them performing, we seem to be in the curious position of
only being able, with any certitude, to apply 'ought' sentences
to ourselves.  In fact, when we judge the behaviour of others, we
do often make such remarks as:  'With such a background what could
you have expected?'  or 'Could a man with his habits have acted
otherwise?'  We are much less likely to exonerate ourselves in this
manner;  and, indeed, it sounds odd to say:  'I know I did wrong,
but with my past history how could I have done anything else?'  It
sounds odd because we are in a position to know whether we could
have avoided a certain action or not and if we could not, we
would not characterise it as morally wrong.  While we take our
intentions and our limitations into account in any self-appraisal,
others judge us as we judge them — strictly in terms of the objective results of our acts;  and what seems to us a relatively
free expression of some intention appears to others as but one
act in a completely determined series of actions and consequences.
   There is thus room for considerable difference between what we
think of ourselves and what others think of us.  Since our 'amour
propre' is constantly threatened by the opinions others have of us
based on our naked acts, existentialist writers have even gone so
far as to call other people our personal hell.  But, of course,
this conclusion is derived more from conditions of life in
capitalist society where all men are in competition with each
other than from the analytical problem of moral judgment associated
with such conditions.
   This discrepancy which complicates the question of morality is
precisely like the problem of other minds which has so absorbed the
attention of analytical philosophers.  The same sort of distinction
between ourselves and others in respect to an analysis of moral
actions also appears in an analysis of mental facts.  If we say

that we are in pain, we are referring more to our awareness of
suffering than to any overt signs of it;  but if we say that others
are in pain, all the statement can mean literally is that they display certain expressions or that their bodies are in a certain
physical state.  Propositions about personal feelings thus have a
different meaning for those who make them and for those to whom
they are addressed.  Just as we found that we only seemed able to
make moral judgments about ourselves, so by the same sort of
analytical approach we can only assume the existence of our own
minds.

This analogy helps us to see where we have gone wrong.  The
view that everyone is shut up incommunicado within the confines of
his own private experience is one that is flatly contradicted
every time a philosopher tries to express it in any way whatsoever.
It is not possible to develop a solipsistic theory with consis-
tency because for anyone to say that only he can experience mental
states is false if the person saying it is anyone but ourselves.
Since we know that we experience mental states, we merely have to
be able to imagine anyone else holding the view that only he can
experience them to realise that the view is wrong.

Our mistake on the ethical plane, as on the epistemological,
consists of starting from an unreal basis — ourselves as isolated
individuals arrived at by a Cartesian abstraction.  If reality were
mechanical, like a watch, it could be dismantled and reassembled,
and we could stand apart from it and deal with all the bits and
pieces by means of a disjunctive, classificatory logic.  It is
this way of looking at moral questions which fails to see how the
social whole is present in both the motive and effect of any
action, in both the individuality and sociality of any actor, so
that they are all linked together in a net of internal relations.
This inability to grasp the ways in which the social whole is
present in any particular entity, so that it is seen as independent
of the whole, as a mere abstraction, is itself characteristic of
capitalist ideology.  As we have seen before, the split between
production and consumption reaching its greatest extent under capitalist commodity exchange results in ideologists of the system
being more involved with prices, money, ideas which are all abstractions than with concrete reality which is the raw material workers
shape into useful objects with particular qualities.  Furthermore,
capitalism's promise to free the human individual from all forms
of political subjection by replacing social ties with economic
ones has had the effect of 'atomising' society as far as any fellow
feeling is concerned and this is reflected in these extreme forms
of analytical thinking.  Once an entity has been isolated by this
kind of thinking as an abstraction, its uniqueness, that is, all
the particular ways it is linked to other things within the whole,
disappears and what is left is its superficial resemblance to other
abstractions which can be arbitrarily lumped together.(6)  Intelligence degenerates into mere classification — as an ideological
counterpart of assembly line work, in factory or office, in which
the sense of shaping materials for human use or of administering
the distribution of useful things is lost in repetitive, undifferentiated and, in itself, meaningless motion.

Because for the working class, as for the system's spokesmen and apologists, capitalism can inhibit valid modes of thought, far from representing any degree of liberation, as compared with other forms of labour, it represents their alienation under conditions of wage slavery. They are separated from their work because they play no part in deciding what is to be produced and how, which represents a break between the individual and his life activity; they are separated from their own products appropriated and disposed of by others, which represents a break between the individual and the material world; they are made to compete with one another for goods and even for the right to work at all, which represents a break between man and man. All these divisions can be reflected in fragmented and disconnected ways of seeing things. But in so far as resistance is generated by capitalist relations and the working class in its own defence begins to realise that its unity is its only strength and that it must reverse all attempts to divide and atomise it, there is the beginning of an ethic of its own opposed to the ethics of capitalism, a start toward replacing the false ideology of capitalism with its own proletarian ideology, which is Marxism.

Putting actions back into their social context is not enough to get at their moral significance: we must also put ourselves firmly back into the society in which we developed in order to understand the conditions of moral conduct. As Marx puts it: 'What is to be avoided above all is the re-establishing of "society" as an abstraction vis-a-vis the individual. The individual is the social being.'(7) Man's very senses only become human to the extent that their objects have become social, human objects — objects emanating from man for man.

The senses and enjoyments of other men have become my own appropriation. Besides these direct organs, therefore, social organs develop in the form of society; thus, for instance, activity in direct association with others has become an organ for expressing my own life, and mode of appropriating human life.(8)

It is only through our relationships with others that we have obligations at all and, therefore, only in society that we can hope to find the meaning of 'ought' sentences and that element of freedom they presuppose. 'Only in association with others has each individual the means of cultivating his talents in all directions. Only in a community therefore is personal freedom possible.'(9) To 'construct' other moral beings like ourselves out of the obligations we happen to feel or on the basis of particular actions we merely observe, like the 'construction' of the universe out of private sense data, is a perverted sophistication which reverses the real order of our developing awareness within a social context.

Once we realise that it is ourselves and others as moral agents within society, and not this or that individual act, which must be the starting point for an investigation of ethical concepts, we can begin to understand the relation between motive and results. As long as attention was concentrated on the isolated act, the impulse to perform it and the effect actually achieved appeared quite distinct. But when the object of study becomes the moral

agent acting over a period of time within a social context, this
distinction between motive and effect turns into a relationship
between what can only be separated at the cost of the meaning of
each.  Their separation is a result of that split we have come to
recognise as between man as maker or doer and man as enjoyer or
appraiser which is a characteristic of man in commodity-exchanging
society particularly in its extreme capitalistic form — the origin
of the breach between the subjective and objective or between
theory and practice which takes the ideological form of a breach
between idealism and mechanical materialism.

In the case of specific acts the motive for them seems to be
'given', almost as part of the situation with which we are confronted;  and the intention to produce certain results has no
scope within which to operate.  But over a longer period of time
we can intend to be animated by different motives and may even
succeed, within limits, in changing the nature of the impulses
which move us.  The injunctions that prompt isolated acts are
addressed solely to the will, urging the choice of this or that
explicit alternative almost as an end in itself;  but over a
longer period of time, there is at least room for reason to review
and criticise these discrete decisions in the light of an overall
direction or purpose.  While any particular act may be more or less
typical of our general moral attitude, the sum of our actions over
a lifetime cannot but express that attitude faithfully, together
with all its modifications in the course of our development.  In
fact, the total consequences of everything we have done simply is
our morality in a final resolution of intentions and results.  It
is not by this or that specific action that we expect our fellow
men to judge us, nor even by this or that thing we say about ourselves at any particular period, but by a way of life revealed in
the totality of the difference our being alive has made to others.
'The criterion for judging subjective intention or motive is social
practice and its effect.'

But the question of just how free we are actually to change the
nature of the impulses that move us and to modify our conduct in
the light of an overall direction or purpose is not a question we
can pursue in respect to individuals alone.  Robinson Crusoe on
his island was only free in respect to one choice — to survive or
perish, a freedom shared with every living thing.  There are clear
statements of the Marxist view of the capacity of people to change
themselves, which is the greatest freedom possible, but always in
a social context, as when Mao Tsetung says:  'The epoch of world
communism will be reached when all mankind voluntarily and consciously changes itself and the world.'(10)

For man in class-divided society reality is inevitably mediated
by class.  We must see how this affects the question of moral
freedom.


FREEDOM AND CLASS INTEREST

It is not possible to arrive at any proper conception of morality
by starting from a particular act performed by a certain person at
a precise moment in time.  But once the nature of morality has been

understood in its social and temporal aspects, then individual
acts can be considered in moral terms.  We have seen how an
appreciation of productive relationships interacting through time
gave us the meaning of 'value' as a measure of the effort to
create useful goods;  and we were thus able to understand what was
involved in making a value judgment about any particular object.
An appreciation of socially-determined human relationships imposing obligations on individuals throughout their lifetime gives
us the meaning of morality as the measure of the effort to act in
accord with these obligations;  and this standard, once formulated,
can be applied to individual actions.  Men enter into associative
production to make things which sustain life and thus create value.
Men at the same time, through these same productive relationships, make society and in making society they make themselves
and thus create morality.

Because production for use is mediated in capitalist society
by production for the profit of a capitalist class, the relationship between usefulness in the broadest sense and value simply
in terms of the amount of labour constructively employed becomes
distorted.  As much value is incorporated in the shoddy, frivolous
and even harmful things it pays capitalists to palm off on people
as in the things society really needs.  To describe as 'goods',
we said, cheaply-made articles which quickly break in use or
improperly-tested drugs and medicines with dreadful side-effects
or the proliferation of objects like motor cars which make whole
cities uninhabitable or all the sensationalist, pornographic
trash which passes for culture in our capitalist world seems to
do violence to our language.  When this kind of distortion occurs,
we can only see how a proper relationship between utility and value
can be restored by a moral consideration of the kind of society
we are making through the sorts of things we are producing and
the way they are distributed.  The social obligations which are
our evidence for freedom of choice and our occasion for acting
morally are not just so many opportunities for kindly, polite or
considerate behaviour in our personal relationships, but, ultimately, our responsibility for creating a society with a certain
quality of human life and, in the process, for creating not only
ourselves but generations to come.  The real proof of some degree
of freedom is goal-setting and beyond the aim of mere communal
sustenance there is, as evidence of our freedom to judge and act,
the overall end of the quality of society we want for mankind.

Just as labour can be misdirected in the interests of a selfish
minority into the creation of disvalues instead of values, so
moral effort, the mere amount of spiritual energy exercised in
the attainment of some goal, can operate partially on behalf of
a selfish minority and to the detriment of the quality of life in
human society in general.  Like the ingenuity and physical effort
that may go into the making and distribution of useless, wasteful
or harmful objects are the devotion and courage of, for example,
missionaries who pave the way for the conquest and exploitation of
primitive peoples, of officials and police who support an unpopu-
lar and oppressive regime, of teachers untiring in their efforts
to inculcate imperialist ideas of racial supremacy.  Even though
these actions will have the 'moral' approval of the selfish

exploitative minority in whose interests they are performed, they
are as far from being 'right' as are addictive drugs furtively
sold from being 'goods'.  Only a moral critique of the class
relationships within a particular society or within the capitalist system generally can enable us to judge what the moral
language in use really means.

But to talk about the quality of life of mankind in general is
to beg the question.  As was pointed out before, humanitarianism
cannot stretch across the gulf between exploiters and exploited
without losing any real content.  The social circumstances in
which humanitarianism could be meaningful have to be created.
The only form of moral commitment that does not degenerate into
some vague utopian dream of a better world is embracing the
interests of the exploited in the struggle to end exploitation.
Marx specifically denounces any prescription of the socialist
ideal of 'an association in which the free development of each is
the condition for the free development of all' which neglects or
ignores the struggle of one class with the other and concerns
itself not with 'the interest of the proletariat, but the interests
of Human Nature, of Man in general, who belongs to no class, has
no reality, who exists only in the misty realm of philosophical
fantasy.'(11)  And Mao Tsetung makes the same point:

Is there such a thing as human nature?  Of course there is.
But there is only human nature in the concrete, no human
nature in the abstract.  In class society there is only human
nature of a class character;  there is no human nature above
classes.(12)

If the evidence for some degree of freedom is the capacity to
set ourselves goals, either immediate ones concerned with our own
well-being or the ultimate one of improving the quality of life in
society and, of course, of improving ourselves in the process,
then anything which makes such a goal realisable, like class
involvement in the struggle which is necessary if society is to
be changed, cannot be considered a denial of freedom but rather a
condition of its practical exercise.  But we must look a little
deeper still into this question of how the freedom of choice
implicit in the concept of 'ought' can be reconciled with the
social determination of our moral obligations.

One sense such freedom might have has already been suggested
by the analysis of what is meant by commending an object as 'good'.
Just as some man-made article can be better than it need have
been because of the extra labour and craftsmanship bestowed on it,
so an action performed in accord with a particular standard of
morality may go beyond what is strictly required.  Even if this
extra effort can be analysed in terms of early training or personal
traits, even if the motivation can be traced to a desire to be
thought well of or to deserve some special reward, still the difference between it and a more conventional response can only be
described in moral terms as a free exercise of will over and
above the norms required.  Socialism has its moral heroes who
are an inspiration to others in the world-wide class struggle
against the exploitation of man by man.  As Mao Tsetung says:
'Countless revolutionary martyrs have laid down their lives in the
interests of the people, and our hearts are filled with pain as

we the living think of them.'

Often something more extraordinary than this is meant by
freedom of choice — the possibility of acting in quite unexpected
ways, and by 'unexpected' is meant in ways which are irrelevant to
anything the actor really wants.  It is assumed that conduct dic-
tated by personal interest is rational but neither moral nor free,
and freedom would consist in a person's capacity to perform, if
he so chose, actions which were contrary to his own interests.
But 'interest' itself is a term which can have a very different
significance in a different social context.  In primitive tribal
groups the distinction between individual and communal interests
hardly exists.  As we have seen, the idea of private as contrasted
with public interest is largely bound up with the projection of
the ego in the development of private property;  and extreme individualism is closely associated with the rise of capitalism which
substitutes for human relationships a cash nexus, which dicho-
tomises society more neatly than ever before into exploiters and
exploited and which, even among the class of exploiters themselves,
turns each man's hand against all others.  Only in such a highly
competitive society does 'interest' come so exclusively to mean
rights asserted against everyone else.

And yet even in an  atomised society like ours a mother may
risk her life to save her child.  This does not mean that she acts
against her own interests but that her interests include the well-
being of her child.  In socialist countries like China and Albania
people voluntarily accept limitations on the production of consumers goods to increase the output of production goods which will
raise the standard of living of the next generation;  and they do
this not by way of acting against their own interests but by extending their own interest to cover those as yet unborn.  This use
in the general interest of a surplus by the state when state power
is in the hands of the people in no way resembles the appropriation of surplus-value by a tiny capitalist class whose very decision to invest any of it at all in expanding production depends
on the expectation of further profits accruing to them alone.
Acting on behalf of class interest may mean supporting the 'right'
of a minority to exploit the vast majority or it may mean identifying oneself with the class of those who in emancipating themselves from exploitation put an end to exploitation itself.  The
former interest involves a double check on freedom, not because it
is grounded in considerations of class, but of an exploitative
class which means, in the first place, the bondage of the vast
majority of the people and, in the second, since that bondage can
only be enforced by severe restrictions on the liberty of all who
might revolt, limitations also on the liberty of the very minority
in whose interest the oppression is maintained.  'Those who enslave
others cannot themselves be free.'

'Interest', then, has an indefinite extension ranging from the
self-assertive egoism of a single individual to a concern for
fellow workers everywhere, and in classless society, for humanity
itself.  It refers to whatever commands our sympathies as practically expressed in purposeful action.  The idea that freedom involves acting against one's interests would really mean, therefore,
that only random, arbitrary and pointless acts could be free.  And

yet if impulsive acts of this kind are unconscious, spontaneous and instinctive, thus providing no opportunity for reasonable direction toward a considered goal, they seem farthest removed from any area of freedom; and a deliberately purposeless act is inconceivable since even its performance simply to prove the possibility of such acts would give it point enough to keep it from qualifying.

Indeed, the development of class consciousness, which for the working class can only be revolutionary consciousness, does not arise spontaneously and irrationally out of the conditions of capitalist society. For this development there must not only be the sense of the unjust and illegitimate character of the existing social order but also the recognition of the possibility of a social order on an entirely different basis. This development cannot be generated automatically within the material and intellectual confines of the very system to be superseded but comes about from a new organisation of total human experience, including the existing exploitative system, presented to the working class and assented to as belonging to it in a way that the false consciousness acquired within a system coloured through and through by the interests of a capitalist class never could. In this recognition of and acceptance of its own revolutionary ideology and its social implications the working class demonstrates an element of rational and moral choice at the deepest level. As Lenin says: 'Class political consciousness can be brought to the workers only from without, that is, only from outside of the economic struggle, from outside the sphere of relations between workers and employers.' (13) The economic struggle can be conducted by trade unionists but this is not yet revolutionary struggle which depends on being able to generalise all manifestations of tyranny, oppression and injustice into a single functional picture of an exploitative society, which Marxism first did for the working class and the Leninist party of a new type continues to do, keeping ever before workers 'the world historic significance of the proletariat's struggle for emancipation'.

We have already seen how the peculiar notion of freedom as spontaneous, unconditional and utterly irrelevant arises. The division of labour which leads through the development of classes to those mainly involved in mental tasks being primarily concerned with the consumption side of the productive process, tends to arrest their thinking at the idealistic phase of the process of knowledge, the phase in which concepts become detached from their roots in material reality. These 'free' ideas which can be juggled with, transposed and recombined suggest the possibility of actions which would be 'free' in the same sense. The equivalent of ideas completely abstracted from the objective world would be actions without effects; but actions can only be performed in the objective world and can never have that sort of detached meaninglessness, like a kind of pornography of activism. They can never be anything but the final phase of the process of knowledge, bringing all ideas down to earth again and subjecting them to the rigorous critique of reality.

The same idealistic attitude is responsible for another distorted view of freedom which ends in a similar kind of frustration.

Subjective states such as happiness or equanimity are seen, like
abstract ideas, as somehow separate from the objective conditions
which they normally reflect.   Thus detached, they can be set up
as goals to be achieved on their own without attempting to do anything about material circumstances.   We are free, it is argued,
to attain peace of mind or contentment with our lot whatever those
circumstances may be.   But quite apart from the fact that it is
one thing to rise superior to petty vexations afflicting us and
quite another to be calmly detached about other people starving
to death, this striving for purely subjective goals proves
psychologically self-defeating in the end.   Those who pursue
happiness with the greatest persistence are the least likely to
find it.   The wish merely to have a clear conscience carries with
it a sense of guilt.   The unhappiness of hedonists and the moral
doubts of monks who must realise that the slightest assurance of
their own salvation can cost them that hope are each in their
way the penalty of chasing shadows.   Marxism, just as it does not
merely attempt to change moral ideas themselves but also the social
conditions from which those ideas arise, gives no warrant for
seeking solace in subjective states.   It counsels instead of any
such utopianism the active effort to achieve objective ends with
such states as satisfaction, contentment or happiness being realised as the by-products of the concerted struggle with one's
fellows for a better society.
   Although the obligations we feel are conditioned by the type of
society we live in and by our class allegiance in that society,
this could only be considered a fatal limitation on our freedom
of action if it could be reasonably argued that we should be able
to make up our own sense of obligation just as we please and
without reference to what anyone else might expect of us.   The
very word 'obligation' indicates a link or tie with something
outside ourselves and not, therefore, subject to our private
whims.   Marxism does not forge our links with the class to which
we belong by our role in the productive process, but in revealing
the nature of that link it helps to make conscious the social
springs of our actions and the social ends those actions serve;
and only conscious actions can be free.   Freedom to live according
to the particular ethical standard apposite to our circumstances
is the bare minimum for acts to be considered moral at all.   In
showing how that standard came to apply through an understanding
of the social conditions which gave rise to it, in providing the
material criteria by which it can be judged in terms of the quality
of social life it implies, and in calling on us in the fellowship
of our class relations with all who are exploited to change those
very social conditions, thereby coming to recognise quite different
obligations from those acquired simply by the accident of being
born into and of growing up in particular surroundings, Marxism
opens up a whole new vista of freedom.
   This potential freedom is inseparable from the social force
whose mission it is to bring about the classless society of
communism because only when there is no exploitation of man by
man can man be truly free.
   The proletariat carries out the sentence which private
property, by creating the proletariat, passes upon itself,

> just as it carries out the sentence which wage labour, by
> creating wealth for others and poverty for itself, passes
> upon itself.  If the proletariat triumphs, this does not
> mean that it becomes the absolute form of society, for it is
> only victorious by abolishing itself as well as its opposite.
> Thus the proletariat disappears along with the opposite which
> conditions it, private property.(14)

That is to say exploitative class rule disappears because it is
based on the ruling class's proprietorial grip on the means of
production.

> Only in communist society, when the resistance of the capital-
> ists has been completely crushed, when the capitalists have
> disappeared, when there are no classes (i.e. when there is no
> difference between members of society as regards their rela-
> tion to the means of production), only then 'the state ...
> ceases to exist' and it 'becomes possible to speak of
> freedom'.(15)


FREEDOM AND PREDICTION

Critics of Marxism contend that freedom is incompatible with
historical materialism.  If, they argue, Marxism claims to be a
science of society capable of making necessary predictions such
as the supersession of class-divided society by a co-operative
society without classes, it cannot at the same time issue a valid
call to ethical action in pursuance of such a goal.  If the
capitalist system of exploitation is inevitably doomed, then it
cannot be anybody's duty to bring about its end.

These critics, either intentionally or inadvertently, have mis-
taken historical materialism for some form of mechanical deter-
minism which prescribes the lines of human development as
ineluctably as metal rails fix the route of a train.  In assuming
that Marxism relegates consciousness to a mirror-like role of
merely reflecting what would be happening whether or not consciousness existed they suppose that there is no room for human volun-
tarism.  But Marxism is nothing like that.  The determining
agency is a specifically human reality.  The material base of a
society, which is the preponderant influence in shaping the ideas
and attitudes of people in that society and guiding their future
actions, is simply a system of human relationships.  'History
itself is nothing but the activity of men in pursuit of their
ends.'(16)  'Freedom is won by the people through struggle...'
and 'the people, and the people alone, are the motive force in
the making of world history.'(17)  To say, therefore, that if a
particular system of exploitation is doomed, no one can have the
duty of bringing about its end is like saying that, because a cure
for cancer will one day be found, research workers need not bother
to go on looking for it.  One is not, in either case, speaking of
something which will happen in spite of men's actions but of something which will be brought about through that very agency.

Marxist predictions are not about an inescapable fate that is
to overtake mankind — though the end of exploitation may well
seem to capitalists like the cooling off of the sun;  nor, on the

other hand, are they mere pious hopes for the future in the form
of imagining ideal utopias or of encouraging men to behave differently without in any way changing the circumstances that incline
them to behave as they do.  Marxist predictions are about what men
will do, based on a knowledge of what they are, and what they are
depends on the productive relationships they have entered into in
order to sustain and enrich human life:  it also includes what it
is possible for them to become on the basis of understanding those
relationships well enough to be able to change them — and thus
change themselves.  Such predictions are more complicated but no
different in kind from the anticipation that men at a particular
stage of development, confronted with an enormous boulder denying
them access to a fertile valley will sooner or later organise themselves in such a way that, with the help of simple tools like stone
hammers and crude levers, the boulder will be broken up and removed.
Our being able to anticipate the clearing away of the obstruction
does not represent a constraint on those men's freedom of action
but an understanding of its basis.

Such predictions on the scale of vast social movements, depending on an understanding of the complex productive relationships of
an entire society, can only be made at a stage in those productive relationships when the possibility of profoundly altering them
already exists.  Indeed, a proper appreciation of historical
development in general is a result of the extent to which men are
able to enter into those developments and take a class-conscious
active part in shaping their own destiny, of the extent to which,
history having made men, men begin to make history.

This connection between understanding historical developments
and being able to enter into and control them explains one form the
criticism of Marxist prediction takes.  History itself appears
quite different to a class which has enjoyed power and feels itself
threatened than to a class which is gathering its strength to
assert itself positively on the world stage.  A class which is
losing its control of historical processes is bound to view those
processes as inimical, as something imposed on them in spite of
their own will.  The spokesmen of such a class would like to deny
that any pattern can be found in history because any pattern they
can discern is working against the interests they represent.  And,
since they are no longer identified with a class making history,
they really do find it more and more difficult to understand
history's course.  It has become alien and malign to them.  The
same class apologists, who at the period of capitalism's ascendancy saw history as a steady progressive advance, now, in capitalism's decline, dismiss the very idea of progress and describe
history as just 'one emergency following on another'.

At the peak of bourgeois power their historians could praise the
revolutions which laid the basis for it;  but at a time when social
change could take that power away from them, all change becomes
suspect — even that change in the past from feudalism to capitalism.
'You can't change human nature!' is not so much, with them, a statement of fact as a despairing plea.  If it was previously possible
for a dominant class to be overthrown, it might happen again;  and
in order to deny that such a change will ever occur in the future,
it becomes necessary to deny that real social change has ever

occurred at any time, the world having always really been frozen in
a timeless, changeless Platonic state.  According to scholars like
Wittfogel the West has always been 'free', while from the time of
ancient hydraulic societies like Egypt or China down to the present
the East has always been totalitarian:  no change of any significance
has ever taken place in either hemisphere;  and the Cold War ought
to be dated from the last Ice Age!(18)

Even if change were conceivable, it could only, from the point of
view of the capitalist class and its hirelings, be for the worse.
Tinkering with things as they are to effect a few minor adjustments
is as much as they dare contemplate.  'Piecemeal technology' or
'social engineering', superficial tampering which leaves everything
basically as it is, are the terms used by Karl Popper in the course
of his futile attempts to make social democracy philosophically
respectable.(19)  Since history is assumed to have no discoverable
pattern, all change is blind, its consequences quite unforeseeable,
only the utterly irresponsible could ever embark on a course of
radical alteration.  The reason sometimes advanced in support of
this petty reformism is that any prediction of major change is bound
to have its prior influence on society, thus destroying the objectivity of the prediction.  An example given of the futility of fore-
casting future social events is that if a fall in the price of shares
in three days' time were predicted, everyone connected with the
market would sell before that time causing an earlier decline and
thus falsifying the prediction.  Anyone relying on the accuracy of
the forecast would have been badly caught out.  While this may be
one of the trivial truths of the basically static world of 'piecemeal technology', there are countries where, on the basis of Marxist
predictions of real social change, that kind of gambling in commodities has been done away with altogether.

Marxists would certainly not deny that predicting the overthrow
of an exploiting class is bound to have its prior influence of pro-
voking that class into frantic efforts to falsify the prediction,
whether by disproving it on paper or in fact.  A great deal of
economic and sociological writing since Marx's time has been devoted
to demonstrating just how wrong he was, and the constant succession
of books which finally demolish his work is a fine tribute to
Marxism's creative growth as the ideology of the working class.
There have also been those whose reaction to Marxism, as in the
case of Keynes for example, was to try to eliminate some of the
more vulnerable aspects of capitalism while preserving its basic
exploitative character.  What can be categorically denied is that
any amount of subtle argument or improvised tinkering can save a
system whose demise has been predicted on the grounds of a critical
internal contradiction — the conflict between capitalist class and
working class which can only be resolved by the ascendancy of that
class which can do without the other and, in dispensing with the
other, ends the exploitative relationship between men in society.
The only way the capitalist ruling class can meet the challenge
of that kind of prediction is by removing that crucial contradiction
which would mean, since it cannot get rid of the working class,
eliminating itself, thus anticipating not falsifying the prediction.
Capitalists, apart from those who jump out of skyscrapers in a
stock market crash, prefer to take refuge in Louis XIV's attitude,
'it'll last out my time!'

Criticisms of Marxist prediction which take the form of trying to prove that in tipping its hand Marxism allows itself to be circumvented are based on the belief that ideas determine material conditions and therefore that combatting the idea of material change, through being forewarned of it, is tantamount to preventing change itself.   Such idealism, as we have so often noted, is the characteristic attitude of a class no longer in the ascendant — and particularly of the apologists for that class who by the very nature of the clerical tasks they are paid to perform tend to be cut off from reality.   These spokesmen may not call themselves idealists, but the empiricism they advocate is as different from the practical Baconian philosophy of trial and error of a more hopeful period of bourgeois history as is their attitude of deploring real change from an earlier belief in progress.   An empiricism of observation alone, which is all social democracy can claim by way of philosophical justification, divorced from experimental social practice, can prove nothing about the future of anything and ascribes its own short-sightedness to history's inscrutability.   Far from being what it pretends, a method for securing tentative social advance, neo-empiricism realises its purpose in putting a check on all change whatsoever;   and it betrays its non-materialist character not only in reducing reality to ideal elements like sense-data but also in the utterly sterile and scholastic nature of its formulations generally, often tipping over into a jejune mysticism.   The argument that no prediction can be absolutely correct in every detail and therefore no real social change can ever be envisaged no matter how bad things get shows up this so-called empiricism to be, in effect, as static an idealism as the philosophical foundations of Plato's arrested Republic.

If one prong of the critical attack on historical materialism takes the form of denying the possibility of valid prediction in the name of random, irrational and unplanned 'freedom', the other maintains that if prediction is possible there must be laws of social development, and if there are such laws, if Marxism is a science, then it can have nothing to do with morality and has no right to urgent expressions of the 'ought' type.   Social conduct, explained in terms of class interests rooted in the material conditions of life, is thus no more moral than obeying the law of gravity.

This argument ignores the distinction Marxism makes between history which is the account of men's actions in pursuit of their aims and the physical sciences which describe the pre-existent natural stage on which these actions take place.   This is the distinction between the two kinds of knowledge, knowledge of the struggle for production which grows out of the contradiction between man and nature and knowledge of class struggle which grows out of contradictions within society, a distinction which itself represents a contradiction between the forces of production and the relations of production.

Both knowledge of the struggle for production, the physical sciences, and knowledge of class struggle, the social sciences, have their laws;   but while the laws of physics operate with a regularity independent of whether anyone is aware of them or not, the laws of social development, which are simply the pattern of changing human relationships, while independent of what any individual man or class

of men would like them to be, are nonetheless affected by men's
consciousness of them.  Where subject and subject matter are the
same, a more thorough knowledge of the subject matter cannot but
be accompanied by and interlinked with changes in the subject.
Consciousness develops in the context of a pre-existent natural
world;  human consciousness develops in the context of social
being;  individual consciousness develops in the context of class
consciousness;  but while logical and temporal priority belong to
the context, the relationship between context and development,
between ground and emergent is dialectical, not mechanically deterministic.  Once consciousness develops in some material context, it
belongs to a larger whole including both, both being internally
related within that whole.  There is no warrant in dialectical
materialism for dealing with causality in unilinear terms of single
effects following single sufficient causes, like stations on a
railway line with a stop called 'consciousness' coming after some
stop called 'economic facts' and therefore unable to react back
on them.

Consciousness is not mechanically determined by any single thing
in the social context in which it develops nor is it part of any
one-way causal chain;  but the entire social situation gives rise
to it, conditions it, shapes and influences it and, in short,
determines that the range of its reactions back on that social
situation will be limited to what is meaningful within the larger
whole including both situation and awareness of it.  The idea of
changing society, therefore, does not arise till the material conditions of that society as described by the laws of social development are ripe for it.  That is why Marx limits the scale of conscious action in a society which has discovered the law of its own
movement to 'shortening and lessening the birth-pangs' of a new
order.(20)  Such a new order does not originate in an ideal conception but is generated out of contradictions both within the
social organisation it replaces and between that social organisation
and the total world-wide productive experience of the working
masses.  These contradictions which are in the process of weakening
that older form of society and strengthening the forces which are
to change it can be set down with all the scientific rigour displayed in the classics of Marxism-Leninism, those classics themselves being simply the theoretical formulation of the historical
experience of the working masses in struggle.  Once men understand
this process of change involving them in their class character, once
they appreciate the possibilities it holds of a better society, they
then become agents for actualising those possibilities the old
society is pregnant with in the quickest and most painless way,
even setting aside immediate and personal interests which may attach
them to the old order to act in the name of their class interest to
realise the new.  Though the idea of the new society originated in
the contradictions of the old, it cannot be born without the conceptualisation of it by the working class which, changing and being
changed by revolutionary action, is both mid-wife and new born
child.  'Without a revolutionary theory there can be no revolutionary movement.'(21)  This is the not inconsiderable area of moral
action staked out by the Marxist conception of predictable social
change.

Of course, it cannot be denied that a social change which is to free the working class from the yoke of capital is at the same time a curtailment of the liberty of capitalists. 'Free enterprise' is nothing but the liberty to exploit the labour of others. Just as 'freedom of the press' is the freedom to buy up newspapers and journalists in the interests of creating a public opinion hostile to change; or just as prohibitions against workers' enforcing union discipline are called 'freedom of work'. To the ideologists of capitalism any change which diminishes the prerogatives of those for whom they speak is bound to seem totalitarian; but a struggle to free the working masses of the world, even at the expense of those who exploit them, obviously deserves to be described as liberative. Lenin explains how the freedom of the vast majority can only be won at the cost of the freedom of their oppressors.

Simultaneously with an immense expansion of democracy, which for the first time becomes democracy for the poor, democracy for the people, and not democracy for the money bags, the dictatorship of the proletariat [that is, the assumption of state power by the working people] imposes a series of restrictions on the freedom of the oppressors, the exploiters, the capitalists. We must suppress them in order to free humanity from wage slavery.... (22)

Dialectical materialism is the dynamic pattern of change and growth in the objective world and, since minds developed in that world, it is also the form of the relationship between subject and object, between thought and action, between consciousness and the material conditions in which it arose and on which it in turn reacts. Dialectical materialism, in short, takes its character from the nature of changing reality as extended in time and may be contrasted with any conceptualisation involving, as the method of investigation, an attempt to stop the whole process in order to have a closer look, obtaining thereby a view of reality as static and dead on which it would be impossible to act.


FREEDOM AND TIME

We have already touched on the importance of extension in time for an understanding of individual morality. An analysis of specific acts at a particular moment did not yield any element we could designate as moral, and only when we considered the agent in a given social context over a long enough time span to embrace major life purposes as manifest in action were we in a position to appreciate the nature of moral choice. Value gives us the history of an object in its social context. Morality gives us the history of an act in its social context.

Kant has described man as living in two worlds, the phenomenal and the noumenal. In the former he is subjected to the necessity of natural law and, since every event is inevitably linked to its cause, there is no scope for human freedom and hence no possibility of moral action. But through his mind he belongs also to the transcendental realm of pure reason which exists behind the mere sensuous appearance of the phenomenal world; and in this realm he is free because he is capable of responding to the dictates of

universal reason which legislates for things as they really are.
Every action can be explained deterministically insofar as its
results occur in the physical world of strict causation; but it
may also be free if it is motivated by purely rational considerations which do not originate in that physical world.  In other words,
for Kant as for all idealists, freedom only exists in the second
idealistic phase of the process of knowledge and cannot survive
translation into social practice.

What suggested this Kantian solution to the problem of necessity
is the experience we seem to have of past and future — the
encountered and unalterable past where necessity reigns absolute,
and the free and undetermined future which is the realm of moral
choice.  The present seems to stand as an instant without duration
between what has already been irrevocably done for all time and
what is still a matter of free election.  Once we dichotomise time
in this way, even if we try to extend experience of the past into
the future by planning to bring about a certain effect, the very
act of setting up an end to be realised becomes itself a part of
the past the moment it has been willed and thus subject to an
unbreakable causal chain, as is also the case with each means
toward the attainment of that end as it comes to be employed and,
eventually, with the end itself.  By this account freedom takes on
the illusory character of a distant mirage which always disappears
as soon as we get to it.  Indeed, all time necessarily becomes an
illusion if it is simply the infinite repetition of an instantaneous
present equalling zero.

We have learned to recognise such anomalies as an indication
that things which are dialectically related within a more comprehensive whole are being treated as separate entities.  We also know
that this analytical tendency is connected with the distinction
between production and consumption which class division, particularly in the final capitalist stage of commodity exchange, turns
into an almost unbridgable gulf — a gulf appearing in our present
instance as the absolute bifurcation between past and future.  The
exploiting class, whose very title to the property holding on which
its rule is based lies in the past, becomes completely identified
with a conservative effort to keep that past from ever changing;
and the exploited class, whose liberation lies in the future, sees
its mission as the destruction of the past in order to achieve its
freedom in a new society.

This same account of the realm of necessity and the realm of
freedom as the difference between past and future is also related
to the distinction between the world of nature described by the
physical sciences and the world of men described by the social
sciences.  Necessary regularities in the natural order make the
past dominate the future, while the possibility of transforming
social organisation enables the future to dominate the past.  But
this is also, as we have already noted, the distinction between
the two kinds of knowledge, knowledge of the struggle for production and knowledge of class struggle, which can be expressed as the
distinction between the forces of production and the relations of
production which, in turn, takes us back again to that original
distinction between production itself and consumption.  All these
distinctions within a given whole link as well as divide, identify

as well as distinguish, universalise as well as particularise; but in the false ideology which underwrites separatism in the drive to perpetuate class difference, exalts individual interests against social interests and knows only the tactic of divide and rule, these distinctions become absolute and generate such familiar philosophical problems as the irreconcilable split between mind and body or between man and nature or between freedom and necessity, which are all reflections of the class conflict between rulers and ruled, exploiters and exploited, capitalists and workers.

The consciousness on which freedom depends cannot be tied to an instantaneous present, helplessly watching the endless transformation of the undetermined into the determinate. Its field is rather an effective present which is simply the measure of time between ideal objective and actual accomplishment which it is possible to grasp. The extent of its reach is precisely what distinguishes man from other animals; and this distinction is grounded in the material fact that men, unlike animals, 'produce their means of subsistence'.(23) Consciousness thus originates as the mental correlate of the productive process of drawing on past experience to create goods to meet future needs by postponing present satisfactions. In terms of discrete instants consciousness is quite inconceivable. As an effective present consciousness implies that the spurious isolates of thoroughly necessitated past and completely free future must be seen in their dialectical relationship as qualifying each other in the course of purposive action to achieve some end. Necessity qualifies freedom, 'men do not make their history as they please'; but necessity does not devour freedom, men do 'make their own history'. Normative judgments relating to actions which ought to be performed are logically possible as well as factual propositions referring to what is already the case; and their relationship is maintained through this effective present which consciously combines elements of past and future.

The content of this consciousness is the total experience of producible effects in the minds of the working people of the world, the mass knowledge which is liberated for limitless creativity by class emancipation and which is appealed to in the mass line, 'from the masses to the masses'. Beyond the productive effects achieved in this or that kind of society is the effect of altering society itself which consciousness can only bring about when it is class consciousness, when to the content of consciousness is added the ideological form peculiar to the class position of workers in a particular society, turning them from mere receptacles of productive experience into a dynamic social force, which is what Marxism-Leninism is and does. What this amounts to is the revolutionary combination in a specific class of workers in a specific social situation of the two kinds of knowledge, knowledge of the struggle for production and knowledge of the class struggle.

Though firmly rooted in the material conditions of life Marxist morality demonstrates that it is more than the passive response to a given social situation precisely to the extent that it includes the notion of changing that very situation. This notion can only signify that consciousness in its class form, which is the only way it can be effective in class-divided society, is a dynamic moment in the process of history, that consciousness in this socially effective role is itself an alteration in being, an enormous broadening of the scope for purposive action which represents a yet more expansive consciousness.  This is not to suggest, of course, that ideas in themselves effect any changes but only that in revealing the objective nature of a situation which is not itself static they also show something more — what it is possible through social practice for that situation to become;  and it is in taking up an active attitude in their class identity toward this possibility, still lying outside a present social context though realisable through a conscious extrapolation of its current laws of development, that Marxists find their warrant for moral judgment and action.

Few philosophers would wish to deny the pattern of necessity and freedom in our individual lives appearing to us as an extended present within which a planned course of action has meaning.  Without predictable regularities based on experience of the past, planning would be pointless;  without an element of freedom drawn from the future, choice would be impossible.  And yet, as we noticed before, critics of Marxism often seem to agree that when we turn from individual to social action no such pattern is discernible. No regularities in history, nor any trends of development in the organisation of societies are there for us to study and learn from. Either there is no change at all and the appearance of it is illusory or change is completely 'free' in the random sense that any social formation can arbitrarily succeed any other.  This would be a meaningless 'freedom' since we could not hope to bring about a better state of affairs by a course of rational social action.  Indeed it would be pointless on this reading of the matter so much as to pass any opinion at all on the existing state of affairs;  and it is unlikely that we would ever have acquired so otiose a faculty as a capacity for judgment.

But these critics are quite prepared to accept the conclusion that history is meaningless — such is their dislike for what a meaningful history might hold in store for the exploitative class they serve. They will allow us to study the past as long as we are careful not to draw any lessons from it, for that would be to court the error of historicism.  We must not, in other words, try to make sense of the life of a society by applying to it the concept of an effective present which enables us to make sense of our own individual lives. And yet 'history is nothing but the activity of men in pursuit of their aims';  and if history is essentially meaningless, so are the lives of all of us who make it.  It is rather a heavy price to ask us to pay for their fear of social change.


THE DIALECTICS OF FREEDOM AND THE RELATION BETWEEN BASE AND SUPERSTRUCTURE

Some degree of freedom is presupposed in making normative judgments and acting on them.  Ultimately the possibility of this freedom must be found in the essential nature of reality and the manner in which growth, development, change take place.  Obviously if there is no change or if all change is illusory, then there is no possibility of freedom, and morality, in the sense of anything incumbent

on people to do which they need not necessarily do, is also an
illusion.  The Marxist dialectic of knowledge is the consciousness of the dialectical nature of reality itself.  'The law of
contradiction in things, that is, the law of the unity of opposites, is the fundamental law of nature and society and therefore
also the fundamental law of thought.'(24)  It is because there is
internal contradiction in every single thing that there is motion
and development.  'Contradictoriness within a thing is the fundamental cause of its development, while its interrelations and interactions with other things are secondary causes.'(25)  This motion,
development, change is not simply things being pushed around by
external forces like billiard balls knocked about on a table but
is generated internally by the contradictions inside things.
'External causes are the condition of change and internal causes are
the basis of change and external causes become operative through
internal causes.'(26)

In its negative aspect freedom is simply a thing's not being
acted upon by outside forces to which it responds inertly.  In
its positive aspect freedom is the novelty that is created by
qualitative changes resulting from alterations in the balance of
opposites within a thing.

> In each thing there is contradiction between its new and its old
> aspects, and this gives rise to a series of struggles with many
> twists and turns.  As a result of these struggles, the new
> aspect changes from being minor to being major and rises to
> predominance, while the old aspect changes from being major to
> being minor and gradually dies out.  And the moment the new
> aspect gains dominance over the old, the old thing changes
> qualitatively into a new thing.  It can thus be seen that the
> nature of a thing is mainly determined by the principal aspect
> of the contradiction, the aspect which has gained predominance.
> When the principal aspect which has gained predominance changes,
> the nature of a thing changes accordingly.(27)

This struggle of opposites which with 'many twists and turns'
brings forth the new in revolutionary change is found throughout
nature and society and is reflected in our very thinking, thinking
itself being just such a novelty arising from qualitative changes
in the productive struggle between man and nature.  The combination
of thinking or consciousness with the degree of freedom generated
by revolutionary change from within makes morality possible.

Contradiction is universal, therefore the possibility of freedom
in the sense of the new coming into being through a self-generated
resolution of opposites acting within a particular context is all
pervasive.  Mao Tsetung gives examples of this revolutionary character of social change.

> The contradiction between the proletariat and the bourgeoisie is
> resolved by the method of socialist revolution;  the contra-
> diction between the great masses of the people and the feudal
> system is resolved by the method of democratic revolution;  the
> contradiction between the colonies and imperialism is resolved
> by the method of national revolutionary war;  the contradiction
> between the working class and the peasant class in socialist
> society is resolved by the method of collectivisation and mech-
> anisation in agriculture;  contradiction within the Communist

Party is resolved by the method of criticism and self-criticism;
the contradiction between society and nature is resolved by the
method of developing the productive forces.(28)

Where contradictions are antagonistic, as in the case of the conflict between proletariat and bourgeoisie whose very definition as
classes is that the one exploits the other, the only resolution is
the elimination of the one, as a class, by the other.  Where the
contradiction is not necessarily antagonistic, because not expressing a fundamental opposition of class interests, as between workers
and peasants, the resolution is found in changing the conditions in
which the opposition was rooted.  Being able to distinguish antagonistic and non-antagonistic contradictions is one of the most
important aspects of dialectical thinking in the political sphere.

Freedom has been described by Hegel as the appreciation of
necessity;  but in spite of Engels' acceptance of the formula(29)
Marxists can no more take over this conception uncritically than
they could take over without standing it on its materialist feet the
Hegelian dialectic.  If consciousness is simply the passive privilege
of becoming aware of the latter part of a historical pageant already
written out to its final curtain, and if that play of ideas is
beyond criticism from or intervention by the audience who merely
applaud the working out of triadic progressions, then freedom can
indeed be no more than the consciousness of necessity but in what
sense is it still freedom?  Such an account of history as the
inevitable categorical unfolding of self-evolving thought has
nothing to do with Marxism.  Indeed, it could be said in terms of
the dialectical materialist theory of knowledge that just as
Hegelianism absorbs empiricism as one moment in the dialectic of
mind, Marxism absorbs the dialectic of mind as one moment in the
thinking process of self-conscious matter.

Freedom as the consciousness of necessity does apply in the realm
of the physical sciences, the realm of knowledge acquired by the
struggle for production as, for example, when consciousness of the
necessity of the law of gravity and the fixed properties of an air
stream enables men to construct aeroplanes and soar above the earth,
not in defiance of but in intelligent compliance with natural law.
But this does not apply in that realm of knowledge acquired through
class struggle, the social sciences, which is also the realm of
morality.  If, for example, men conscious that a revolutionary
change from capitalism to socialism is imminent hastily set about
acquiring the kind of qualifications they hope will assure them
success and influence in the new social situation, they are not,
in fact, intelligently complying with social law to rise above
circumstances but condemning themselves to the unfreedom of having
no part to play in a revolutionary change which only occurs because
there are others who choose, in an exercise of freedom, to reject
the extreme self-interest of bourgeois morality and anticipate the
new morality of socialism in which individuals no longer seek nor
enjoy that kind of success and influence.  While a freedom acting
through a knowledge of natural laws, whose necessity operates in
spite of men, is sufficient for the production of value, morality
presupposes a freedom acting through a knowledge of social laws
whose necessity operates through men, which actually brings about a
new situation where new laws apply and the agents themselves are

profoundly changed.   'Morality serves the purpose of helping human
society to rise to a higher level and to get rid of the exploitation of labour.'(30)

Knowledge and morality, while closely connected in their derivation from the material conditions of men's social existence, are
not identical.  As we have often remarked, the productive process
is also the process of knowledge.  If we prove in social practice
the correctness of our conception of some natural phenomenon by
reproducing it ourselves and making it serve our own purposes, we
have knowledge that is certain beyond anything we could ever know
in terms of some passive 'copy' theory of the relationship between
idea and reality.  What we can actually make we thoroughly understand and in the productive process of making, object and subject
interpenetrate each other in a mutually transformative way that does
not leave over, as inexplicable isolates, the dichotomies of mind
and matter or man and nature.  The Kantian ungraspable thing-in-
itself becomes, once we are able to produce it, a thing-for-us.(31)
Similarly, if we can apply our knowledge of the laws of society's
development to hasten the advent of a better system of productive
relationships with a fairer and more efficient ordering of social
effort, we have acted morally in a sense that goes beyond any mere
compliance with customary ethical rules.  For in the activity of
changing the conditions of social existence we also change ourselves:  changing ourselves is the greatest freedom we can know
and where freedom is greatest there the highest form of morality is
possible.  But if knowledge and morality are distinguishable, they
are also closely related.  What, morally speaking, ought to be the
case in terms of human fraternity and co-operation also make up
the ideal relations of production for the greatest possible application of man's productive force which is reflected in an enormous
increase in knowledge.

Since morality depends on freedom and since freedom depends on
consciousness, we must decide as a moral issue whether consciousness is merely the awareness of dialectical changes which would
have worked themselves out along the same lines anyway or whether
it is itself a moment in that dialectic which must be taken into
account in the course of subsequent developments.  Marxism, dialectical materialism, as we have seen, subscribes to the second of
these alternatives:  consciousness does react on the material conditions that gave rise to it, and the sort of freedom which morality
presupposes is an emergent aspect of matter's having, at a particular stage of development, become conscious.  This historical
development is recapitulated in each specific example of the dialectical unity of theory and practice.  We start with a concrete
situation which is like the objective material conditions prior to
the origin of consciousness;  that situation is reflected in abstract
thought, like the appearance of consciousness on the natural scene
and those thoughts take the form of an ideal theory about the initial
situation;  that theory is then validated or refuted by application
through social practice to the situation with which the process
began, and this final stage represents consciousness reacting on
material reality.

We have seen how at various stages of this process different
philosophical attitudes, representing the partial experience of this

or that social class, provide an adequate account of only one particular moment, and now we can see how freedom is accommodated by
these attitudes.  The concrete situation as passively reflected in
ideas can be described in terms of mechanical materialism and freedom does not appear at this level at all.  The subsequent phase of
active thought shaping abstract ideas into a theory about the situation can be seen as idealism, and freedom, in the sense of a release
from the bare 'givenness' of the original circumstances, comes into
the picture at this point;  but so far it is the freedom of a purely
conceptual movement without any actual consequences.  In the act of
applying this theory to the posited situation, the freedom of conception is subjected to the stern criticism of objective conditions
and only such elements of novelty are retained as can be incorporated
into whatever new situation develops out of the first.  If these
objective conditions are physical, the result of this process is
the transformation of things in conformity with natural law which is
production at the level of action and knowledge at the level of
consciousness.  If the conditions are social, the result is the
transformation of society in conformity with the laws of man's
productive relationships which at the level of consciousness is
freedom and at the level of action is political change and, combined together, are social morality.  The freedom this morality
implies does not have the limitless but ineffective scope of pure
thought:  it has the narrower but practical range of thought acting
in a material context.

We have also seen how these various phases are expressed in
different languages.  The language of the first phase is purely
descriptive — empirical propositions about objective conditions as
merely reflected in consciousness.  The language of the second
phase is either logical, drawing deductive conclusions from abstract
formulations, or imaginative, spinning out ideal fantasies about
what might be.  Only in the final phase do we get prescriptive sentences in the form of value or normative judgments with their
implicit imperatives that some object ought to be approved as
worthy of choice or that some action ought to be performed as productive of good results.  This moral 'ought' has been prepared for
by the appearance of an ideal freedom in the preceding phase.  It is
because Marxism stresses the interconnectedness of the whole process
and does not take the various phases as separate alternatives that
it can be at once a science of society, a logic of social consciousness and a call to action.  All these languages can be found
in 'Capital' and the other classics of Marxism-Leninism which contain descriptions of how a particular form of society actually
functions, shows logically the nature of that society's inner contradictions and laws of development, goes on to judge that society in
moral terms and to call for revolutionary action on the part of
the class whose mission it is to change it.

Sometimes Marx is only concerned with describing people in terms
of their economic functions.

I paint the capitalist and the landlord in no sense 'couleur
de rose'.  But here individuals are dealt with only in so far as
they are the personifications of economic categories, embodi-
ments of particular class-relations and class-interests.  My
standpoint, from which the evolution of the economic formation of

society is viewed as a process of natural history, can less
than any other make the individual responsible for relations
whose creature he socially remains, however much he may subjectively raise himself above them.(32)

And in the same passage he also makes moral judgments of the same
class of people.  'The peculiar nature of the material it [political
economy] deals with, summons as foes into battle the most violent,
mean and malignant passions of the human breast, the furies of
private interest.'(33)

Kautsky chides Marx for letting 'the influence of the moral
ideal break through his scientific research' since 'science stands
above ethics and its results are just as little moral or immoral
as necessity is moral or immoral.'(34)  For Kautsky the only part
ethics has to play is in providing the proletariat with the morale
for carrying out economic changes on the basis of a purely scientific analysis.

This absolute distinction between scientific and ethical man
was the sign of Kautsky's conversion to the revisionist creed of
supposing that social change would come about automatically without
the need for revolutionary struggle.  All we have to do is wait for
social trends which are going the way we want to go anyway to sweep
us to victory — a programme of sheer opportunism.  Kautsky also
shows his contempt for the working class in treating the moral ideal
as a kind of fairy tale to make them behave as they are supposed to.

Revisionism began with Bernstein who not surprisingly spent some
time in Britain where he became familiar with the social democratic
ideas of the Fabians.  'Revisionism' is, really, a misnomer for a
movement which was eventually to achieve its greatest 'success' on
behalf of bourgeois reaction by restoring capitalism in the Soviet
Union.  'Revisionism' suggests that it is merely a distortion or
reworking of Marxism.  In fact, it is nothing but the ideology of
capitalism disguised under pseudo-revolutionary rather than a
pseudo-democratic mask.  If social democracy is bourgeois morals
and politics wearing a cloth cap, revisionism is bourgeois morals
and politics decked out in odds and ends of Marxist terminology.
Bourgeois morality exemplifies the naturalistic fallacy of assuming
that members of a society in each pursuing his own individual self-
interest will somehow bring about the moral result of the good of
the whole.  Revisionist morality commits the same fallacy in
assuming that contradictions working themselves out automatically
will bring about all the moral consequences of a socialist revolution without anyone's being put to the inconvenience of actually
revolting.  Just as bourgeois morality cannot conceive of anyone's
acting other than on the basis of immediate selfish interests so
revisionism sees the working class as capable only of responding to
material incentives.  It is manipulative rather than liberative and
its typical political form is a bureaucracy acting on behalf of the
working class because it knows better what is good for them — never
the capture and consolidation of state power by the workers themselves.

It is true that in the intellectual effort to explain the material
foundations of life and thought Marx sometimes uses expressions
which look like an economic deterministic approach to social existence and which would be incompatible with any expressions of moral

indignation at crimes against the working class or any summons to
that class to liberate itself.  And sometimes in throwing out all
the claptrap of bourgeois morality Marx seems to be discarding
morality in any form.  But these are only a few remarks taken out
of the context of the vast amount of his writings.  The overall
import of his work is unmistakably that dialectical materialism
allows full scope for a call to action which is at once practical
and ethical, a call not just to interpret the world but to change
it.

As Engels has expressed this point:

According to the materialist conception of history, the ultimately determining element in history is the production and
reproduction of real life.  More than this neither Marx nor I
have ever asserted.  Hence if somebody twists this into saying
that the economic element is the only determining one, he
transforms that proposition into a meaningless, abstract, sense-
less phrase.  The economic situation is the basis, but the
various elements of the superstructure:  political forms of the
class struggle ... constitutions established by the victorious
class ... judicial forms, and even the reflexes of all these
actual struggles in the brains of the participants ... also
exercise their influence upon the course of the historical
struggles and in many cases preponderate in determining their
form.(35)

The relation of the material base of society and the superstructure, 'the legal, political, religious, esthetic or philosophic —
in short, ideological forms', is expressed this way by Stalin:

The superstructure is born of the base, but this does not at
all mean that it only reflects the base, that it is passive,
neutral, that it is indifferent to the fate of its base, to
the future of classes, to the character of the structure.  On
the contrary, having come into the world, it becomes a mighty
active force, actively helping its base to develop and grow
stronger, taking all measures to help the new order to ruin and
liquidate the old economic base and the old classes.(36)

This relationship between base and superstructure is particularly
crucial during the transitional period between capitalist and communist society, the socialist period.  Based on the experience of
the Paris Commune Marx had written:

Between capitalist and communist society lies the period of
the revolutionary transformation of the one into the other.
There corresponds to this also a political transition period in
which the state can be nothing but the revolutionary dictatorship of the proletariat.(37)

The reason for the necessity of this working-class dictatorship is
that class struggle does not suddenly cease with the capture of
state power by the working class.

The abolition of classes requires a long, difficult and stubborn
class struggle, which, after the overthrow of capitalist rule,
after the destruction of the bourgeois state, after the establishment of the dictatorship of the proletariat, does not disappear, but merely changes its forms and in many respects
becomes fiercer.(38)

The revisionist line on this transitional period as developed by such traitors to the working class as Khrushchev is that class struggle ends with the revolution and there is no need for a dictatorship of the proletariat.  Furthermore, since the superstructure is simply the passive and mechanical reflection of the material base, once the material base has been technically altered from capitalist to socialist by the expropriation of the private owners of the means of production, socialist man will be automatically produced like a product coming off an assembly line, with the speed of this production being regulated by material rewards and punishments.  This is the policy which undermined socialism in the East European Peoples Democracies and was advocated in China by Liu Shao Chi and his followers.

Marxism-Leninism, on the contrary, recognises that during the transitional period there must be a cultural revolution complementing the political revolution which destroyed the economic base of exploitative society, that if the superstructure, the ideology, is not also revolutionised so that it is thoroughly socialist and in accord with the socialist economic base, then it will react on that base in a corrosive and destructive way and allow the restoration of capitalism.  Objectively, revisionism which refused to make a revolution on the grounds that socialism could come about automatically sets about, once the revolution has been made, destroying its achievements on the grounds that a socialist society can best be built by bourgeois methods.

The working class having made the revolution must also remain in firm political control of socialist development at all levels of society — cultural as well as economic.  'The proletariat must exercise all-round dictatorship over the bourgeoisie in the realm of the superstructure, including the various spheres of culture.'(39) It is precisely in such spheres as education, publication, administration and propaganda work that the bourgeoisie using its cultural privileges in the previous regime to gain a foothold in the new socialist regime regroups for the purpose of subverting it.  Hence the moral summons to the working class during the Cultural Revolution in China for the defence of socialism:  'Fight self-interest. Criticise revisionism.'  In other words, the working class must fight selfish bourgeois habits and customs within themselves at the same time that they expose revisionism as bourgeois counter-revolution and smash it.  Emancipation of the working class means not only overthrowing the exploitative system of capitalism but also eradicating within themselves all vestiges of bourgeois egoistic morality.

One of the lessons Marxists have learned from the practical experience of consolidating a working-class revolution is that the transitional period will necessarily last longer than was previously anticipated, both because the new socialist country is surrounded by hostile capitalist countries eager to intervene and restore capitalism and because the conquest of bourgeois customs and attitudes internally is a protracted struggle.  Even Lenin who in addressing the Youth Leagues in 1920 thought that many of his audience in twenty years' time would be living in communist society seriously underestimated the duration of the struggle.  The Chinese and Albanians talk in terms of ten generations.  As Mao

Tsetung says:

Socialist society covers a considerably long historical period.
In the historical period of socialism, there are still classes,
class contradictions and class struggle, there is the struggle
between the socialist road and the capitalist road, and there is
the danger of the capitalist restoration. We must recognise the
protracted and complex nature of this struggle. We must heighten
our vigilance. We must conduct socialist education. We must
correctly understand and handle class contradictions and class
struggle, distinguish the contradictions between ourselves and
the enemy from those among the people and handle them correctly.
Otherwise a socialist country like ours will turn into its
opposite and degenerate, and a capitalist restoration will take
place. From now on we must remind ourselves of this every year,
every month and every day so that we can retain a rather sober
understanding of this problem and have a Marxist-Leninist line.
(40)

What is involved in this whole question of a cultural revolution
is an understanding of the relationship between material base and
ideological superstructure and an appreciation of the dialectical
character of this relationship. Unless it is possible for the consciousness of men, having comprehended the laws governing their
social being, to play at certain times a decisive role in social
development, then there is no possibility of the kind of freedom
presupposed by moral action and hence no morality. There would not
then be any legitimate grounds for urging workers in capitalist
countries to mobilise their forces in order to emancipate themselves
and the world from exploitation nor for urging the workers and
peasants of China to 'fight self-interest and criticise revisionism' in order to safeguard socialism.

Mao Tsetung explains this dialectical relationship between base
and superstructure and also demonstrates the circumstances in which
one or the other predominates as the decisive factor.

True, the productive forces, practice and the economic base
generally play the principal and decisive role; whoever denies
this is not a materialist. But it must also be admitted that in
certain conditions, such aspects as the relations of production,
theory and the superstructure in turn manifest themselves in the
principal and decisive role. When it is impossible for the
productive forces to develop without a change in the relations
of production, then the change in the relations of production
plays the principal and decisive role. The creation and advocacy
of revolutionary theory plays the principal and decisive role in
those times of which Lenin said, 'without a revolutionary theory
there can be no revolutionary movement'. When a task, no matter
which, has to be performed, but there is as yet no guiding line,
method, plan or policy, the principal and decisive thing is to
decide on a guiding line, method, plan or policy. When the
superstructure (politics, culture, etc.) obstructs the development of the economic base, political and cultural changes become
principal and decisive. Are we going against materialism when
we say this? No. The reason is that while we recognise that in
the general development of history the material determines the
mental and social being determines social consciousness, we also —

and indeed must — recognise the reaction of mental on material
things, of social consciousness on social being and of the superstructure on the economic base.  This does not go against
materialism;  on the contrary, it avoids mechanical materialism
and firmly upholds dialectical materialism.(41)

In other words, it is precisely in revolutionary situations that
this reaction of relations of production on forces of production,
of consciousness on being, of superstructure on base occurs as part
of the dynamic of change and releases in the process that degree
of freedom necessary for the highest moral endeavour of those making
the revolution.  This dialectical relationship can be compared with
the mechanical accounts of Bukharin and various bourgeois writers
who find the main motive of social development in such forces of
production as levels of technology without appreciating the tremendous liberating effect on the forces of production of a revolutionary change in the relations of production.  It can be compared with
the revisionists for whom the economic base always predominates and
who, as a consequence, make the most appalling economic blunders —
like turning large tracts of Siberia into a dust bowl precisely
like capitalist farming in the USA.

The Proletarian Cultural Revolution in China has been one of
the greatest vindications in social practice of the truth of
Marxism-Leninism as creatively developed by Mao Tsetung.  If the
October Revolution demonstrated for the first time in world history
that it is possible for the working class under correct leadership
to capture state power and lay the foundations of a socialist
society, the Great Proletarian Cultural Revolution proved that the
working class having seized state power can, again under correct
leadership, hold on to it and go on to construct socialism by
their own efforts in the teeth of revisionist and bourgeois
hostility.


A FREE SOCIETY

If Marx had one compelling motive for identifying himself completely
with the working class in order to devote his life to leading them
out of the bondage of wage slavery, it was his feeling about freedom as the supreme good.  This is why he was never interested in
petty schemes for the redistribution of wealth or the amelioration
of the conditions of the poor.  The issue was always that of establishing the social foundation on which the major task of man, social
production, could be carried out in conditions of human dignity,
which could only mean that man must enter voluntarily into relations of co-operative production with other men, thus changing
labour 'from merely a means of life to life's principal need'. Such
a free realm in which there was no exploitation of man by man could
only come into existence when not only the material base of exploitation had been blown sky high but also ideas and habits of centuries
of class-divided, exploitative society had been washed from men's
minds.  Moreover, while justice may be something that is rendered
to men, freedom is something they can only win for themselves. It is
not something which can be achieved on their behalf by any élitist
grouping.  Every form of acting on behalf of people will always

turn into another form of their exploitation.

A decision of the Central Committee of the Chinese Communist
Party concerning the Proletarian Cultural Revolution puts the point
clearly:

> The only method is for the masses to liberate themselves, and
> any method of doing things on their behalf must not be used.
> Trust the masses, rely on them, and respect their initiative.
> Cast out fear. Don't be afraid of disorder.... Let the masses
> educate themselves in this great revolutionary movement and learn
> to distinguish between right and wrong and between correct and
> incorrect ways of doing things.

There is no way except through mass involvement in revolutionary
practice for the working people to learn to make these distinctions.
'What is correct always develops in the course of struggle with what
is wrong. The true, the good and the beautiful always exist in
comparison with the false, the evil and the ugly and grow in struggle
with the latter.'(42)

Marx was always concerned with the dialectic of necessity and
freedom, the relation between the physical compulsion of man's
basic needs and the liberative energy that man as a socially productive being might display in meeting them.

> Just as the savage must wrestle with nature to satisfy his
> wants, to maintain and reproduce life, so must civilised man,
> and he must do so in all social formations and under all possible
> modes of production. With his development this realm of physical
> necessity expands as a result of his wants; but, at the same
> time, the forces of production which satisfy these wants also
> increase. Freedom in this field can only consist in socialised
> man, the associated producers, rationally regulating their inter-
> change with Nature; and achieving this with the least expendi-
> ture of energy and under conditions most favourable to, and
> worthy of, their human nature. But it nonetheless still remains
> a realm of necessity. Beyond it begins that development of human
> energy which is an end in itself, the true realm of freedom,
> which, however, can blossom forth only with this realm of neces-
> sity as its base.(43)

Even communist society is not to be thought of as a final stage
of human development in which all contradictions are resolved and
from which, therefore, no further advance is possible. There would
still be contradictions as, for example, between the new and the
old, the known and the not yet known, present and future demands;
but since such contradictions would no longer break out along class
lines in an exploitative situation they would no longer be antagonistic. Marx does not describe communist society as the end but
the beginning of history, true history made by men freely and consciously in co-operative pursuit of their aims; and everything
leading up to it, the various forms of class-divided society with
their strife and blindness and inhumanity, must be regarded from
this perspective as a prehistoric period.

We have the enormous advantage over Marx's contemporaries of
being able to study Marxist-Leninist ideas in terms of their actual
application in social practice — not as yet, of course, in communist society but certainly in the transitional society of socialism which lies between successful working-class revolutions and the

achievement of full communism.  What is said here of Albania as a
free socialist society could also have been said of China or of
Vietnam, as it progressively liberates itself from the brutal and
contemptible efforts of the USA to impose capitalism by force, but
with less precise detail simply because the author has spent so much
less time in China and none at all in Indo-China.

The first thing that has to be said in respect to the political
basis of popular freedom in Albania is that, the property grounds
for the exploitative class of landlords and comprador capitalists
having been swept away by the revolutionary war of liberation, the
working class enjoys and exercises real state power.  This is reflected throughout society with workers controlling the factories
and the farms where they work and deciding the aims for the overall
economic five-year plans which they achieve with such enthusiasm
because they recognise the goals as their own — the plans have
'the mark of the people on them'.  They decide all questions dealing
with the defence and the expansion of socialist relations in all
spheres of life.

Recently when it was agreed that education should be 'revolutionised' to bring it into accord with the socialist base and
enable it to serve the needs of the people better, there was a
nation-wide forum lasting for a whole year during which all teachers,
all students from the ninth year on and the whole working class,
as parents concerned with the proper training of their children in
socialist ways of life and as workers concerned with the qualifications of recruits to production, were free to make any suggestions
they liked.  In this country of a little over two million people
there were 21,000 meetings attended by 600,000 people, or more than
half of the adult population, at which contributions were made by
160,000 individual citizens.  All proposals offered whether they
were contradictory or not, provided they were not at variance with
general socialist principles, were collected in a document which
was then resubmitted to the mass for further discussion and eventually the reorganisation of the whole educational system on the
widest possible basis of agreement was set in motion.  This is the
mass line, 'from the masses to the masses' in operation.  'They
corroborated in practice', the head of the Central Committee for
the Revolutionising of Education said at the end of the public
consultation, 'the principle that the socialist revolution forges
ahead through class struggle with the active participation of the
masses who are not only the object but also the subject of the
ideological and cultural revolution.'

This maximum exercise of democracy to arrive at popularly agreed
decisions combined with the organisation and determination to carry
out decisions once arrived at is democratic centralism which is the
social form of the dialectical relationship between freedom and
discipline.  It is the principle which is realised in every organisational structure in the country from the Party of Labour itself
down to the smallest residential collective for ensuring the proper
management of a single block of flats.  It is the guarantee in
every area of society that the people do rule and rule in an orderly
way.  It is as far removed from bourgeois democracy, 'deciding once
in three or six years which member of the ruling class was to mis-
represent the people in Parliament',(44) as a system of co-operative

production to meet people's needs directly now and in the future, is from a system of production geared solely to the profits to be reaped by a capitalist class.

It is because state power is vested in the working people and serves no other interest that the people enjoy freedom from the restraints and fears that beset all workers who are not in control of their own destiny.  No one in the whole of Albania (or China or North Vietnam) has to worry for a moment about ever being out of a job, going hungry, lacking decent living quarters, having the best medical care free of charge when he is ill and a comfortable pension when he retires, nor of ever being deprived, as long as he lives, of the fullest opportunity of contributing whatever he has to offer for the improvement and enrichment of the life of the community.  There is no taxation, no inflation, no economic crisis of any kind. Prices steadily go down and real wages steadily go up.  It must sound like Utopia to workers anywhere in the capitalist world, but when workers themselves govern in their own interests why should things be any other way?  Albania and China have the only stable currencies in the world because they are the only countries where the source of value, human labour, receives its full reward and rising production is reflected in improved living conditions of the creators of value.

The freedom of genuine working-class democracy manifests itself in an infinite number of ways.  In every factory, agricultural co-operative, school, office, or community centre of any kind is to be found a bulletin board on which any individual or collective is free to charge any other individual or collective, including the management or directorship, with mistakes, inefficiency or inade-quacy.  Criticisms have to be answered satisfactorily and failure to do so, in the case of managers, can result in dismissal.  Com-plementary to this will be another bulletin board on which outstand-ing achievements or extraordinary services to the people are men-tioned for commendation.  Fear of the sack no longer existing, and income differentials amounting to no more than one to two over the whole of society, the major form of motivation is socialist emula-tion and the fact that the growth rate of the Albanian economy is the highest in Europe is material evidence for its efficacy, though the quality of life based on co-operation rather than competition is its real justification.

Freedom is meaningless without discipline.  Membership of the Party of Labour, which is the highest distinction a citizen can enjoy, confers no privilege but that of being of greater service to one's fellow citizens.  Recently when a new block of flats con-structed by voluntary labour was opened there was no question in anybody's mind but that the flats on the less comfortable side of the building would naturally go to any Party members.  Justice is as democratic as every other institution.  Judges are popularly elected and, like all other democratically-elected officials, sub-ject to recall.  Ordinary citizens from any area of work sit on the bench for a fortnight on a rota basis and have equal power with the judge in all judicial decisions.  But more and more in Albania infringements of socialist discipline or crimes against socialist property are dealt with through discussion sessions and agreed correction within the various collectives.  The courts have less and less to do and there is no society in the world where the police force is so little in evidence.  Discipline there is, but it is a discipline the people impose on themselves.  People can be told how to make a revolution or build socialism;  but no one can do it for them or in spite of them.  A socialist society must always, therefore, be an inner-directed society.  Restraint must be the self-restraint that comes from the democratic practice of criticism and self-criticism.  Self-discipline is only possible where social ends are those the people themselves have fixed, and social morality only exists in any full sense when people are free to choose the kind of society they want to make and to make it relying on their own efforts.

Of course, proletarian democracy has another face which is turned toward class enemies of the working people, toward those who would revive bourgeois ways of thinking and feeling as a prelude to diverting the country from its socialist course and restoring capitalism.  This is the face of the dictatorship of the proletariat.  Nor is there any softness in Albania's readiness to defend from foreign foes the independence which has cost the lives of so many heroes and heroines and entailed such sacrifices among the people generally.  The armed services, also an example of proletarian democracy with their absence of rank or status symbols, are in a constant state of preparedness and all young people take their turn at military training.  There could be no better proof of the stability of Albanian society and the correct relationship between people and their own state than the fact that all citizens possess weapons and know how to use them.  The working class in Albania is an armed proletariat;  and the defence of socialism within and of national sovereignty without rests on the tested fighting qualities of workers who still, and for many years to come, in the slogan of the Party of Labour, will have to build socialism with pickaxe in one hand and rifle in the other.

The principle of the mass line is the pattern of socialism. Democratic centralism is the organisational form of the mass line. From the extended membership of the Party of Labour of Albania flow to the centre in the most democratic way the ideas, opinions and aspirations of individuals based on their experience of class struggle.  These ideas, opinions and hopes are concentrated in the Party line.  This line is then given back to the membership for general implementation.  This is not a once-for-all process but is continuous.  And as with the Party so in every other form of organisation — the people's state in relation to all workers in fixing the norms of the five-year plans, the factory management or collective farm leadership in respect to the workers in these productive centres, down through local government and the various front organisations like women or youth or even children to the committee and residents of a single housing unit.  Power is in the hands of the working class.  It flows inwardly, democratically, to a central authority and outwardly again as an agreed line of action to the working people.  A line of action for the people takes the form of stern prohibitions to all those whose interests are not those of the people:  the dictatorship of the proletariat is simply the mass line as it appears to enemies of the working class.

This mass line, which at the level of organisation is democratic centralism, at the level of understanding is simply the Marxist theory of knowledge.

Take the ideas of the masses (scattered and unsystematic ideas) and concentrate them (through study turn them into concentrated and systematic ideas), then go to the masses and propagate and explain these ideas until the masses embrace them as their own, hold fast to them and translate them into action, and test the correctness of these ideas in such action.  Then once again concentrate ideas from the masses and once again go to the masses so that the ideas are persevered in and carried through. And so on, over and over again in an endless spiral, with the ideas becoming more correct more vital and richer each time.(45)

The Marxist conception of truth is inseparable from the mass line because the only source of correct ideas is social practice, the practical experience of the people down the ages in the struggle for production and in class struggle.  Only those who learn from the masses have anything to teach the masses.  Just as value judgments are the tribute we pay to the labour of fellow men, so our regard for right thinking is the respect we pay to their hard-won know-ledge.  'It has to be understood that the masses are the real heroes, while we ourselves are often childish and ignorant, and without this understanding it is impossible to acquire even the most rudimentary knowledge.'(46)  These correct ideas from social practice, once they are 'concentrated and systematised', are then 'grasped by the masses' and 'turned into a material force'. 'Communists must be ready at all times to stand for the truth, because truth is in the interests of the people;  communists must be ready at all times to correct their mistakes because mistakes are against the interests of the people....'(47)  A regard for the masses is a regard for truth and a regard for truth is a regard for the masses.

In the organisational form of democratic centralism, criticism is the democratic aspect, the right of everyone to speak his mind. Self-criticism represents the centralist aspect, the discipline of the individual in accepting the mass line once democratically estab-lished.  This principle is expressed in the new constitution of the People's Republic of China adopted in January 1975, by the Fourth National People's Congress:

Speaking out freely, airing views fully, holding great debates and writing big character posters are new forms of carrying on socialist revolution created by the masses of the people.  The state shall ensure to the masses the right to use these forms to create a political situation in which there are both centralism and democracy, both discipline and freedom, both unity of will and personal ease of mind and liveliness, and so help consoli-date the dictatorship of the proletariat.(48)

The unity of theory and practice takes the same form of the mass line.

Start from perceptual knowledge and actively develop it into rational knowledge;  then start from rational knowledge and actively guide revolutionary practice to change both the sub-jective and the objective world.  Practice, knowledge, again practice, and again knowledge.  This form repeats itself in endless cycles, and with each cycle the content of practice and knowledge rises to a higher level.  Such is the whole of the dialectical-materialist theory of knowledge, and such is the

dialectical-materialist theory of the unity of knowing and
doing.(49)

The only solution to the problem of whether theory corresponds to
objective reality is

to re-direct rational knowledge to social practice, apply
theory to practice and see whether it can achieve the objectives
one has in mind.... Idealism and mechanical materialism, opportunism and adventurism are all characterised by the break between the subjective and the objective, by the separation of
theory from practice.(50)

This is the pattern of socialism:  everywhere this pulsating
motion from extremities to centre and from centre back to extremities again in a never ending dialectic of revolutionary development.  The same kind of basic pattern appears in capitalist society
under bourgeois rule;  but it is a very different pattern.  In
spite of any pretensions to democracy on grounds of expediency,
bourgeois art, philosophy, science, politics are élitist and indi-
vidualist.  They deny importance to the masses.  The masses, in
their work, are commodities, in their needs, consumers, and in the
use economic imperialism often makes of them, cannon fodder.  The
general pattern is an exploitative metropole surrounded by an
exploited hinterland — factory management and workers, city and
countryside, capitalist government and wage earners, metropolitan
country and colonies.  Everything in the way of culture, knowledge,
programmes of action are presumed to flow out from the centre;
nothing is supposed to flow back again but loot, surplus-value.
The centre in this capitalist pattern is like a large brain with no
good red blood flowing to it — and, progressively, no rational
orders issuing out from it either.

Chapter 4

# MORALS AND POLITICS

INTRODUCTION

The fact that the social existence of men, particularised in the
form of their involvement in the productive process, largely
shapes without mechanically determining their ethical attitudes,
means that Marxism cannot expect any qualitative change in society
based on the moral efforts of individuals acting within the range
of their own personal relationships.  Their very conceptions of
what is 'right' in respect to those personal relationships will have
been profoundly influenced by the mode of production or specific
form of exploitation in their society and by their own position as
belonging to the class of exploiters or exploited.  In a situation
where growing contradictions in the basic mode of production, which
as we have seen are always, ultimately, class contradictions, people's reactions in the moral crisis which is part of the general
economic crisis are inevitably coloured through and through by
what side of the class contradiction they are on.

   In such a period of moral crisis, among those who fear or
hate change and see the world as teetering on the brink of disaster,
there may be an immediate decline in the standards of personal
relationships either from a sense of panic and an attitude of
'sauve qui peut' or from a sense that nothing matters any more and
one might as well take whatever pleasure one still can regardless
of others.  On the other hand, there may be a time lag between the
corruption of personal relations and the deterioration in the ethical standards of a whole class, but without that differential in
the rate of demoralisation serving as any check on the general
decadence.  Certain of the leaders in fascist Germany are reputed
to have been kindly fathers and husbands but it in no way affected
their responsibility for extermination centres in which thousands
were brutally slaughtered nor does it mitigate history's judgment
of them.  In any case the regime's encouragement of delation within
the family by suborning children in the Hitler Jugend to inform
on their parents soon subverted any tiny salients of decency left
in Nazi society so that, as in South Africa today, it is very
difficult to imagine any good person who would not have been under-
ground, in prison or dead.

Marxism is by no means unconcerned with the morality of such
individual relationships as those between husband and wife, parents
and children, fellow workmates and close friends.  Indeed it is the
poisoning of those relationships which is part of its indictment of
capitalism.  But the understanding that these relationships are
inevitably stunted or fostered, weakened or strengthened by the
prevailing social climate means that real concern about their
quality has to take the form of creating the atmosphere in which
they can flourish.  That is to say, it calls for a material foundation of society which can support wholesome, happy, mutually bene-
ficent personal relationships — not just in this country or that,
not just among this class or that, but among all people without
distinction.

The small, isolated, ingrown bourgeois family with its complex-
ridden relationships is not the inevitable and eternal context of
human development.  Just as Marxism sees a progression in social
organisation from primitive communism through various forms of class-
divided society to a consciously planned communism at a higher
level, so it envisages corresponding changes in the family — from
its natural integration in the tribal community through the social
forms which reflect, in the position of women or the treatment of
children, different types of exploitation to the re-integration of
the family in the organised co-operative life of a commune.

It is, of course, just as absurd to hold the Teutonic-Christian
form of the family to be absolute and final as it would be to
apply that character to the ancient Roman, the ancient Greek, or
the eastern forms which, moreover, taken together form a series
in historic development.  Moreover it is obvious that the fact
of the collective working group being composed of individuals
of both sexes and all ages, must necessarily, under suitable
conditions, become a source of humane development;  although in
its spontaneously developed, brutal, capitalistic form, where
the labourer exists for the process of production and not the
process of production for the labourer, that fact is a pesti-
ferous source of corruption and slavery.(1)

An Albanian, asked why family relations were so strong and happy
in his country answered simply:  'Because there is not the slightest
economic compulsion on any member, from birth on, to remain in the
family group.'

A critique of personal relations in bourgeois society can only
take the practical form of a call for, in Lenin's words, 'a
morality which serves the purpose of helping human society to rise
to a higher level and to get rid of the exploitation of labour.'
It is a call for a new society in which warm personal relationships
will not be at odds with relations of production based on private
ownership, selfishness and competition but will complement, deepen
and personalise relations of production based on common ownership,
regard for others and co-operation.

The old society was based on the principle:  rob or be robbed,
work for others or make others work for you, be a slave owner or
a slave.  Naturally, people brought up in such a society imbibe
with their mother's milk, so to speak, the psychology, the habit,
the concept:  you are either a slave owner, a small employee, a
small official, an intellectual — in short, a man who thinks
only of himself, and doesn't give a hang for anybody else.(2)

This call for the establishment of the very conditions in which higher ethical standards can be realised is itself supremely moral;  but it can only be answered in terms of political activity. Such a social change cannot be brought about by individual changes in personal relationships, though political activity devoted to transforming society has its moral implications for the area of personal relationships.  Intimate associations in the family or among friends are not unaffected by the concerted political struggle to achieve a better ordering of social life.  Indeed, it is to the extent that people dedicated to changing the very foundations of society are capable here and now of beginning to act on the moral principle of a lively concern for others which will be character-istic of that new society and of having all their relationships profoundly influenced by that principle that such a better ordering of society will actually be achieved.

But this call for changing society cannot, effectively, take the form of a vague summons to people to show more regard for each other and observe a more humanitarian attitude in their conduct.  As we have seen, the gulf between exploiters and exploited is so great that no general humanitarian principles can stretch across it mean-ingfully.  There is no morality which can unite in a common pattern of social behaviour people born to live out their pitifully short lives on the verge of starvation and those whom privilege insulates from every natural discomfort, between those whose lives depend on selling their capacity to labour as dearly as they can and those who are in a position to traffic profitably in the labour of others. The acceptance of such differences by subscribing to any system of belief which ignores them, explains them away or justifies them is the negation of morality.  Genuine humanitarianism has to start with the demand for an end of the exploitation of man by man, which immediately turns it into the morality of a class.

All morality is class morality.  One is either for an existing exploitative social arrangement or against it.  There is no third possibility.  Any attempt to retreat into personal relationships and let the rest of the world go hang, any attempt to opt out of existing society and establish some small communal enclave merely commits one to tacit support of the status quo, a hanger-on of the exploiting class.  Setting up such opt-out communes is like trying to organise 'workers' control' in a particular factory while leaving the capitalist context intact:  it is only a device for deluding any workers not clever enough to see through it.  Try 'cultivating your own garden', if you are so privileged as to be able to do so, and you are likely to find anyway that the plants are all dying from the pollution it profits somebody to create and nobody to remedy, or defoliated because some wild defenders of the existing system think an urban guerrilla may be hiding there.  As a system like capitalism is more and more in conflict with the objective progressive laws of human development, actions in its name inevitably become increas-ingly immoral.

Marx describes the difference between exploitative societies and a society from which exploitation has been eliminated in terms of the class relationships of individuals.  Whereas in all exploita-tive societies the individual could only participate in the life of the community as a member of some class, 'in the community of

revolutionary proletarians, who establish their control over the
conditions of existence of themselves and the other members of
society, the individuals participate as individuals.'(3)   Since
the state is simply the governmental form of the domination of the
exploiting class, the ending of class-divided society with the
elimination of exploitation means the 'withering away of the state'.

If the state is the product of irreconcilable class antagonisms,
if it is a power standing above society and increasingly alienating itself from it, it is clear that the liberation of the
oppressed class is impossible not only without a violent revolution, but also without the destruction of the apparatus of
state power which was created by the ruling class and which is
the embodiment of this alienation.(4)

What this means in ethical terms is that in all class-divided
society effective morality can only take a political form.   In
communist society, when classes no longer exist because the very
ways of thinking and habitual actions of an exploitative system
will have been eradicated by many post-revolutionary generations of
applying the socialist principles of 'curing the sickness to save
the patient' and 'learning from past mistakes to avoid future ones',
when all institutional forms of class rule and the force to back it
up have long disappeared, then politics will take the form of
morality.


ALIENATION AND SURPLUS VALUE

The moral crisis of the capitalist world reflecting the deepening
economic crisis and exacerbating it is as widely attested as it is
superficially accounted for.  That something pretty fundamental is
wrong is generally agreed, but the care with which pundits in
various fields overlook the obvious causes to pick out and elaborate
what are not causes at all but further symptoms of the malaise
proves that most of them are afraid that the only cure is, from
their point of view, worse than the disease.  It is like those international conferences on, say, pollution before socialist Chine let
a little light into their deliberations, where all sorts of figures
showing the extent of deterioration would be discussed and the un-
industrialised countries would be warned by the industrialised
countries exploiting them not to make their mistake of becoming
industrialised, but not one word would be said about the simple
fact that social cost can never be a major consideration under
capitalism and that there are no quick profits to be made out of
cleaning up after some dirty, money-making raid on the world's
resources.

There is a good deal in the writings of contemporary social
scientists about the alienation of modern man, his sense of
estrangement and frustration, his inability as he becomes more and
more isolated to communicate with others at all.  Different theories
are proposed to account for this feeling of 'homelessness' which
turn out to be just a list of additional consequences:  life has
become too complex for the individual to do more than resignedly
fill in the forms which fix his place in an increasingly corporatised
state;  the conventional morality of a stagnant social system has

made men 'other-directed' instead of 'inner-directed' as they were
supposed to be in more adventurous times;  science has outstripped
wisdom and looms threateningly as a monster out of control;  or
contractual relationships which engage men in limited capacities
have replaced those natural groupings to which they belonged as
whole persons.  Philosophical movements like existentialism reflect
this same sense of alienation and the absurdity of life, usually
concluding that it is just the way life is and we must learn to
live with it.  The same sense is to be found in all high-brow
current literature with countless writers whining about their
essential loneliness in the midst of a 'population explosion' and
trying to communicate to us the incommunicability of human experience

Marx's use of the term 'alienation', his uncovering of its roots
in social existence and his tracing of its relations with other
aspects of the material conditions of specific men in their productive relationships, shows his own development from a petty bourgeois intellectual with compassion for oppressed people to a spokesman for, because through active involvement in their class struggle
a member of, the working class.  Socialism, the ideology of the
working class, does not arise spontaneously among workers.  It is
the application to their own experience in class struggle of the
theoretical formulations of the world-wide experience of the social
relations of production down the ages.  It is in this sense that
Lenin speaks of class political consciousness, what makes the proletariat a class-for-itself, as coming to workers from without,
that is, from outside of the sphere of relations between workers
and employers.(5)

> The theory of socialism grew out of the philosophic, historical
> and economic theories that were elaborated by the educated
> representatives of the propertied classes, the intellectuals.
> According to their social status, the founders of modern scien-
> tific socialism, Marx and Engels, themselves belonged to the
> bourgeois intelligentsia.(6)

But only as 'proletarianised' by sharing in the struggles of the
working class, by taking the lead in founding the first Workers
Internationale, was Marx able to apply 'philosophic, historical
and economic theories' to the experience of the working class in
the first capitalist country and give to workers a revolutionary
theory which they could recognise as their own on the basis of the
mass line.

Hegel uses the word 'alienation' in connection with the ideal
process of creativity.  The act of creation is to some extent a
self-diminution on the part of pure Mind or Spirit, a derogation
from its own unity and perfection in order to project a natural
world which has a quality of 'otherness' about it as alienated
from its maker.  In much the same way, man exteriorises his own
powers in institutions and objects which are similarly 'other' to
his essential nature as pure consciousness.  Moreover, although as
generalised man he is responsible for this extension of his being
in forms of social life and objects of production, in his individual capacity he cannot recognise them as his own creations and
seems to move in a foreign world in which he is a bewildered alien.

Marx recognised the validity of 'alienation' as a description
of the state of man in Western society;  but in his earliest writings

he criticises and rejects Hegel's derivation of the term.  A man
is not mere consciousness:  he is an objective being whose consciousness reflects his existence.

> A being who is objective acts objectively, and he would not
> act objectively if the objective did not reside in the very
> nature of his being.  He creates or establishes only objects,
> because he is established by objects — because at bottom he is
> nature.  In the act of establishing, therefore, this objective
> being he does not fall from his state of 'pure activity' into a
> creating of the object;  on the contrary, his objective product
> only confirms his objective activity, establishing his activity
> as the activity of an objective natural being.(7)

If man was alienated, it was not because of some ideal consequence of the act of creation as such:  it was because of the specific conditions of production at some historical period of social
development.  In not realising that man naturally expresses himself
in productive social effort and in not appreciating that other forms
of society are possible than the one developing in the Germany of
his day, Hegel extrapolated from alienation of human labour under
capitalist exploitation to the eternal character of all creative
effort.  Alienation thus was identified with all objectivising
activity whatsoever and must remain man's fate as long as he is
involved in the necessity of production.

The problem of alienation conceived simply as a state of mind
requires only an ideal solution.  Hegel argues that the idea of
private property is transcended by the idea of morality;  but as
Marx points out, this dialectic of thought leaves objective reality
precisely where it was before.  'In order to abolish the idea of
private property, the idea of communism is completely sufficient.
It takes actual communist action to abolish actual private property.'(8)  The Hegelian concept of annulling what is estranged
from man by appropriating it for himself can only become positive
once this appropriation is seen, not as an ideal process in which
consciousness annihilates the 'otherness' of the objective world,
but as an actual appropriation of the products of man's labour
through a communistic suppression of private property.  'Private
property' is Marx's expression for the objects produced by alienated
labour which reaches its culmination in capitalist society.  It
explains his statement that the 'division of labour and private
property are ... identical expressions:  in the one the same thing
is affirmed with reference to activity as is affirmed in the other
with reference to the product of the activity.'

It need hardly be said that what is being referred to is not
personal possessions but the kind of property whose ownership
establishes class dominance.  All the empty talk about 'managerial
revolutions', 'property-owning democracies' and the like is just
so much dust-raising to obscure the palpably unjust fact that in all
capitalist countries something in the order of a half to two-thirds
of the wealth in property is in the hands of less than 5 per cent
of the population.  As capitalism shifts unprofitable but necessary
industries onto the backs of taxpayers, mainly workers, with high
compensation charges on them as well, and adds insult to injury by
calling such nationalisation 'socialism', the gulf between property
owners and the propertyless is by no means diminished.  But the

communism following on the suppression of private property as the
objective sign of alienation cannot be based on general envy in
which avarice merely re-establishes itself in another form consti-
tuting the essence of competition, a kind of levelling down which
Marx calls 'crude communism', but must be based on the common
need of men in their productive relationships to reclaim themselves
through the things they have made.

This appropriation is necessary because man's sense of alienation is rooted in the fact that

the object which labour produces — labour's product — confronts
it as something alien, as a power independent of the producer....
The worker is related to the product of his labour as to an
alien object';(9)

and 'the more the worker spends himself, the more powerful the
alien objective world becomes which he creates over against himself
and the poorer he himself — his inner world — becomes.'(10)   And
it is not only the produced object that is alienated from the
worker but his very activity of production itself.

Finally the division of labour offers us the first example of
how, as long as man remains in natural society, that is as long
as cleavage exists between the particular and the common interest,
as long therefore as activity is not voluntarily but naturally
divided, man's own deed becomes an alien power opposed to him
which enslaves him instead of being controlled by him.(11)

In the early 1840s Marx developed his ideas on man's alienation
in respect to the objects of his labour as an analogy with the
estrangement in the realm of consciousness which takes a religious
form.

In religion the spontaneous activity of the human imagination,
of the human brain and the human heart, operates independently —
that is, operates on him as an alien, divine or diabolical activity — in the same way the worker's activity ceases to be his
spontaneous activity.   It belongs to another;  it is the loss
of his self.(12)

This other under whose 'service, domination, coercion and yoke',
the activity of the worker is performed becomes progressively in
history as well as in Marx's writings the capitalist who determines
the form, conditions and intensity of labour, the nature, quality
and quantity of its products and even whether or not it will take
place at all.

The gods by this analogy are the effects of man's intellectual
estrangement, as private property is the effect of his alienated
labour.   'The more man puts into God, the less he retains in himself.   The worker puts his life into the objects;  but now his life
no longer belongs to him but to the object.'   And to the very
extent that the object of his labour, which becomes alienated labour
in the act of selling his labour-power to another, 'the greater the
product, the less he is himself'.(13)   There is thus for Marx at
this stage a connection between atheism and communism:  in the one
case what is involved is man's reappropriation of the products of
his own consciousness;  in the other, it is the reappropriation of
the fruits of his own objective labours.   'Just as atheism, being
the annulment of God, is the advent of theoretic humanism so communism, as the annulment of private property, is the justification

of real human life as man's possession and thus the advent of
practical humanism.'(14)  But the negative idea of 'annulment'
only applies to the stage of transition from alienated to socialist
life.  Once the real existence of man and nature has been reasserted
in practical, sensuous and perceptible terms,

> when man has become for man the being of nature, and nature for
> man as the being of man, the question of an alien being above
> nature and man has become impossible.  Atheism has no longer
> any meaning, for atheism is a negation of God, and postulates
> the existence of man through this negation;  but socialism as
> socialism no longer stands in need of such a mediation....
> Socialism is man's positive self-consciousness, no longer mediated
> through the annulment of religion, just as real life is man's
> positive reality, no longer mediated through the annulment of
> private property.(15)

If man's labour is alienated because its products do not belong
to him in any sense, and if those products are turned into money,
then money is the universal form assumed by the alienated ability
of mankind.    In this role of representing man's productive
capacity money arrogates to itself the right of pronouncing which
of man's actual needs can be realised and which cannot.  Since a
demand on the part of one without money is a mere thing of the imagination, ineffectual and objectless, money thus becomes the arbiter
between the real and the unreal.  'The difference between effective
demand based on money and ineffective demand based on my need ...
is the difference between the imagined which exists merely within
me and the imagined as it is outside me as a real object'(16) —
the difference between Kant's real and imagined hundred thalers.
Money is the common medium which turns an image into reality and
reality into a mere image.  As the outward form of value by which
all things are exchangeable, it is also, in itself, the general
confounding of all things, including natural and human qualities.
As the effective link between man and man it is the determinant
of all human relationships.

'Money is the pimp between man's need and the object, between
his life and his means of life.  But that which mediates my life
for me, also mediates the existence of other people for me.  For
me it is the other person.'(17)

> Every product is a bait with which to seduce away the other's
> very being, his money;  every real and possible need is a weak-
> ness which will lead the fly to the glue pot — general exploi-
> tation of communal human nature.  Just as every imperfection in
> man is a bond with heaven, an avenue giving the priest access
> to the heart, every need is an opportunity to approach one's
> neighbour in the guise of the utmost amiability and say to him:
> Dear friend, I give you what you need;  but you know the 'conditio
> sine qua non';  you know the ink in which you have to sign your-
> self over to me;  in providing for your pleasure, I fleece
> you.(18)

And if every need exposes one to having his very substance taken
away from him, the basis is laid for that morality of extreme
asceticism and miserliness which actually characterises a period
of primitive accumulation.

> Self-denial, the denial of life and of all human needs is its
> cardinal doctrine. The less you eat, drink and read books;  the
> less you go to the theatre, the dance hall, the public house;
> the less you think, love, theorise, sing, paint, fence etc.,
> the more you save — the greater becomes your treasure which
> neither moths nor dust will devour — your capital. The less
> you are, the more you have;  the less you express your own life,
> the greater is your alienated life — the greater is the store of
> your estranged being.

And even in periods of conspicuous consumption the nature of money
can blight the very pleasure it makes possible and end in a kind of
pecuniary Oblomovism.

> All the things which you cannot do, your money can do. It can
> eat and drink, go to the dance hall and the theatre;  it can
> travel, it can appropriate art, learning, the treasures of the
> past, political power — all this it can appropriate for you ...
> yet being all this, it is inclined to do nothing but create
> itself;  for everything else is after all its servant. And
> when I have the master ... I feel no need of the servant.(19)

There is not much asceticism about these days but man, that is,
'affluent man' is as alienated in his pleasures as he formerly was
in his hoarding. Even among those who have very little of it, money
can create its illusions by screening, as it were, the relationship between master and man, between exploiter and exploited.  'In
imagination individuals seem freer under the dominance of the bourgeoisie than before, because their conditions of life seem acci-
dental.  In reality of course they are less free, because they are
more subjected to the violence of things.'(20)

Alienated labour is the source of estrangement among the exploited
classes of society;  but the alienated ability of mankind in general,
which takes a monetary form, gives all men a sense of estrangement.
'The worker is alienated in his life;  but the non-worker, the
bourgeois intellectual, is alienated in his thought.'(21)  He, too,
is a victim in a world of alienation which strikes at each man or
group of men through precisely what is dearest to them, so that the
transcendence of estrangement appears to each in a different guise.
Comparing various countries at the time he was setting down these
early reflections, Marx comments on how their citizens tend to
view the overcoming of alienation in terms of the respective form of
estrangement which is dominant in each:  in Germany through a philosophical extension of self-consciousness;  in France through a
political realisation of equality;  in Britain through a practical
application of economic theory. And these of course — German
philosophy, French socialism and British political economy — are
the three strands woven into the texture of Marx's own views at this
juncture. But in so far as he already finds the real roots of
alienation in commodity production, which dehumanises the worker in
turning him also into a commodity, and brutalises the capitalist
in making him a dealer in men, Marx has isolated the common source
of estrangement in all exploitative societies where commodity exchange is the main economic relationship.

It was his preoccupation with the actual material foundations of
society that enabled Marx to criticise the social ideas of those
whom in thinking about society abstractly, merely reproduced in

theoretic form their own alienation.  Starting with economic
relationships themselves, instead of with the manner in which they
might be reflected in this or that individual consciousness, he
succeeded, even at this early stage of the development of his ideas,
in making a substantial contribution to the new science of sociology.

The history of industry and the established objective existence
of industry are the open book of man's essential powers, the
exposure to the senses of human psychology. Hitherto this was
not conceived in its inseparable connnection with man's essential being, but only in an external relation of utility,
because, moving in the realm of estrangement, people could only
think man's general mode of being (religion or history in its
abstract-general character as politics, art, literature etc.)
to be the reality of man's essential powers and man's species-
activity.  We have before us the objectified essential powers of
man in the form of sensuous, alien, useful objects, in the form
of estrangement, displayed in ordinary material industry....
Since all human activity hitherto has been labour — that is,
industry — a psychology for which this, the part of history
most contemporary and accessible to sense, remains a closed
book, cannot become a genuine, comprehensive, and real science.
(22)

In the relationship between private property and alienated labour
Marx already in the 'Economic and Philosophic Manuscripts of 1844'
had recognised both the essential character of capitalism and the
means by which it might be overthrown.

From the relationship of estranged labour to private property
it ... follows that the emancipation of society from private
property, etc., from servitude, is expressed in the political
form as the emancipation of the workers;  not that their emancipation alone was at stake but because the emancipation of the
workers contains universal human emancipation — and it contains
this, because the whole of human servitude is involved in the
relation of the worker to production, and every relation of
servitude is but a modification and consequence of this
relation.(23)

A similar claim for a materialistic explanation of alienation is
made by Sartre when he takes as his point of departure the scarcity
of nature and the needs of man.(24)  But this is, in fact, a different approach from Marx's derivation from productive relations.
Why the emphasis on the scarcity of nature rather than on its
abundance, on the needs of man rather than on his productive capacity except that Sartre betrays the consumption bias which is
typical of the intellectual who is cut off from any actual experience of the productive process and for whom the objective world is
not something to be actively transformed by labour but something
to be passively dependent on for the satisfaction of wants.  For
such a person, as we have noted before, economics is the outlay of
limited means on available goods for whose purchase he competes
with others.  It has little to do with entering into co-operative
relations with others in order to produce those goods.  Thus
Sartre's starting point is Malthusian rather than Marxist and
enables him to deduce certain characteristic existentialist conclusions.  'On the basis of scarcity the menace of man for man

reveals itself:  man is the Being by which man is reduced to the
state of a haunted object.' The 'population explosion' is the
current pop form of this nightmare.

It is true, as Sartre states, that a large proportion of the
people of the earth are tragically undernourished;  but to argue
from this that 'scarcity is the fundamental human relationship
both in respect to nature and other men' is to regard a situation
created by imperialist exploitation, which is only capitalist exploitation in its international form, as the basic human condition
and to ignore the example of China where a quarter of the world's
population, once chronically subject to famine, now feed themselves
well under socialism.  Sartre's thesis conceals the class differences between exploiters and exploited and offers us instead a
fatalistic scheme of social existence in which all men are each
other's enemies in an endless competition for too few goods.
'Singular man' thus confronts in the context of society the Other,
this Other being the needs of all those men which would rob him of
his own satisfaction.  From this 'singular man', completely alienated
and frustrated at every turn by the malign 'otherness' of the people
and objects around him, it is impossible to go forward to any conception of social forces which could revolutionise the system of
competition and exploitation.  It is not class struggle which is for
Sartre the motivation of history but the existentialist, or bourgeois
concept of the individual in a life and death battle with the 'other'
— rather like the zo-omorphic accounts of human society, territorial
imperatives and so forth, which are our equivalent of the anthro-
pomorphic accounts of animals in the Middle Ages.  'Thus the comprehension', Sartre says, 'of the enemy is always more immediate than
the comprehension of the ally, since, naturally, the material conditions of scarcity decide what kind of comprehension is possible.'
Struggle is the basic human activity but the struggle has no purpose
but bare survival — which is a tragic conclusion for a man as
sympathetic to the plight of the oppressed as Sartre to be driven to.

It was because Marx took his stand firmly on the solid base of
man's 'objectified essential powers in ordinary material industry',
of man's labour which sums up all human activity, that sociology
since, in the work of Weber, Durkheim, Mead, Mannheim and so many
others has been, either openly or implicitly, 'a debate with Marx'.
(25)  Much of what Marx wrote during the period of the 'Economic and
Philosophic Manuscripts' has been found acceptable by sociologists
who would certainly reject with alarm any positive prescription for
action which would actually transform society.  Hence the great
popularity of Marx's early writings with revisionists.  As long as
communism could be described in such general terms as 'the real
appropriation of the human essence by and for man, the complete
return of man to himself as a social being — a return become conscious, and accomplished within the entire wealth of previous
development', as long as communism was, in short, a form of humanism
to which men, in spite of any question of class interest, could pay
lip-service, sociologists could profess to find Marxism illuminating
and perceptive.  They could declare with Marx that the 'only alternative to the socialisation of the individual mind and character is
its alienation'.(26)  But socialising actual property by forcefully
expropriating capitalist owners as one of the conditions for this

socialisation of individuals would be another matter.  The idea of
humanising productive relationships is a perfectly acceptable
subject for discussion;  but the demonstration that humanism is an
empty concept as long as class divisions persist and that they can
only be ended by a proletarian revolution tends to stimulate remark-
ably the critical faculties of ideologists who associate themselves
with the interests of the ruling class.

In his early writings can be found most of Marx's leading ideas
in embryonic form;  but they have not yet acquired the concentrated,
systematic structure of his mature work.  They are philosophical
jottings about the material conditions of life rather than a science
of society rigorously deduced from those conditions as a result of
experiencing them directly as a member of the class with whose
interests he identified himself completely.  In the 1844 Manuscripts Marx has already grasped the basic principle that there is
no human essence apart from 'productive forces and social forms of
intercourse' and that 'all history is nothing but the continuous
transformation of human nature' but he still includes statements
about man in the abstract, about man's essential powers, and he
still sometimes speaks of 'alienation' as affecting mankind in
general, irrespective of class, as though the original division of
labour were like some universal fall from grace.  Four years later,
in 'The Communist Manifesto of 1848',he firmly rejects all such vague
references to 'Human nature, to Man in general, who belongs to
no class, has no reality, who exists only in the misty realm of
philosophical fantasy.'(27)  And in the 'Theses on Feuerbach' he says:
'Human nature is no abstraction inherent in each separate individual.  In its reality it is the ensemble of social relationships.'
(28)

'Alienation' as something that happens to all men in commodity-
exchanging societies in which money mediates all relationships is a
term Marx uses less and less in his mature work.  He speaks instead
of the effects of alienated labour-power which have a clear class
reference.

The exercise of labour-power is the worker's own life-activity,
the manifestation of his own life.  And this life-activity he
sells to another person in order to secure the necessary means
of subsistence.  Thus his life-activity is for him only a means
to enable him to exist.  He works in order to live.  He does
not even reckon labour as part of his life, it is rather a sacrifice of his life.(29)

The loosely expressed 'universal emancipation contained within
the emancipation of workers' of the 'Manuscripts' becomes the clear
statement of revolutionary mission in the Manifesto:

The proletarians cannot become masters of the productive forces
of society, except by abolishing their own previous mode of
appropriation, and thereby also every other previous mode of
appropriation.  They have nothing of their own to secure and
fortify;  their mission is to destroy all previous securities
for, and insurances of, individual property.... The proletariat,
the lowest stratum of our present society, cannot stir, cannot
raise itself up, without the whole superincumbent strata of
official society being sprung into the air.(30)

In 'Capital' the word 'alienation' hardly appears at all, not
that Marx had changed his mind about the range of social phenomena
previously comprehended under that term but only that he had found
ways of describing them which were more specifically related to the
historic task of the working class.  Throughout the existence of
class-divided society the products of labour have never wholly
belonged to those who made them and have thus, to some extent, stood
over against their makers as alien objects.  It remained for capitalism in the commoditisation of labour-power itself to dispossess
workers completely, not only of the product of their labour but of
the very tools of their trade so that no work could be done except
on the terms of the purchaser of labour-power.  What is doled back
to workers in wages, when they are fortunate enough to be in
work at all, is determined by the subsistence rate based on the
value of necessary commodities for a particular time and place and
leaves over for the capitalist surplus-value, the substantial difference between the total value produced and that portion of it
which keeps the work force alive.  The drive for surplus-value
sums up the whole motivation of capitalism and engrosses all the
vaguer sociological characterisations of capitalist society as
profit-seeking, acquisitive, competitive or atomistic.  The concrete
fact of surplus-value not only indicates the precise form of exploitation but also, unlike looser qualifications, designates exactly
who exploits whom.

Surplus-value, as the appropriation through ownership and control
of the means of production of this huge difference between goods
produced by the working class and goods consumed by it, a difference which increases with every rise in working-class skill so that
'human progress' under capitalism can be measured by the greater
amount of wealth appropriated by the capitalist, simply is the law
of capitalism.  Capitalism cannot be changed unless this basic
economic law of the appropriation of surplus-value has changed; and
any claim that capitalism is gradually turning into something else,
as long as this law remains in operation, is mere terminological
quibbling.

Monopolisation may have introduced a minor distinction between
ownership and managerial control in vast corporations but the
personnel of the ruling class overlaps these categories which are
both, in any case, equally devoted to the pursuit of surplus-value.
The state, which in capitalist society is simply 'the executive
committee for managing the affairs of the whole bourgeoisie', may
have had to intervene more and more to preserve the system as
economic crises grew in severity, taking over and running at the
expense of the public, mainly the working class, those essential
industries in which surplus-value was small or non-existent so that
private ownership could go on reaping large profits from those industries in which surplus-value was high;  but this by no means represents any kind of socialism nor any change in the basic nature of
capitalism.  Surplus-value is the key to the capitalist character
of states which may look very different superficially — colonial
clients of imperialist countries or imperialist countries themselves, bourgeois democracies or corporate states like fascist Italy
or Germany.  Nothing that happens to countries from the outside can

change this basic nature — only an internal change which puts an
end to the private appropriation of surplus-value.  When the whole
armed state and military administration of Germany was smashed,
there among the rubble was capitalism, which had invented Hitler to
begin with, still seeking surplus-value and only requiring the plasma
of money from the capitalist USA to rise out of the ruins as fat and
greedy as ever.

As we have seen, the capitalist drive to amass surplus-value
means that the quantity and quality of commodities actually produced in a given situation directly depends not on human needs but
on expectations of profit.  Those whose labour creates value determine neither by their material demands nor by their conscious will
the direction of the productive process.  Even those who do control
production in their own class interest do not have the same degree
of control over the market where this interest and the general
effective demand for goods must be resolved in the conversion of
commodities into profits.  Neither monopolisation nor the intervention of the capitalist state can change the anarchic nature of
a system of production based not on supplying people's needs but
on exploiting them;  and to the ordinary deprivation of the working
class in being robbed of surplus-value is added the incidental
hardship of economic crises the capitalist class is powerless to
prevent.  Both classes pay tribute, but by no means in anything
like equal proportion, to a state of society in which the process
of production has the mastery over man instead of being controlled
by him.  These two classes are quite clearly distinguishable at all
times by the fact that only one of them, the working class, in that
it must offer for sale on the market its own value-creative ability,
assumes itself a commodity form.

The pernicious influences and distortions of vision affecting
men in societies based on commodity-exchange Marx describes as
'commodity fetishism'.  Commodity fetishism, which involves
ascribing value to things simply as they are in themselves rather
than as the products of human labour, covers the same social phenomena as were previously referred to by the more generalised term
of 'alienation' but now made more specific as particularly relevant
to the final stage of commodity production under capitalism.  If
surplus-value provides the key to the exploitative class relationships of capitalist society, commodity fetishism complements it as
a general illusion resulting from the absolute pervasiveness of
commodity relations throughout capitalist society.  Since value is
the common element in all commodities as produced by human labour,
and since that labour in all class-divided societies is more or less
alienated labour, alienation as an affective state is produced
generally along with the production of commodities.  Only under
capitalism and the fullest development of commodity production can
value, as a social product, presupposing the dissolution of all
previous relations of production not completely dominated by exchange, appear in its strict sense as the product of labour completely alienated from the labourer himself by the outright purchase
of his labour-power.  And it is this absolute alienation which is
reflected in 'commodity fetishism'.

In commodity-exchanging society the social character of men's
labour appears to them as an objective value stamped on the product

of that labour.   'A definite social relation between men thus
assumes, in their eyes, the fantastic form of a relation between
things.'(31)   But these things which embody their relationship with
other men in society neither belong to them nor were produced at
their instigation, and so the relationship itself tends to become
incomprehensible, what Marx calls a 'social hieroglyphic'. Membership in society determines the very nature of the individual human
being, but this membership as mediated by things has become a
mystery to him.   To find an analogy for this strange plight of man
in commodity-exchanging society, Marx returns to his earlier comparison of the '1844 Manuscripts', reformulated in the light of his
intervening studies in political economy:

> We must have recourse to the mist-enveloped regions of the reli-
> gious world.   In that world the productions of the human brain
> appear as independent beings endowed with life, and entering
> into relations both with one another and the human race.   So it
> is in the world of commodities with the products of men's hands.
> This I call the Fetishism which attaches itself to the products
> of labour, so soon as they are produced as commodities, and which
> is therefore inseparable from the production of commodities.(32)

Commodity fetishism as a particular form of the various aspects of
estrangement Marx had noted previously he describes thus:

> The mode of production in which the product takes the form of a
> commodity, or is produced directly for exchange, is the most
> general and the most embryonic form of bourgeois production.
> It therefore makes its appearance at an early date in history,
> though not in the same predominating and characteristic manner
> as now-a-days.   Hence its Fetish character is comparatively easy
> to be seen through.(33)

But when we come to its highest development under capitalism, this
appearance of simplicity vanishes.   What was only one area of
social existence and could be compared with other areas relatively
untouched by exchange relationships comes to pervade the entire
framework of life in society, leaving no alternative standard by
which its influence might be judged.   Just as all the general
characteristics of capitalist society disappear only when the law
of surplus-value has been abrogated, so commodity fetishism, or
man's sense of alienation in capitalist society, will only vanish
when production is planned for use, directly determined by the
real needs of society, and not for exchange.

Under socialism, the transitional stage to communism, the law of
value ceases to be the sole regulator of the proportions of labour
distributed among various branches of production because it is
limited in its operation by the social ownership of the means of
production and by the law of the balanced development of the national
economy in the interest of the working masses.   As Stalin put it in
'Economic Problems of Socialism in the USSR' written in 1952:   How
else would it be comprehensible that 'our light industries, which
are the most profitable, are not being developed to the utmost and
that preference is given to our heavy industries, which are often
less profitable, and sometimes altogether unprofitable'?   Or the
same could be said of the cultivation of land in Albania which in
capitalist terms would be highly 'uneconomic'.   Under full communism the law of value loses its function as a regulator of exchange

relations entirely because exchange relations themselves no longer
exist.

> Value, like the law of value, is a historical category connected
> with the existence of commodity production.  With the disappear-
> ance of commodity production, value and its forms and the law
> of value also disappear.  In the second phase of communist
> society, the amount of labour expended on the production of goods
> will be measured not in a round about way, not through value and
> its forms, as is the case under commodity production, but directly
> and immediately — by the amount of time, the number of hours,
> expended on the production of goods.  As to the distribution of
> labour, its distribution among the branches of production will
> be regulated not by the law of value, which will have ceased
> to function at that time, but by the growth of society's demand
> for goods.(34)

Value will have disappeared because it will no longer be projected
as a distinguishable aspect of things by production for exchange
and will have been reabsorbed into the integral process of production for use.

In the transitional period of socialism some commodity-exchange
continues as between agricultural co-operatives and the state pur-
chasing agency.  This is because co-operative ownership is not yet
full state ownership in the name of the whole people as is the case
with factories, mines or, of course, state farms.  Until the commodity form of goods disappears entirely society cannot move from
the socialist productive relationship 'from each according to his
ability, to each according to his work' to the communist productive
relationship 'from each according to his ability, to each according to his need'.  In the latter case labour has become so free and
products so abundant that needs no longer have to be directly
connected with work done.

'Economic Problems of Socialism in the USSR' was Stalin's last
theoretical work and it was an attack on revisionism.  In it he
anticipates many of the arguments the Chinese and Albanian communists were to level at Khrushchev and the other revisionists who
usurped state power and began the restoration of capitalism.  In
an article on The Basic Economic Law in 1962 Stalin is taken to
task for suggesting 'that in the course of communist construction
commodity and money relations outlive themselves and retard our
progress toward communism.'  It is argued instead that 'in the
expansion and perfection of production the fullest use should be
made of commodity and money relations, in keeping with the new
content they acquire under the socialist system'(35) — an apology
for capitalism in pseudo-Marxist terminology.

In suggesting that the expansion of production and the higher
standard of living attendant on it, without at some stage the
liquidation of commodity and money relations, can of itself bring
about communism the revisionist author of the article on the Basic
Law, and indeed all the so-called liberalisers who set about dis-
mantling socialist economies, fly in the face of Marx's conception
of the altered relations of production in communist society.

> The labour of the individual is taken from the start as social
> labour.  Therefore whatever the specific material form of the
> product which he creates or helps to create may be, that which

he has bought with his labour is not a special specific product,
but a specific share of the communal production.  For this reason
he has no special product that he has to exchange.  His product
is not an exchange value.  The product does not have to be
translated into a specific character form in order to acquire
a universal character for the individual.  Instead of a division
of labour, necessarily ending in the exchange of exchange value,
we would have an organisation of labour, which results in the
participation of the individual in communal consumption.(36)
Or, in ethical terms, communist morality is not based simply on the
availability of plenty, but also on the conditions of human dignity
and freedom in which that plenty is produced by conscious, self-
expressive labour.

This concern with the commodity from its inception in the division
of labour and the beginning of class differences through the development of commodity production which, with the appearance of labour-
power in the market place as itself a commodity, leads to capitalism
and on from there to the disappearance of the commodity with the
end of exploitative relationships in communist society takes us
back to the point from which we started in an attempt to define the
word 'good'.  Indeed the method of our procedure can be seen, in
a sense, as the reverse of Marx's development from the writing of
the 'Manuscripts' to the publication of 'Capital'.  He succeeded in
giving his philosophical ideas about the ethics of social organisation the concise, scientific form of an economic analysis of a
particular type of society, its network of inner relationships and,
as a result, what it was capable of being turned into.  We have
been trying to release from that systematic contruct, under the
guidance of Marx and his successors in developing working-class
ideology, its philosophical implications in order to gain a better
understanding of morality in general and the ethical problems of
our own times in particular — not as an intellectual exercise but
in answer to an urgent social need in a period of crisis.


THE WORKING CLASS AS THE AGENT OF SOCIAL CHANGE

Economic exploitation gives the working class its incentive to
revolt against existing conditions;  a state of crisis in those
conditions provides the occasion;  and the consciousness of the
possibility of some other ordering of society in which the role of
workers would no longer be that of wage slaves lends political
direction to the revolutionary impulse.  This is Lenin's revolutionary situation:  when the ruling class can no longer rule in the
old way and the working class is no longer prepared to let itself
be ruled in the old way.  The latter condition implies that the
working class has become a class-for-itself and is no longer simply
a class-in-itself, that is to say, it has become a class with its
own ideology which for the working class can be no other than the
revolutionary establishment of socialism with the final ending of
exploitative relations of production.  This means that there has
to be an ideological revolution by which the theory of scientific
socialism grips the working masses and becomes a material force
before there can be a political and economic revolution.  In this

ideological revolution is generated the morale which enables the
working class to endure a protracted war, achieve ultimate victory
over its class enemies and smash the capitalist system of class
exploitation.

The basic class division between workers and capitalists is the
main contradiction in capitalist society and conditions the whole
outlook of these two forces in their irreconcilable opposition.  As
we have seen in our analysis of commodity-exchanging society, the
division between work done and satisfactions enjoyed results in
very different experiences for those who sell their labour-power
under pain of deprivation of satisfactions and those who traffic
in the labour-power of others.  A class which does no physical
work and is mainly concerned with manipulating intellectually as
well as physically those who do, a class for whom reality is constantly filtered through the abstract spectacles of prices, stock
quotations and unit costs and only handles reality through the kid
gloves of money easily acquires the illusion that ideas command
the existence of things, that desires, with ready cash as their
ponce, create the substance of their own fulfilment.  Workers can
have no such illusion.  To them useful articles are always the
result of specific labour and desires are only satisfied to the
extent that labour-power has been sold.  This idealistic illusion
of a non-productive ruling class can be expressed in economic
terms as the distorted view that money, from being simply a measure
of the equivalence of values as created by a common human labour,
appears actually to have called that labour into being.  An abstraction thus seems to be the real source of all value.  If more money
is to be made in exporting capital abroad than in making things at
home, then the thing to do is just stop making things and only
make money.  Carried to such extremes this distorted vision in-
capacitates a ruling class and its ideologists for coping with real
social issues.  Money and the abstract speculation which is its
ideological reflection, instead of being recognised as the by-
products of a system of commodity exchange, are seen as its main
stays, and, as such, are invoked in defence of the system.  Difficulties arising from contradictions in the material basis of society
can either be 'bought off', or 'thought' out of existence.

The working class can never really forget the connection between
utility and value, no matter how obscured it may have become behind
the movement of commodities.  Because they themselves have largely
assumed the qualities of a commodity by having to sell their labour-
power in the market, they preserve within their own nature, however
unconsciously, that essential relatedness of the amount of work done
and the worth of things made.  For them duty and pleasure, reason
and emotions are not driven so far apart as is the case with members
of a class whose nature is essentially that of buyers of the labour
and services of others.

In daily working contact with their physical environment industrial workers certainly cannot but be aware through their own
muscles and their own brains of the real origin of all our values
and the ultimate source of all our knowledge.  Tell a worker with
calloused hands that the world beyond his finger tips may be an
illusion and his response is likely to be that of Doctor Johnson's
to Berkeleian idealism — only more personally directed.  Working-

class ideology is slower to develop among so called white-collar
workers who also sell their labour-power but whose conditions of
work often involve them in a more isolated capacity dealing with
abstractions, but once they do begin to grasp the ideology of their
own class that very familiarity with abstractions may deepen their
theoretical understanding of it.  The capitalist class, on the
other hand, more and more detached from the workshop, mill or mine
where muscle and brain transform nature and quite unlike the early
masters who remained in close association with a small number of
workers at the point of production, increasingly loses touch with
reality.  In cutting themselves off completely from the productive
process they are cutting themselves off from the source of correct
ideas.  They are being by-passed by the epistemological transmission
belt of the knowledge-producing mass line — from the perceptual
experience of the working masses to conceptualisation in theory
and then back to the masses again for verification in social practice.

> Where do correct ideas come from?  Do they drop from the skies?
> No.  Are they innate in the mind?  No.  They come from social
> practice, and from it alone;  they come from the three kinds
> of social practice, the struggle for production, the class
> struggle and scientific experiment.(37)

A large factory in London has wasted two years trying to apply an
industrial process thought up by a junior executive whose career
depends on its success which any worker on the shop floor could
have told management was not on from the start.  Multiply that
sort of thing in workplaces all over the country, indeed, all
over the capitalist world and you have one of the ways in which
relations of production are inhibiting growth of the forces of
production.

With the socialisation of the labour force, the gathering together of workers in ever larger factory complexes, there has
inevitably been a socialisation of the thinking and habits of
workers.  They realised from their own daily experience of class
struggle in these mass conditions that their unity was their
strength, that an injury to one must be regarded as an injury to
all, that their shop-floor leaders must be protected from victimisation by the class enemy.  Extreme individualism they recognised
as the characteristic of those too selfish to join a union and fight
the employer but willing to accept any advances others might win
by their sacrifices, the outlook of the bourgeois spy in their midst,
of the scab.  As victims of an exploitative system they learned to
hate not just their own exploitation but exploitation as such.  Their
sense of class unity embraced workers in other lands, becoming the
only real internationalism against the international crimes of imperialism — 'workers of the world unite'.

Thus in the womb of capitalism has been developing another
morality, a morality as different from the rugged individualism and
selfish acquisitiveness of capitalist ethics as the conditions of
the working class differ from those of the bourgeoisie.  That is
not to say that workers always act in accord with these ideals:  a
regimen from which no one ever departs is not morality but natural
law.  But it is a morality that honestly declares its class character as serving the interests of workers, the vast majority of citizens.  The bourgeois morality of individual selfishness pretends to

be universal but it no more applies to those whose exploitation
yields the profits for capitalists to be selfish about than
bourgeois democracy has ever meant that the working class could
vote on the question of whether it was to be exploited or not.
The bourgeois morality of individual selfishness serves the
double purpose of both providing an apology for actions of the
capitalist class on the grounds that self-interest is the only
form of social motivation that works and also offering an argument
against social change on the grounds that human nature never alters
and the most that people can do is change one lot of exploiters
for another.

It was on the basis of this working-class morality of the factory that Lenin formulated the principle of democratic centralism.

> Is it really so difficult to understand that, before a decision
> has been taken by the centre on a strike, it is permissible to
> agitate for and against it, but that after a decision in favour
> of a strike (with the additional decision to conceal this from
> the enemy) to carry on agitation against the strike is strike-
> breaking? Any worker will understand that.(38)

And this principle of democratic centralism originating in the
discipline and democracy of the factory is the organisational form
of Lenin's party of a new type, the political conscience of the
working class.

> We have already more than once enunciated our theoretical views
> on the importance of discipline and how this concept is to be
> understood in the party of the working class. We define it as
> unity of action, freedom of discussion and criticism. Only
> such discipline is worthy of the democratic party of the ad-
> vanced class. The strength of the working class lies in organi-
> sation. Unless the masses are organised, the proletariat
> is nothing. Organised — it is everything. Organisation means
> unity of action, unity in practical operations.... Therefore the
> proletariat does not recognise unity of action without freedom
> to discuss and criticise.(39)

This work place origin of the idea of the communist party led
one of the Mensheviks to complain that Lenin seemed to look on
the party as though it were a 'huge factory', to which Lenin
replied:

> This dreadful word of his at once betrays the mentality of the
> bourgeois intellectual unfamiliar with either the practice or
> the theory of proletarian organisation. For the factory, which
> to some seems a bogey, represents that highest form of capitalist
> co-operation which has united and disciplined the proletariat,
> taught it to organise, and placed it at the head of all other
> sections of the toiling and exploited population. And Marxism,
> which is the ideology of the proletariat trained by capitalism,
> has been, and is, training unstable intellectuals to distinguish
> between the factory as a means of exploitation (discipline based
> on fear of starvation) and the factory as a means of organisa-
> tion (discipline based on collective labour united by the condi-
> tions of a technically advanced form of production). The
> discipline and organisation which come so hard to the bourgeois
> intellectual are easily acquired by the proletariat just because
> of this factory schooling.(40)

In so far as the working-class movement is not completely
dominated by working-class ideology expressed in a vanguard communist party, 'the most advanced and resolute section of the working class', having 'no interests separate and apart from the proletariat as a whole',(41) that movement will inevitably be influenced by two bourgeois tendencies disguised as working-class
ideas.  When no revolutionary organisation exists, though the
revolutionary movement is growing, 'we observe two opposite extremes which, as is to be expected (when we look at the matter
dialectically) meet, that is, absolutely unsound Economism and the
preaching of moderation and equally unsound, excitative terror.'(42)
These two tendencies may be characterised as opportunism or reformism on the one hand and anarchism or adventurism on the other.  As
Lenin says:  'Anarchism was not infrequently a kind of penalty
for the opportunist sins of the working-class movement.  The two
monstrosities complemented each other.'(43)  This can be seen in
the rise of various Trotskyite anarchic groupings as a result of
the revisionism affecting many so-called 'communist' parties,
particularly after the betrayal of socialism in the Soviet Union.
As Lenin points out these two 'monstrosities', reformism and adventurism, are two sides of the same coin.  Though they often clothe
themselves in revolutionary language, they are equally counter-
revolutionary in effect, the one by deterring workers from fights
they can win, the other by luring workers into fights they cannot
win.  In every struggle in which workers are involved, from the
factory or office right up to the country as a whole or, even,
the international arena, they will always be presented with these
two equally false alternatives, the ultra-leftist one of raising
the stakes to an impossible level for that stage of conflict or
the rightist one of finding some excuse for not fighting after all.
    Lenin also describes opportunist reformism as 'economism'.  It
is in the bourgeois interest to try to separate the economic demands
of the working class from any political movement.  A failure in the
working class to revolutionise its ideology will result in avoiding the issue of all out class conflict by seeking themselves the
sort of division between economics and politics which serves the
interests of the capitalist ruling class.  This was what led workers
in Britain to create the Labour Party as their political representa-
tive in Parliament while they concentrated on their struggles under
trade union leadership for economic demands within the capitalist
system — the essence of social democracy.  But economics and
politics cannot be divided — any more than the forces of production can be separated from the relations of production.  Politics
delegated by the working class to somebody else will always become
politics united with somebody else's economic interests.  And
every struggle which workers push through to the end themselves
has political implications — particularly in the latter stages
of capitalist development when the employing class has to rely
more and more on the state to prop up failing industries with public money and to cripple trade unions legally or absorb them into
the bourgeois state apparatus.  Workers in Britain are finding that
the monster they created in the Labour Party is capitalism's most
obedient servant when it comes to enforcing wage-cuts and trying to
destroy the defensive organisations of workers against such attacks.

The tactics of workers, whether in the jungles of Asia, Africa
or Latin America or in the cities of the advanced capitalist
countries, in order to avoid the two alternatives of opportunism
and adventurism at a time when the class forces ranged against them
are relatively stronger, have to be guerrilla tactics.  Workers have
to learn to avoid confrontations with superior forces either in the
case of imperialist armies occupying their countries which parti-
sans might inadvertently encounter head on or the power of the
capitalist state which workers might challenge in a general strike
before they are ready to make such industrial action on a national
scale part of a revolutionary strategy.  They have to learn to
concentrate their forces for the main blow, to be mobile and flex-
ible, able to operate in self-reliant detachments with great
initiative and ingenuity without losing sight of the general plan,
have  to use the enemy's weapons, whether material or ideological,
against him.  They must have secure bases, deep in the forest or in
a completely-organised factory, office or school from which they
can operate.

In Britain the oldest working class in the world is, probably,
the best organised for this kind of struggle in a highly industrialised country.  The essence of it is to counter the employers'
attacks of laying off workers where profits are low by withdrawing
their labour where profits are high.  They have developed in their
defensive fight against redundancy and closures such tactics as
occupying factories and holding to ransom the capitalists' assets
like goods and machinery.  Indeed, their very success in this
limited kind of industrial warfare has been a factor in their failure up to now to develop revolutionary class consciousness believing
that it might always be possible to win concessions within the
system without having to attack the system itself.  While guerrilla
tactics win battles, they do not win wars.  For final victory they
must be integrated in a revolutionary strategy as the means of
mobilising and training the workers' revolutionary army.

The employing class in Britain can no longer afford a working
class able to win any concessions at all and increasingly relies
on the capitalist state to change the rules of the game, like
outlawing free collective bargaining, thus demonstrating the inability of 'the ruling class to rule in the old way'.  And for all
the many decades of organised struggle by the working class in
Britain in defence of its standard of living within the confines
of the capitalist system, for all the millions of words of sociologists about the alleged affluence of the working class in capitalist society making non-sense of Marx, British workers in terms
of their miserable share of the wealth they produce and of still
enjoying the right to work at all at the mercy of employers and
their state machine are not really any better off.  After two
hundred years of class struggle over wages and conditions they
can still be thrown on the scrap heap of unemployment in their
hundreds of thousands as of no further use to humanity.

A situation in which the working class no longer lets the
bourgeoisie rule in the old way is a revolutionary situation, but
every revolutionary situation is also a counter-revolutionary
situation.  The ending of the political truce of social democracy
because the ruling class can no longer afford it and the working

class repudiates it leaves the working class with no alternatives but going forward through revolution to socialism or sinking back under the weight of fascist counter-revolution.  Fascism is simply capitalism in extremis — a final morbid state in which all class struggle is ruthlessly put down by force.  The ruling class no more wants fascism which is a flagrant denial of all its ideological pretensions than it wants massive unemployment which yields no surplus-value but, ultimately, it can continue its political domination in no other way.

The world context of workers' revolutionary movements is very different from October 1917.  Not only has the working class in China and Albania fought off all attempts internally or externally to undermine their socialist systems but also one of the two major imperialist powers, the USA, has been thoroughly defeated on the field of battle by the Vietnamese people and the other people of Indo-China and its forces rolled back to permit the development of socialist societies there.  It is true that the Soviet Union, where revisionism has subverted the workers' state established by the October Revolution, has emerged as the other major imperialist power, contesting and sharing world hegemony with the USA, and proving itself a threat to the independence of the under-industrialised countries, the more so since the revisionist usurpers have not entirely used up the material advantages and international confidence they inherited from the period of socialist development. But on the whole the Chinese are surely justified in saying of the world today that 'revolution is the main trend'.

Dialectical materialism finds the dynamism of change in the contradictions within a thing bringing about, by internal causation, qualitative differences which turn the thing into something else.  External causes, the relations with what is outside the thing, provide the conditions of change, favouring or inhibiting it and thus operating through that internal revolution which transforms the thing.  The world, itself divided into capitalist and socialist blocs in every part of which there is class struggle between the bourgeoisie with its capitalist outlook and the working class with its socialist outlook, provides the general background of socialist revolutions; but an actual working-class revolution can only be achieved by the capture and transformation of state power within a particular country where

> the proletariat which is much more numerous than the bourgeoisie and grows simultaneously with it but under its rule ... gradually gains strength, becomes an independent class playing the leading role in history, and finally seizes political power and becomes the ruling class.(44)

'The proletariat of each country must, of course, first of all settle matters with its own bourgeoisie.'(45)

The perspective of social change in our own era is developed by Mao Tsetung out of the correct explanation of imperialist contradictions given by Lenin and Stalin.

> When the capitalism of the era of free competition developed into imperialism, there was no change in the class nature of the two classes in fundamental contradiction, namely, the proletariat and the bourgeoisie, or in the capitalist essence of society; however, the contradiction between the two classes became

intensified, the contradiction between monopoly and non-monopoly capital emerged, the contradiction between the colonial powers and the colonies became intensified, the contradiction among the capitalist countries resulting from their uneven development manifested itself with particular sharpness, and thus there arose the special stage of capitalism, the stage of imperialism. (46)

At what point the fundamental contradiction between the proletariat and the bourgeoisie will result in a revolutionary reversal of their position depends on where the particular form of that fundamental contradiction is sharpest.

We have seen how a polarisation of class forces in modern capitalist countries results in the splitting of society 'into two great hostile camps, into two great classes directly facing each other: Bourgeoisie and Proletariat.'(47)  In the colonial and semi-colonial world a similar polarisation takes place when a revolutionary civil war develops to the point of threatening imperialism through the domestic reactionaries by whom it rules whereupon imperialism sends in its own armed forces to help the domestic reactionaries directly.

At such a time, foreign imperialism and domestic reaction stand quite openly at one pole while the masses of the people stand at the other pole, thus forming the principal contradiction which determines or influences the development of the other contradictions.(48)

The fact that in the imperialist phase of capitalism the latter polarisation has first reached the extreme form of a principal contradiction every member of society was aware of being involved in is a factor in determining the locus of the earliest working-class revolutions in the colonial and semi-colonial world rather than in the oldest industrialised countries.  But already in the last quarter of the twentieth century with the completion of class polarisation in a country like Britain and with capitalism in a general state of crisis this locus is likely to move westward and it would be fitting if the first capitalist country in the world were also the first major industrialised country to have a socialist revolution.

In those cases of colonial polarisation where the masses of the people confronting an imperialist aggressor have represented an alliance of classes including a large peasantry under the leadership of a relatively small working class, the revolution has had to be carried out in two stages.  The first stage, that of the establishment of a people's democratic dictatorship which would unite all classes even bourgeois elements prepared to resist the foreign invaders on a broad programme of national liberation, social justice and land reform, had to precede a subsequent stage of establishing a dictatorship of the proletariat which could then proceed to the building of a socialist society.  This, Mao explains, 'is a special historical feature, a feature peculiar to the revolution in colonial and semi-colonial countries and not to be found in the revolutionary history of any capitalist country.'(49)  Where the polarisation of classes is a result of the simplifying of class antagonism to that between capitalist class and workers, as in Britain, the working class goes directly for socialism under a proletarian dictatorship established in a one stage revolution.

In the first case of polarisation, under colonial conditions,
the national question predominates to begin with and the class
question then comes to the fore in determining whether the liberated
country is to develop self-reliantly on a socialist basis under working-class rule or slip back into some form of neo-colonialism.   In
the second case of polarisation, in developed capitalist conditions,
the class question predominates to begin with and the national question is then raised as the ruling bourgeoisie, unable on its own
to solve the class question to its permanent advantage, seeks to
internationalise the class struggle, as the British ruling class
has done in forcing Britain into monopoly-capitalist alliances like
the European Economic Community.   This leaves the working class as
the only defender of national integrity and independence.   Nationality in the broadest sense is simply the essential genius of working people who in a particular place over a considerable period of
time have developed their peculiar skills and arts for the enrichment of life both materially and spiritually one of whose products
is their language.   The bourgeoisie exploited this nationality to
build their capitalist state — just as they used working people to
defeat feudalism, and then disenfranchised them.   Once the bourgeoisie have no further use for nationalism, since profit knows no
nationality, it is for workers who developed it down the centuries
as their particular form of co-operative value-creativity to liberate it, thus freeing their own genius, skill, courage, intelligence
and initiative for the service not only of themselves but of a whole
world from which exploitation has been eliminated.

The question of whether a revolution requires one or two stages
depending on whether capitalist relations of production have reached
their full extent or not is like the problem of the continuous
revolution Marx had to deal with in connection with countries like
Germany or Russia where there were proletarian movements but no
bourgeois revolution had taken place.   Just as Mensheviks mechanically insisted that every single country had to pass through the
stages of feudalism and capitalism before coming to socialism, so
their spiritual heirs, Trotskyites, have denied that any working-
class revolution could take place in the poorer countries of Asia,
Africa or Latin America because they did not have a large urban
proletariat and that any revolutions that did occur could not
possibly be working class — as if peasants who under working-class
leadership adopt a working-class ideology of socialist revolution
and fight for it right to the end do not make themselves working
class in the process!   There are, of course, differences not only
in the stages working-class revolutions pass through but also in
the ideological preparation for them as between semi-feudal countries
where relations of production however grossly exploitative are still
human relations and developed capitalist countries where commodity
exchange and such reflections of it as commodity fetishism have
reached their full extent.   In the first case the ideological revolution reaches its height after liberation and the seizure of state
power as the popular democratic dictatorship of the period of
people's war is changed into the dictatorship of the proletariat in
all fields, cultural as well as economic;   in the second case there
has to be a considerable ideological revolution within the working
class to expel an alien ideology from workers' minds before they can

mobilise themselves under their own ideological banners for the
revolutionary seizure of power.

Would-be leftists have tried to counterpose the working-class
struggles in the colonial territories to working-class struggles
in the metropolitan countries, but in so doing they were really
carrying out the divide-and-rule policy of the imperialists, the
common enemy of workers everywhere.  As Lenin has said:

> The revolutionary movement in the advanced countries would in
> practice be a sheer fraud if, in their struggle against capital,
> the workers of Europe and America were not closely and completely
> united with the hundreds upon hundreds of millions of 'colonial'
> slaves who are oppressed by capital.(50)

But as was pointed out before, the best service workers in the
imperialist countries can perform for their fellow workers in the
underdeveloped countries is to make a revolution at home.  'In
proportion as the exploitation of one individual by another is put
an end to, the exploitation of one nation by another will be put
an end to.'(51)

The existence of socialist countries like China and Albania, with
a foreign policy of proletarian internationalism toward all in
struggle against capitalism, has a double advantage for workers
everywhere.  It reassures them about the feasibility of workers'
seizing and holding on to state power, since the largest Asian
country and one of the smallest European countries pretty well
cover between them the whole range of possibilities.  And it means
that the reasonable voice of socialism is heard in international
councils exposing the role of capitalist exploitation in relation
to such questions as pollution, the so-called population explosion,
the widening gulf between the richer and the poorer countries and
so forth.  Because real social change depends on 'the contradictions within a thing bringing about, by internal causation, qualitative differences', because 'external causes can only operate
through internal causes', it is not possible to export socialist
revolutions nor to impose them from above.  Since, therefore,
socialist countries can never be involved in interfering in another
country's internal affairs, however sympathetic they may be to the
embattled working class there to whom they will have made available
the lessons of their own successful, self-reliant struggle, proletarian internationalism is compatible with peaceful co-existence.
Peaceful co-existence is the maintenance, based on non-interference,
respect for territorial integrity and trade on equal terms, of
correct state relations between countries having different social
systems.  At the same time the armed masses of socialist countries
will tolerate no infringement of their sovereignty whatsoever.

Since the whole political point of a socialist revolution is the
investing of the working people with real state power, so that they
do take their destiny into their own hands, there is no question
of ever carrying out a revolution on their behalf, of imposing
socialism from above.  They make the revolution themselves and they
make it when they are ideologically and materially strong enough
to do so.  There are no short-cuts by way of coups, putsches or
conspiratorial plots — only the protracted struggle of developing
the self-conscious, independent movement of the immense majority,
in the interest of the immense majority'.  The revolution itself is

not an unfortunate necessity imposed on men by the intractable
nature of social change:  it has intrinsic value as the assertion
through united action by the vast majority of a common human dignity hitherto suppressed and also it is the only training ground
for the subsequent tasks of carrying out the building of a socialist
society on the basis of democratic centralism.

> this revolution is necessary, therefore, not only because the
> ruling class cannot be overthrown in any other way, but also
> because the class overthrowing it can only in a revolution
> succeed in ridding itself of all the muck of ages and become
> fitted to found life anew.(52)

The struggle to end exploitation is not a necessary evil but an
eloquent expression of all that is best in the consciously
achieved solidarity of exploited peoples everywhere.  And just as
material values are measured by the labour incorporated in them,
so moral values can only be estimated in terms of the amount of
human thought and effort involved in their realisation.

Marxists are often criticised for holding the view that the end
justifies the means and therefore countenance, if they do not
actually encourage, the use of violence.  The violence of revolutionary force is only the other face of the violence of counter-
revolutionary repression inherent in the existing situation, and
since the latter form of violence goes uncriticised, one must
assume that it is not really the means which are being objected
to but the end — the abolition of the exploitation of man by man.
Revolution is the expression in social practice of the working
class's detestation of a system that degrades human beings and
uses them only for the purpose of profit-grubbing. 'Clearly the
weapon of criticism cannot replace criticism of weapons, and
material force must be overthrown by material force.  But theory
also becomes a material force once it has gripped the masses.'(53)

After all, what can justify any means except the end?  And yet
because the end also conditions the means of attaining it, Marxism
categorically rejects, for any short-term organisational advantages
in this place or that, any methods which break the unity and
fellowship of the international working class.  This means it
regards all forms of chauvinism which try to substitute for class
unity some spurious and vicious order, like 'all us whites together' or 'all us British together' or 'all us males together', as
weapons the capitalist class employs in its incessant efforts to
divide and rule the working class.  The morality of means must be
considered in terms of a normative judgment about ends;  and the
evidence is overwhelming that the effort to preserve a system incorporating obvious injustices denies itself the use of no weapons, no matter how vile and destructive, while the effort to
reorganise society on a more equitable basis shows, in the midst
of struggle, a concern for the quality of future life with every
liberated area becoming a promise of the socialism to be.  The
ends, exploitation of the many by the few or emancipation of the
many, colour through and through the respective means used.

Violence does not only take the form of forcible detention or
corporal punishment or mass killings, though no system of exploitation has ever been able to dispense with such means either explicitly
or implicitly.  Millions upon millions of people living at a bare

subsistence level are also the victims of violence even if no guns
are being fired at them.  If a man is sitting on another man's
chest, their relationship may appear to be non-violent — until
the man on the bottom tries to get up.  Pity for the victims of
this kind of violence which is not combined with active detestation of its perpetrators is utterly futile.  Peace movements which
fail to specify the source of aggression in the contradictions of
capitalism or which would put a halt to all social disruption at a
stage when so many millions live under conditions of intolerable
economic oppression are tools of an exploiting class.  Nuclear
blackmail has been one of the ways US  imperialism aided and
abetted by the neo-imperialists of the Soviet Union have tried to
terrorise people into acquiescing in a grossly unfair distribution
of the world's goods.  Like any blackmail, the submission to the
threat of the H bomb, which has been elevated in western countries
to the most terrible form of commodity fetishism, gives no
assurance of avoiding the blow and increases the demands of the
criminals.  It remained for the People's Republic of China, a
country where commodity exchange is being progressively eliminated,
to remind the world that people are more important than weapons,
even the so-called ultimate ones, and then, in the interests of
the world's people, to break the US-USSR nuclear oligopoly by
developing such weapons themselves, alone declaring that they would
never use them first and continuing to demand their total abolition.

The revolutionary force which Marxism sanctions as the only way
to liberate people from economic bondage and establish the basic
conditions for genuinely moral relationships is not directed at
individuals but at a class and the state institutions which maintain its domination.  The enemies of revolution, all those who
have something to lose or think they have something to lose in the
abolition of injustice and exploitation, try to raise the cost of
social change to a figure civilised people would be unwilling to
pay.  Lies are propagated about the liquidation of kulaks amounting to mass murder;  but the liquidation of a class of exploiters
by no means implies the elimination of individual members of that
class — only the destruction of the social basis which enabled
them to exploit others.  The class of criminally negligent motorists, for example, could be eliminated without a single person's
being subjected to violence — unless, of course, those motorists
insisted on defending their 'right' to drive just as they please.
The truly remarkable thing about the revolutionary transformation
of even so vast a country as China is the economy of force used.
This is because it is directed against the real enemies of the
people who are very few and, as the revolution advances, the confused dupes of those enemies desert in their millions to the
popular cause.

The soldiers of the liberation army adhere to the strictest
moral discipline in relation to the people in whose interest they
fight, not 'taking so much as a piece of thread without paying for
it.'  Indeed, it is the kindly, helpful conduct of these troops
which first convinces the masses that this is an entirely different movement from any of the brutal incursions of soldiers they
have been subjected to in the past.  Even in the treatment of the
enemies of the people the effort is always made to rehabilitate

them — 'to kill the disease in order to save the patient'. This
tends to be obscured by the media in the capitalist world since
the trial and execution by a people's court of one vicious landlord gets more attention than the freeing from serfdom and misery
of millions of peasants.

Reducing politics to the question of individual rights is a
way of evading real political issues, just as stressing the individual act avoids any consideration of the real problems of ethics.
As long as the ruling class can limit political and moral criticism to the rights and duties of the individual they have effectively put their own interested acts as a class beyond the reach
of working-class criticism in social practice.

We have already seen how the full development of commodity
production under capitalism, by substituting money relations for
personal ones and by treating the members of a community as units
competing with each other in the market for jobs and goods, has
the tendency of atomising society and isolating the individual.
This alienated individual can be generalised as the subject of
political study and his abstract rights can be enshrined in the
institutions of bourgeois society — the right to vote or the right
to own property, the right to pursue his own happiness or the right
to think as he pleases. But these abstract rights do not in themselves enable anyone to publish dissident views nor obtain work
paying a living wage nor so much as buy a single loaf of bread;
nor, on the other hand, do they limit in any way the privileges
exercised by those who have amassed the means for turning abstract
rights into material benefits. The capitalist class is not threatened by the isolated individual which capitalism tends, unless
checked by the socialisation of labour, to produce — hence the
concern for the preservation of this harmless product. What the
ruling class has to fear is mass action on the part of the working
class and therefore any institutions which give workers the appearance of expressing their class will while limiting that expression
to some form of 'Parliamentary cretinism' are very useful. And, of
course, whenever there is the slightest chance that such institutions might fall into the hands of the working class, they can
be hastily abolished on the grounds that democracy is in danger!

If only the working class could be persuaded to limit its pro-
test against suffered injustices to casting a vote in secret or
writing to 'The Times'! The ruling class in the name of democracy
is always trying to write into any trade union legislation a provision for a secret ballot before strike action because the individual worker, on his own and subject to all the influences brought
to bear on him not to make trouble, is a very different political
animal from a worker in a mass meeting of his workmates feeling
the strength of class solidarity. At a time when the ruling class
was threatened by mass social action if it could get away with
suddenly calling a general election and persuading everybody to
go off somewhere and cast a secret ballot for something, it would
have nothing further to worry about. In class-divided society
there is always the question of democracy for whom. The existing
social order which the apologists for capitalism describe as
democratic is, from the point of view of the working class, a
dictatorship of the bourgeoisie while the emancipation of the

working class is, as far as the bourgeoisie is concerned, a proletarian dictatorship.  One class's 'open society' is another
class's 'totalitarian state'.

One of the main contradictions of capitalism is that, for
extending its sway or defending what it already holds, it has to
depend on those who are not themselves capitalists.  It is the
essential nature of capitalists as a class to be exploiters.  They
do not exist apart from that exploitative relationship with others.
It is not the essential nature of workers to be exploited but to
transform nature to meet human needs — a task they can perform
infinitely better freed from the exploitative relationship.  The
capitalist class cannot do without workers but the working class
can do very nicely without capitalists.  Capitalism could only
sustain itself indefinitely by ceasing to raise an army of workers
against it by robbing them of surplus-value;  but then the profit
motive having been abandoned, it would have ceased to be capitalism.  All reformism takes the form of saying, in effect, if capitalism were only something other than what it is, it would not be
necessary to change it.

History affords us no example of a privileged minority, as a
distinct class, voluntarily resigning its special position and
sharing its worldly goods with other members of that society,
simply because such a class is by definition those who benefit
from a particular form of exploitation and whose membership of
that class carries with it the ideological conviction of the
'rightness' of that privileged position.  And even if it were conceivable that such a class would be moved to some such act of
general redistribution, it would not satisfy the Marxist condition
for a system of morality based on human relations of freedom in a
society from which exploitation was excluded.  Charity on the
widest scale might mitigate some of the more obvious forms of
distress but it would not alter the relationship between dominant
and subject classes.  Being able to give away goods is itself an
expression of a special position in society, however rarely in-
dulged in by the rich and powerful.  On the other hand, to be
grateful for gifts of what they have made themselves, from the
point of view of the working class, would merely add humiliation
to injustice.

The ruling capitalist class, not just in this country or that,
but all over the world has proved itself as incompetent as it is
corrupt.  It cannot even secure its own position, much less
guarantee any security to the world at large, because it cannot
control the very economic forces it directs in its own selfish
interests.  The working class, though individual members and even
whole sections may vacillate and try in this way or that to opt
out of the role for which history, the sum of human actions, has
cast it, is not, simply by the nature of its relationship to the
means of production, corrupt.  Labour itself cannot be corrupted.
It is the source of all value.  And the working class in so far
as it consists of those who produce value is a creative force which
cannot be corrupted.  It is not power which corrupts.  Power
wielded for the general good by the working masses themselves in
socialist countries does not corrupt but dignifies as the freedom
of people in control of their own future.  It is power wielded

partially, in the service of exploitation which corrupts.

In our era a belief in humanity and a hope for its bright future can take no other rational form than the social homeopathy of working-class revolution — involvement with the value-creators against the despoilers in class struggle to put an end to classes.


## CULTURE AND CLASS STRUGGLE

It remained for capitalism to develop commodity production to the point where it became a cloak for the grossest forms of exploitation and at the same time, for those who penetrated the disguise, suggested the possibility of a society which would have nothing to conceal because no one was being exploited. It is the very impersonality of economic oppression under capitalism which not only permits excessive abuses but seems to put them beyond the reach of moral criticism. If the victimisation of millions of people can be made to appear as the result of the movement of unforeseen forces, then no one need feel guilty about it. Are hundreds of thousands of workers thrown out of jobs bringing misery to their families? Then they have priced themselves out of the labour market by demanding too much in wages for the current state of economic activity, that is all. Are many millions of those living in the capitalist world chronically undernourished if not actually starving? Well, the terms of trade must have moved against primary producers. Are under-developed countries constantly thwarted in their efforts to raise their standard of living by the 'assistance' of the original capitalist powers? Ah, that merely proves that the economic conditions for the 'take-off', when industrialisation gains sufficient momentum to be self-sustaining, are more complicated than was thought and, perhaps, another book ought to be written about it. And of course many many books must be written to show that this kind of economic system, whereby an impersonal market in commodities automatically robbing workers of their livelihood and impoverishing primary producers is 'freedom', while any attempt to assert control over their economic destiny and assume responsibility for their actions, both as they affect themselves and as they affect others, is materialistic bondage — 'the road to serfdom'.

And more books can be written for those who do feel some sense of unease at acquiescing in a system that can only function on the basis of the waste and destruction of resources whether natural or human, comfortable people who wish to add to other luxuries and amenities just one more — a good conscience. But all they are offered on the market are further distractions from having a bad one. Of course these people do not wish to purchase a good conscience at the cost of the very privileges which put them in the market for an easy one. They want peace but not at any price. They want peace in a world still divided into rich and poor — a world, therefore, in which war is inevitable as the means by which imperialist countries hope to preserve that division.

Nor can they close their eyes to it all and seek refuge in a few intimate relationships because in a state of alienation, dominated by objects, those very relationships with others get trans-

lated into relations among things.  And where are they to look for
guidance or relief in this general estrangement?  To psychologists
whose advice is also a commodity?  To writers and artists whose very
works are not only commodities produced for a market and subject to
the same laws as any other articles made to sell but whose talent
also, like the labour-power of other workers, is bought and sold at
current prices, thus transforming them into commodities too.

> This art ... full of the easy gratifications of instincts
> starved by modern capitalism ... is the religion of today, as
> characteristic of [capitalist] exploitation as Catholicism is
> of feudal exploitation.  It is the opium of the people;  it
> pictures an inverted world because the world of [bourgeois]
> society is inverted.(54)

As Bertolt Brecht has remarked of so many contemporary writers, 'The
fact that money-making is never the subject of their work makes one
suspect that ... it may be the object instead.'

How is anyone to find his way through this commodity-world to
the reality behind it when the media of information, the newspapers
we read together with the news printed in them, the programmes we
watch or hear, even education itself, are all commodities offered
on the market.  Everyone is like Midas, desperately needing natural
sustenance and human warmth, yet condemned to turn everything
touched into money — itself merely the most general form commodities can take.  The awareness of the influence on human relationships of commodity exchange was naturally greater when its effects
were first being felt.  Shakespeare writes of:

> That smooth-faced gentleman, tickling Commodity,
> Commodity, the bias of the world...
> This sway of motion, this Commodity...
> This bawd, this broker, this all-changing word.(55)

If life in capitalist countries has become atomised, man set
against man in competition for jobs and the things money can buy,
human relationships changed into monetary ones, perhaps these
effects can be overcome by a new impulse toward social living,
perhaps all that is needed is to recover a sense of belonging to
something greater than oneself, a feeling of 'togetherness' with
others.  But which others?  Psychiatric treatment takes the form
of helping one to adapt oneself to living in the commodity world as
it is — in spite of the fact that it is just that world which is
at the root of individual psychological problems.  Or one can belong
to a corporate society in which exploitation remains the same but
is hidden behind phoney bonds of unity of a racist or nationalist
form and by irrational feelings of hatred and fear toward groups
thought to be more alien than oneself — an involvement based on
gut reactions and thinking with one's blood as extolled by the
later D.H. Lawrence as part of the denial of working-class morality.
Even joining a revolutionary movement simply to lose one's personal
feelings of estrangement by belonging to something, as so many
intellectuals did in the 1930s, is unlikely to have much therapeutic
value and certainly does nothing at all for the movements themselves.  Revolutionary movements of the working class are not substitutes for a religion the individual has precociously lost and
fondly regrets.  A book published some years ago, 'The God that
Failed', is a typical plaint from those who expected to get some-

thing out of communism, some personal uplift or sense of salvation, who hoped thus to recover a lost faith.  What they were
really looking for was revealed by Arthur Koestler in his own
apologia in that book:  'A faith is not acquired by reasoning.
One does not fall in love with a woman, or enter the womb of a
church, as a result of logical persuasion.'  Or perhaps the dessi-
cated individual of capitalist society seeks to undo the alienating
effects of the system through love of the people when, like George
Orwell, he finds that he does not really like them.  As a failed
narodnik he could only vent his bitterness by imagining a utopian
hell of endless suffering for those who had been unable to make him
love them, blaming it all on what he calls a 'socialist' but is
really a degenerate state-capitalist system which, with its drab-
ness, its organised hatreds, its utter pointlessness, its extreme
degree of alienation, is modelled on the developing features of
his own bourgeois society.  Genuine revolutionary activity has
nothing to do with losing oneself in society — only with finding
oneself in society, which means becoming aware with all its implications of belonging to a class capable of changing that society.

   There are two moralities existing contemporaneously in our present world — the one bound up with the decaying economic system of
capitalism, the other founded on the socialism which grows inside
the bourgeois world and in various places has burst forth to
flourish as a new social order.  In Britain the situation is not
entirely dissimilar to that of an earlier Elizabethan period which,
too, was a period of transition, the newer ethics of bourgeois
society co-existing with the tiered order and personal loyalties of
feudalism.  There was considerable ideological confusion as the
result of this moral polarisation under two different standards —
a confusion which was to be found in the minds of individuals as
well as in society itself.  Often a man's sentiments pulled him
one way and his reason another, or his very reason might be divided
against itself.  Sometimes a man might think he belonged to one
party when his actions proved him to belong to the other.  Shakespeare might express a nostalgia for the vanishing order in which
each man knew his place and what it entailed ethically in terms of
relations with those above and below, he might rail passionately
against the universal commodity gold, the 'common whore of mankind'
that 'will make black white, foul fair, wrong right, base noble';
but he actually lived according to the new dispensation of the self-
made man, raising himself by the commoditisation of his great works.

   The idea of betrayal which haunted the minds of those poets and
dramatists returns to us in the scenes of ideological trials, most
evidently at the height of the Cold War when our own Bosolas and
Iagos turned courtrooms into stages and with rhetorical flourishes
and much breast-beating repudiated espoused beliefs and informed
on old friends.  Sometimes this delation could not be accounted
for solely on the basis of bribes offered in the name of the established order.  Violent shifts from one set of standards to another
appear, from one point of view, as incomprehensible malevolence,
from another, as a return to the true faith after dabbling in
heresies.  But then intentions are hard to follow across the trans-
valuation involved in suddenly altering the very standards by
which judgment takes place;  and the actions of such unstable

characters seem quite unmotivated, their explanations no more than
a vain hope that a multiplicity of inadequate reasons will eventually add up to a single sufficient one.

Our times are like theirs also in the wild fluctuations from
the heights of optimism to the depths of despair, depending on an
identification of interest with a world that is being born or one
that is visibly cracking up. Like them there is an obsession with
sexual relationships — partly from the illusion that physical
passion may be the one enduring thing where all else is in flux
and partly from the fact that the disjunction between past and
future in an age of transition precipitates this relationship,
like others, from any natural context — so that it becomes isolated, an act in itself, all important and at the same time, meaningless. Despair itself, the sin against the Holy Ghost, can be
offered as a nicely packaged marketable commodity by writers who
take the alienation of man in bourgeois society, cut off from
other individuals, afflicted with a sense of the meaninglessness
of life, and turn it into the plight of man as such, inhabiting a
grey limbo, like Orwell's political hell which, in fact, is simply
the Catholic cosmogony with god left out.

When these alienated artists do write about the 'people' it is
never a class-conscious worker with some idea of changing things:
it is always a tramp or meth  drinker or perverted criminal, in
short, someone as alienated physically as they themselves are
intellectually. And, of course, understandably popular with the
bourgeoisie are writers as wildly reactionary as Solzhenitsyn, a
kind of avatar of Rasputin who takes readers back to a dark medi-
eval Russia constructed, like Plato's Republic, in such a way that
this time it will not lead to the present, since that present
includes something as disastrous for the enemies of the working
class as the October Revolution.

It is an interesting fact of bourgeois culture that, from the
beginning, the best examples of that peculiarly bourgeois literary
form, the novel, have all been more or less open attacks on bourgeois morality. At a time when there was as yet no vision of a
future alternative to capitalism Balzac, like Shakespeare, could
only find his ideal society in some modified and enlightened form
of feudalism, but his critical understanding of French bourgeois
society, laying bare all its selfish motives and ridiculous aspirations, was so brilliantly reflective of the reality as to make his
books Marx's favourite fiction. 'The Eighteenth Brumaire of Louis
Bonaparte' itself reads like the witty setting of a nineteenth-
century novel of manners. The great English novels of this period
owe their enduring quality to their exposure of the real nature
of bourgeois society underneath all the outward show of success
and material wealth.

From a working-class point of view it is not so much a question
of the area of society dealt with as of the attitude toward
bourgeois values that makes a work progressive. Henry James's
novels of the subtle effects of money on human relationships —
a clever woman who cannot see why her young man should not be the
heir of an ailing millionairess, a rich father who buys an elegant
Italian prince for his daughter, an emissary from wealthy interests in America to an effete Europe who formulates as the only

dignified code of conduct 'not to have got anything out of it for
himself' — these works have a higher political value in spite of
the level of society dealt with than any of the flood of so-called
working-class books and plays by writers, themselves working
class, who have bought their way into bourgeois acceptance by
depicting workers as venal, feckless and promiscuous.  Working-
class heroes are as absent from their work as from that of the
most pretentious and recondite authors who titillate the bourgeoisie with obscurantism passing for profundity.

One can find in all the best literature of the bourgeois period
criticisms of the selfishness and emptiness of bourgeois life;  but
no further great works will be produced on that theme.  It is too
late for any more creative fiction merely criticising capitalist
society:  the great works to come will be born out of the emancipation of the people from exploitation and the glorious human
adventure of building societies which do not rest on anybody's
back.

The Cultural Revolution in China was the kind of soil-turning
and seed-planting out of which these great works will come in
other countries too.  Enver Hoxha describes the development of
Albania's culture in this way:

Our socialist art and culture should be firmly based on our
native soil, on our wonderful people, arising from the people
and serving them to the full.  They should be clear and comprehensible but never vulgar and thoughtless.  Our Party is
for creative works in which the deep ideological content and
the broad popular spirit are realised in an artistic form
capable of stirring profoundly and touching the hearts of the
people, in order to inspire and mobilise them for great deeds.
We must intensify our struggle for a revolutionary art and
literature of socialist realism.... As in every other field, a
sharp class struggle is taking place here also between the two
ideologies — Marxist-Leninist materialist ideology on the one
hand and feudal and bourgeois ideology on the other.  Decadent
bourgeois culture and art are alien to socialism.  We oppose
them and at the same time we appreciate and make use of everything that is progressive, democratic and revolutionary, criti-
cally viewed in the light of our own proletarian ideology.(56)
All morality is class morality.  All culture is class culture.
In the world today all culture, all literature and art belong
to definite classes and are geared to definite political
lines.  There is in fact no such thing as art for art's sake,
art that stands above classes, art that is detached from or
independent from politics.(57)

Furthermore

Revolutionary culture is a powerful revolutionary weapon for
the broad masses of the people.  It prepares the ground ideologically before the revolution comes and is an important,
indeed essential, fighting front in the general revolutionary
front during the revolution.(58)

In that earlier time were in circulation all the ideas from
which Englishmen were to find the courage and resolution to rebel
against their king and by his execution to destroy the last vestiges
of feudalism in the seats of power.  Ralegh  in rejecting a cyclical

view of history enabled men to think of politics as an art or a
science related to changing social and economic circumstances.
Bacon drew from the practice of artisans a scientific philosophy
of nature governed by laws and of man redeeming himself from
error through science.  As Christopher Hill writes of the political
results of such ideas:

> Unless we can expect effects to follow causes in a rational and
> predictable way, leaving room for human freedom, there is no
> stimulus to that moral effort to which Hakewill (and the Puri-
> tans) attached such importance.(59)

George Hakewill, much influenced by Ralegh and, in turn, influencing,
among others, Milton, put it thus in his 'Apologie': 'The first
step to enable a man to the achieving of great designs is to be
persuaded that by endeavour he is able to achieve it.'  He also
expressed the moral indignation of the age at venal courtiers
and judges, at gentlemen who 'strip the backs of the poor, that
they may apparel their walls, and snatch meat from their mouths,
that they may give it to their hawks and dogs.'(60)

Spenser, Ralegh, Pym all asserted the power of humanity to
escape by the use of reason from 'an ineluctable cyclical decline'.
Ralegh's and Bacon's conception of history made the idea of controlled change conceivable.  Just as, subsequently, 'Bacon's former
secretary, Thomas Hobbes, could say that politics was a science
because men made the state, so Harrington could conceive of history
as a science because men could control it.'

These ideas of the first Elizabethan period were the ideological
preparation for the bourgeois revolution which laid the foundation
for the development of capitalism in Britain and of British imperialism abroad.  In this present Elizabethan period all the ideas
are in circulation from which the working class will find the
courage and resolution to make the proletarian revolution.  But
working-class revolutionary culture which is part of the ideological
preparation for revolution itself is not going to be seen on the
screens of television sets or the cinema;  it is not going to be
heard in any Radio Three lecture series nor read in any of the
thousands of books pouring onto the market, particularly in any
of those reviewed by the press.  'The class which has the means of
material production at its disposal, has control at the same time
over the means of mental production.'  No overt censorship is
required to police the interdiction on revolutionary works:  they
can always be rejected on the grounds that they are not commer-
cially viable propositions by film companies, editorial boards,
publishers who all have a vested interest in keeping things as they
are no matter how bad they get.  Indeed, updating that remark of
Phocion's, 'any time you succeed in getting any work published or
performed which receives critical acclaim and wins you material
rewards, look to see in what precise way you have served the
interests of the capitalist class and betrayed your fellow workers.'

The birth of capitalism in Britain, its original home, was so
brutal and represented such a traumatic experience for those who
were uprooted from the countryside and their traditional rural
culture and driven into cities where conditions were appalling that
they were for some time inhibited in their own cultural response to
the new situation.  There was thus a break in British working-class

culture which facilitated the intervention of the bourgeoisie with
a cheap mass-produced pseudo-working-class culture to be fobbed
off on workers in the same double exploitation as that of the
company store which takes back at one door the meagre wages handed
out at another.  Fortunately there are limits to the moral damage
that can be done by meretricious products and the heightened class
consciousness which accompanies industrial action can sweep away
all the rubbish emptied out on workers from every corner.  One
has seen television interviewers dashing frantically from worker
to worker vainly seeking for someone who will put the scab's view
of the strike being covered.

Working-class revolutionary culture is being generated every
day in slogans that reveal the class's humour as well as its political understanding, in the marginalia on management's notices
pinned to factory bulletin boards, in the jokes and stories that
grow out of class struggle and become the currency of any places
where workers congregate.  It is to be found, of course, in the
publications of the Marxist-Leninist party which most capitalist
countries have since Marxism-Leninism is the ideology of the working class.  It will be increased by the enormous strengthening of
the working class by all those teachers, office workers, government
employees, research scientists and the like who have recognised
their own membership in the working class and will bring their own
skills to the expression of the class's social and political
aspirations.

Marxism is not utopian.  It does not portray in glowing colours
some New Jerusalem into which harassed people can wish themselves
without the effort of constructing on sound principles the necessary
approaches.  Nor does it promise quick and easy social results.

A revolution is not a dinner party, or writing an essay, or
painting a picture, or doing embroidery;  it cannot be so
refined, so leisurely and gentle, so temperate, kind, courteous,
restrained and magnanimous.  A revolution is an insurrection,
an act of violence by which one class overthrows another.(61)

What Marxism says in ethical terms is that the free development
and activity of individuals, the possibility of humanising production and laying the foundation of truly moral personal relationships, requires them 'to bring under their own conscious control the material conditions of life, conditions which have previously been abandoned to chance and which have thus acquired an
independent existence over against individuals.'(62)  The ethics
of the very struggle to lay the foundations of a truly ethical
society can be summarised thus:

Our morality is entirely subordinated to the interests of the
class struggle of the proletariat [ because ] only the proletarians, fired by a new social task to accomplish for all
society, to do away with all classes and class rule, are the
men to break the instrument of that class rule — the state,
the centralised and organised governmental power usurping to
be the master instead of the servant of society.(63)

The 'interests of the class struggle of the proletariat' may
seem an inadequate expression of the moral ideal but it contains
by implication all that is necessary in the way of ethical principles for establishing the material base of a higher moral order

of society from which the exploitation of man by man has been
eliminated.  In the concept of 'struggle' is that Marxist thesis
that the point is not simply to understand and interpret the
world but to change it.  In the concept of 'class' is all the
fellowship, brotherhood and common purpose in the form of a common
goal which unites workers all over the world.  Dialectically combined they represent the 'self-conscious, independent movement of
the immense majority in the interest of the immense majority', the
liberation of all men from the slavery of exploitation in any form.

# NOTES

CHAPTER 1  VALUES - THE MEANING OF VALUE-JUDGMENTS

1  David Hume, 'A Treatise of Human Nature', p. 415.
2  Jeremy Bentham, 'Introduction to the Principles of Morals and Legislation'.
3  Marx, 'Capital', vol. III, p. 795.
4  Marx, 'Economic and Philosophic Manuscripts of 1844', p. 74.
5  Marx, 'The German Ideology', p. 164.
6  Marx, 'Capital', vol. I, p. 170.
7  Ibid., p. 171.
8  Lenin, 'Collected Works', vol. XXXVIII, p. 363.
9  Mao Tsetung, 'On Practice', 'Selected Works', vol. I, pp. 290-3.
10  Mao Tsetung, 'Some Questions Concerning Methods of Leadership', 'Selected Works', vol. III, p. 119.
11  Adam Smith, 'Wealth of Nations', p. 13.


CHAPTER 2  RIGHTS - THE MEANING OF NORMATIVE JUDGMENTS

1  Marx, 'The German Ideology', p. 14.
2  John Locke, 'Second Treatise of Civil Government', p. 15.
3  Marx, 'The German Ideology', p. 22.
4  Marx, 'Capital', vol. I, p. 79.
5  Ibid., p. 713.
6  Marx and Engels, 'The Communist Manifesto', 'Selected Works', vol. I, p. 42.
7  Marx, 'The German Ideology', p. 22.
8  Plato, 'The Republic', p. 293.
9  Ibid., p. 287.
10  Ibid., p. 316.
11  Aristotle, 'The Nicomachean Ethics', pp. 222-3.
12  Aristotle, 'Politics', p. 15.
13  Marx, 'Capital', vol. I, pp. 59-60.
14  Aristotle, 'The Nicomachean Ethics', p. 36.
15  Aristotle, 'Politics', p. 37.
16  George Thomson, The Prehistoric Aegean, 'Studies in Ancient Greek Society', pp. 357-8.

17   Aristotle, 'Politics', p. 19.
18   R.H. Tawney, 'Religion and the Rise of Capitalism', p. 53.
19   Marx, 'Critique of Hegel's Philosophy of Right'.
20   Engels, Preface to 'Poverty of Philosophy', p. 13.
21   Marx, 'Theses on Feuerbach', 'Selected Works', vol. II, p. 367.
22   F.H. Bradley, 'Appearance and Reality', p. 327.
23   Marx and Engels, 'The Communist Manifesto', 'Selected Works', vol. I, p. 33.
24   Ibid., p. 35.
25   Mao Tsetung, 'On Contradiction', 'Selected Works', vol. I, p. 313.
26   Engels, 'Herr Eugen Duhring's Revolution in Science', p. 109.
27   Mao Tsetung, 'Rectify the Party's Style of Work', 'Selected Works', vol. III, p. 39.
28   Marx, 'The German Ideology', p. 39.
29   Marx and Engels, 'The Communist Manifesto', 'Selected Works', vol. I, p. 42.
30   Marx, 'The German Ideology', p. 41.
31   Eugene Kamenka, 'The Ethical Foundations of Marxism', p. 129.
32   Marx, 'Critique of the Gotha Programme', 'Selected Works', vol. II, p. 23.
33   Marx, 'Poverty of Philosophy'.
34   Marx, 'The German Ideology', p. 15.
35   Mao Tsetung, as quoted in 'Philosophy is no Mystery', editor's note.
36   Marx, 'The German Ideology', p. 41.
37   Mao Tsetung, 'Talks at the Yenan Forum on Literature and Art', 'Selected Works', vol. III, p. 91.
38   Marx, 'Preface to the Critique of Political Economy', 'Selected Works', vol. I, p. 329.
39   Mao Tsetung, 'On Practice', 'Selected Works', vol. I, p. 301.
40   Lenin, 'The Tasks of the Youth Leagues', 'Selected Works', vol. II, p. 667.
41   Enver Hoxha, 'Report to the Vth Party Congress', p. 177.
42   Mao Tsetung, 'Concerning Methods of Leadership', 'Selected Works', vol. III, p. 119.
43   Stalin, 'The Foundations of Leninism'.
44   Mehmet Shehu, 'On the Experience of the National Liberation War'.
45   Mao Tsetung, 'Unite and Fight to Accomplish the Party's Tasks', 'Selected Works', vol. III, p. 317.
46   Marx, 'The German Ideology'.
47   Lenin, 'Report on War and Peace', 'Selected Works', vol. II, p. 293.
48   Marx, 'Preface to the Critique of Political Economy', 'Selected Works', vol. I, p. 329.
49   Lenin, 'Left-wing Communism, an Infantile Disorder', 'Selected Works', vol. II, p. 621.
50   Marx, 'Capital', vol. I, p. 753.
51   Ibid., p. 754.
52   Marx, 'Critique of the Gotha Programme', 'Selected Works', vol. II, p. 23.
53   Ibid., p. 30.

CHAPTER 3  OBLIGATIONS - THE MEANING OF OUGHT SENTENCES

1  Marx, 'Theses on Feuerbach', 'Selected Works', vol. II, p. 367.
2  Marx, 'Eighteenth Brumaire of Louis Bonaparte', 'Selected Works', vol. I, p. 225.
3  W. David Ross, 'Foundations of Ethics', pp. 159-60.
4  Marx, 'Capital', vol. I, p. 47.
5  Mao Tsetung, 'Talks at the Yenan Forum on Literature and Art', 'Selected Works', vol. III, p. 88.
6  Bertell Ollman, 'Alienation', p. 134.
7  Marx, 'Economic and Philosophic Manuscripts of 1844', p. 104.
8  Ibid., p. 107.
9  Marx, 'The German Ideology'.
10  Mao Tsetung, 'On Practice', 'Selected Works', vol. I, p. 308.
11  Marx and Engels, 'The Communist Manifesto', 'Selected Works', vol. I, p. 55.
12  Mao Tsetung, 'Talks at the Yenan Forum on Literature and Art', 'Selected Works', vol. III, p. 90.
13  Lenin, 'What Is To Be Done?', 'Selected Works', vol. I, p. 201.
14  Marx, 'The Holy Family', p. 52.
15  Lenin, 'The State and Revolution', 'Selected Works', vol. II, p. 201.
16  Marx, 'The Holy Family', p. 125.
17  Mao Tsetung, 'On Coalition Government', 'Selected Works', vol. III, p. 207.
18  Karl A. Wittfogel, 'Oriental Despotism'.
19  Karl Popper, 'The Poverty of Historicism'.
20  Marx, Preface to the First German Edition of 'Capital', 'Selected Works', vol. I, p. 409.
21  Lenin, 'What Is To Be Done?', 'Selected Works', vol. I, p. 163.
22  Lenin, 'The State and Revolution', 'Selected Works', vol. II, p. 201.
23  Marx, 'The German Ideology', p. 7.
24  Mao Tsetung, 'On Contradiction', 'Selected Works', vol. I, p. 345.
25  Ibid., p. 313.
26  Ibid., p. 314.
27  Ibid., p. 333.
28  Ibid., pp. 321-2.
29  Engels, 'Herr Eugen Duhring's Revolution in Science', p. 130.
30  Lenin, 'Tasks of the Youth Leagues', 'Selected Works', vol. II, p. 670.
31  Engels, 'Feuerbach and the End of Classical German Philosophy', 'Selected Works', vol. II, p. 336.
32  Marx, Preface to the First German Edition of 'Capital', 'Selected Works', vol. I, p. 10.
33  Ibid.
34  Karl Kautsky, 'Ethics and the Materialist Conception of History'.
35  Engels, 'Letter to J. Bloch', 'Selected Works', vol. II, p. 443.
36  Stalin, 'Marxism and Problems of Linguistics', p. 5.
37  Marx, 'Critique of the Gotha Programme', 'Selected Works', vol. II, p. 30.

38   Lenin, 'Greetings to Hungarian Workers', 'Selected Works',
     vol. II, p. 481.
39   Mao Tsetung, quoted in 'Peking Review', no. 7, 14 Feb. 1975.
40   Mao Tsetung, 'Address to the 10th Plenary Session, VIIIth
     Party Congress'.
41   Mao Tsetung, 'On Contradiction', 'Selected Works', vol. I,
     p. 336.
42   Mao Tsetung, 'On the Correct Handling of Contradictions Among
     the People', 'Four Essays on Philosophy', p. 115.
43   Marx, 'Capital', vol. III, pp. 799-800.
44   Marx, 'On the Civil War in France', 'Selected Works', vol. I,
     p. 472.
45   Mao Tsetung, 'Concerning Methods of Leadership', 'Selected
     Works', vol. III, p. 119.
46   Mao Tsetung, 'Preface to Rural Surveys', 'Selected Works',
     vol. III, p. 12.
47   Mao Tsetung, 'Unite and Fight to Accomplish the Party's
     Tasks', 'Selected Works', vol. III, p. 315.
48   'The Constitution of the People's Republic of China', Article
     13, p. 20.
49   Mao Tsetung, 'On Practice', 'Selected Works', vol. I, p. 308.
50   Ibid., p. 307.

## CHAPTER 4   MORALS AND POLITICS

1    Marx, 'Capital', vol. I, p. 490.
2    Lenin, 'The Tasks of the Youth Leagues', 'Selected Works',
     vol. II, pp. 669-70.
3    Marx, 'The German Ideology', p. 74.
4    Lenin, 'The State and Revolution', 'Selected Works', vol. II,
     p. 145.
5    Lenin, 'What Is To Be Done?', 'Selected Works', vol. II, p. 145.
6    Ibid., p. 168.
7    Marx, 'Economic and Philosophic Manuscripts of 1844', p. 156.
8    Ibid., p. 124.
9    Ibid., p. 69.
10   Ibid., p. 70.
11   Marx, 'The German Ideology', p. 22.
12   Marx, 'Economic and Philosophic Manuscripts of 1844', p. 73.
13   Ibid., p. 70.
14   Ibid., p. 164.
15   Ibid., p. 114.
16   Ibid., p. 140.
17   Ibid., p. 137.
18   Ibid., p. 116.
19   Ibid., p. 119.
20   Marx, 'The German Ideology'.
21   Roger Garaudy, 'Humanisme Marxiste', p. 68 (my translation).
22   Marx, 'Economic and Philosophic Manuscripts of 1844',
     pp. 109-10.
23   Ibid., p. 82.
24   Jean-Paul Sartre, 'Critique de la raison dialectique'.
25   T.B. Bottomore and Maximilien Rubel, 'Karl Marx, Selected
     Writings in Sociology and Social Philosophy', p. 45.

26  Werner Stark, 'The Sociology of Knowledge', p. 142.
27  Marx and Engels, 'The Communist Manifesto', 'Selected Works',
    vol. I, p. 55.
28  Marx, 'Theses on Feuerbach', 'Selected Works', vol. II, p. 366.
29  Marx, 'Wage Labour and Capital', 'Selected Works', vol. I, p. 77.
30  Marx and Engels, 'The Communist Manifesto', 'Selected Works',
    vol. I, pp. 42-3.
31  Marx, 'Capital', vol. I, p. 72.
32  Ibid.
33  Ibid., p. 82.
34  Stalin, 'Economic Problems of Socialism in the USSR', p. 22.
35  'Voprosi Ekonomiki', no. 1, 1962.
36  Marx, 'Grundrisse', as quoted in 'The Ethical Foundations of
    Marxism', by Eugene Kamenka, p. 56.
37  Mao Tsetung, 'Where Do Correct Ideas Come From?','Four Essays
    on Philosophy', p. 134.
38  Lenin, 'Letter to the Central Committee of the Russian Social
    Democratic Labour Party', 'Selected Works', vol. VI, pp. 329-30.
39  Lenin, 'Party Discipline and the Fight against the Pro-Cadet
    Social Democrats', 'Collected Works', vol. 11, pp. 320-1.
40  Lenin, 'One Step Forward, Two Steps Back', 'Selected Works',
    vol. I, p. 324.
41  Marx and Engels, 'The Communist Manifesto', 'Selected Works',
    vol. I, p. 44.
42  Lenin, 'What Is To Be Done?', 'Selected Works', vol. I, p. 240.
43  Lenin, 'Left-Wing Communism, an Infantile Disorder', 'Selected
    Works', vol. II, p. 580.
44  Mao Tsetung, 'On Contradiction', 'Selected Works', vol. I,
    p. 334.
45  Marx and Engels, 'The Communist Manifesto', 'Selected Works',
    vol. I, p. 43.
46  Mao Tsetung, 'On Contradiction', 'Selected Works', vol. I, p. 325.
47  Marx and Engels, 'The Communist Manifesto', 'Selected Works',
    vol. I, pp. 33-4.
48  Mao Tsetung, 'On Contradiction', 'Selected Works', vol. I, p. 332.
49  Mao Tsetung, 'Introduction to the Communist', 'Selected Works',
    vol. II, p. 287.
50  Lenin, 'The Second Congress of the Communist International',
    'Selected Works', vol. II, p. 660.
51  Marx and Engels, 'The Communist Manifesto', 'Selected Works',
    vol. I, p. 49.
52  Marx, 'The German Ideology', p. 69.
53  Marx, 'Critique of Hegel's Philosophy of Right', 'Early
    Writings'  (Pelican Marx Library), p. 251.
54  Christopher Caudwell, 'Illusion and Reality', p. 107.
55  Shakespeare, 'King John', II, i.
56  Enver Hoxha, 'Report to Vth Party Congress'.
57  Mao Tsetung, 'Talks at the Yenan Forum on Literature and Art',
    'Selected Works', vol. III, p. 86.
58  Mao Tsetung, 'On New Democracy', 'Selected Works', vol. II,
    p. 382.
59  Christopher Hill, 'Intellectual Origins of the English Revo-
    lution',p. 200.

60 George Hakewill, 'Apologie', as quoted by Christopher Hill, p. 200.
61 Mao Tsetung, 'Report on the Investigation of the Peasant Movement in Hunan', 'Selected Works', vol. I, p. 28.
62 Marx, 'The German Ideology', p. 75.
63 Marx, 'The Civil War in France' (first draft).

# BIBLIOGRAPHY

ALTHUSSER, L., 'For Marx', translated by B. Brewster, London: Allen Lane the Penguin Press, 1969.

ARISTOTLE, 'Politics', translated by William Ellis, London: J.M. Dent, 1912.

ARISTOTLE, 'The Nicomachean Ethics', translated by D.P. Chase, London: J.M. Dent, 1911.

AYER, A.J., 'Language, Truth and Logic', London: Gollancz, 1947.

AYER, A.J., 'The Problem of Knowledge', Harmondsworth: Penguin Books, 1956.

BENTHAM, J. 'Introduction to the Principles of Morals and Legislation', 1789.

BERLIN, I., 'Historical Inevitability', London: Oxford University Press, 1954.

BLAKE, W.J.,'Elements of Marxian Economic Theory and Its Criticism', New York: Cordon Co., 1939.

BOEHM-BAWERK, E. von, 'Capital and Interest', translated by W. Smart, London: Macmillan, 1890.

BOTTOMORE, T.B. and RUBEL, M., 'Karl Marx, Selected Writings in Sociology and Social Philosophy', London: Watts, 1956.

BRADLEY, F.H., 'Appearance and Reality', London: Allen & Unwin, 1908.

BROGNARD, A., 'Lutte de classe et morale Marxiste', Paris: A. Brognard, 1969.

CAUDWELL, C., 'Illusion and Reality', London: Lawrence & Wishart, 1946.

'The Constitution of the People's Republic of China', Peking: Foreign Languages Press, 1975.

CROOK, D. and CROOK, I., 'Revolution in a Chinese Village', London: Routledge & Kegan Paul, 1959.

CROSSMAN, R. (ed.),'The God that Failed', New York: Bantam Books, 1952.

DOBB, M., 'Political Economy and Capitalism', London: Routledge & Kegan Paul, 1950.

ENGELS, F., 'Marx and Engels, Selected Works', 2 vols, Moscow: Foreign Languages Publishing House, 1951.

ENGELS, F., 'Herr Eugen Duhring's Revolution in Science', Moscow: Co-operative Publishing Society of Foreign Workers in the USSR, 1934.

EWING, A.C., 'Second Thoughts in Moral Philosophy', London: Routledge & Kegan Paul, 1959.

GARAUDY, R., 'Humanisme Marxiste', Paris:  Editions Sociales, 1957.

GIDDENS, A., 'The Class Structure of the Advanced Societies', London:  Hutchinson University Library, 1973.

GRICE-HUTCHINSON, M., 'The School of Salamanca', Oxford:  Clarendon Press, 1952.

HALL, E.W., 'What is Value?', London:  Routledge & Kegan Paul, 1952.

HARE, R.M., 'The Language of Morals', Oxford:  Clarendon Press, 1952.

HEGEL, G.W.F., 'The Phenomenology of Mind', translated by J.B. Baillie, London:  Allen & Unwin, 2nd ed., 1931.

HILL, CHRISTOPHER, 'Intellectual Origins of the English Revolution', London:  Panther, 1972.

HOXHA, E., 'Selected Works', Tirana:  The '8 Nentori' Publishing House, 1974.

HOXHA, E., 'Report to Vth Party Congress', Tirana:  Naim Frasheri Publishing House, 1966.

HUME, D., 'A Treatise of Human Nature', Oxford:  Clarendon Press, 1896.

KAMENKA, E., 'The Ethical Foundations of Marxism', London: Routledge & Kegan Paul, 1962.

KANT, I., 'Critique of Pure Reason', translated by J.M.D. Meiklejohn, London:  J.M. Dent, 1934.

KANT, I., 'Fundamental Principles of the Metaphysic of Ethics', translated by T.K. Abbott, London:  Longmans Green, 1946.

KAUTSKY, K., 'Ethics and the Materialist Conception of History', translated by J.B. Askew, London:  The Twentieth Century Press, 1906.

LAMONT, W.D., 'The Value Judgement', University of Edinburgh Press, 1955.

LENIN, V.I., 'Selected Works', 2 vols, Moscow:  Foreign Languages Publishing House, 1947.

LENIN, V.I., 'Selected Works', vol. VI, London:  Lawrence & Wishart, 1936.

LENIN, V.I., 'Collected Works', vol. 11, London:  Lawrence & Wishart, 1962.

LENIN, V.I., 'Philosophical Notebooks', 'Collected Works', vol. 38, Moscow:  Foreign Languages Publishing House, 1961.

LENIN, V.I., 'Materialism and Empirio-Criticism', Peking:  Foreign Language Press, 1972.

LOCKE, J., 'Second Treatise of Civil Government', Oxford:  Basil Blackwell, 1946.

LUKACS, G., 'Studies in European Realism', London:  Hillway Publishing Co., 1950.

MAO TSETUNG, 'Selected Works', 4 vols, Peking:  Foreign Languages Press, 1967.

MAO TSETUNG, 'Four Essays in Philosophy', Peking:  Foreign Languages Press, 1968.

MARX, K., 'Selected Works', 2 vols, Moscow:  Foreign Languages Publishing House, 1951.

MARX, K., 'Capital', 3 vols, Moscow:  Foreign Languages Publishing House, 1954-59.

MARX, K., 'Economic and Philosophical Manuscripts of 1844', Moscow:

Foreign Languages Publishing House, 1959.

MARX, K., 'The German Ideology', Parts I and III, New York: International Publishers, 1963.

MARX, K., 'The Holy Family', Moscow:  Foreign Languages Publishing House, 1956.

MARX, K., 'The Poverty of Philosophy', Moscow:  Foreign Languages Publishing House, n.d.

MARX, K., 'The Pelican Marx Library, Early Writings', London: Penguin Books, 1975.

MILL, J.S., 'Utilitarianism', Oxford:  Basil Blackwell, 1949.

MOORE, G.E.,'Principia Ethica', Cambridge University Press, 1903.

OLLMAN, B., 'Alienation:  Marx's Conception of Man in Capitalist Society', Cambridge University Press, 1971.

PLATO, 'Laws', translated by A.E. Taylor, London:  J.M. Dent, 1935.

PLATO, 'The Republic', translated by A.D. Lindsay, London:  J.M. Dent, 1935.

POPPER, K., 'The Poverty of Historicism', London:  Routledge & Kegan Paul, 1961.

PRICHARD, H.A., 'Duty and Ignorance of Fact', London:  British Academy Annual Philosophical Lecture, 1932.

ROBINSON, J., 'Economic Philosophy', London:  Watts, 1962.

ROLL, E., 'A History of Economic Thought', London:  Faber, 1945.

ROSS, W.D., 'Foundations of Ethics', Oxford:  Clarendon Press, 1939.

SARTRE, J.P., 'Critique de la raison dialectique', Paris: Librairie Gallimard, 1960.

SEMMEL, B., 'Imperialism and Social Reform', London:  Allen & Unwin, 1960.

SHEHU, M., 'On the Experience of the National Liberation War', Tirana:  Naim Frasheri Publishing House, 1947.

SMITH, A., 'Wealth of Nations', London:  J.M. Dent, 1910.

SOHN-RETHEL, A., 'Mental and Manual Labour', unpublished manuscript.

STALIN, J.V., 'Works', Moscow:  Foreign Languages Publishing House, 1952.

STALIN, J.V., 'The Foundations of Leninism', Peking:  Foreign Languages Press, 1965.

STALIN, J.V., 'Economic Problems of Socialism in the USSR', Peking:  Foreign Languages Press, 1972.

STALIN, J.V., 'Marxism and Problems of Linguistics', Peking: Foreign Languages Press, 1972.

STARK, W., 'The Sociology of Knowledge', London:  Routledge & Kegan Paul, 1958.

TAWNEY, R.H., 'Religion and the Rise of Capitalism', London: Penguin, 1938.

THOMSON, G., 'Studies in Ancient Greek Society', 2 vols, London: Lawrence & Wishart, 1949-55.

TOULMIN, S., 'The Place of Reason in Ethics', Cambridge University Press, 1950.

VENABLE, V., 'Human Nature:  the Marxian View', London:  Dobson, 1946.

WEBER, M., 'The Protestant Ethic and the Spirit of Capitalism', translated by T. Parsons, London:  Allen & Unwin, 1930.

WITTFOGEL, K.A., 'Oriental Despotism', New Haven:  Yale University Press, 1956.

# INDEX